VIENNESE POPULAR THEATRE:
A SYMPOSIUM

DAS

VIENNESE POPULAR THEATRE: A SYMPOSIUM

DAS WIENER VOLKSTHEATER. EIN SYMPOSION

Edited by
W. E. Yates
and
John R. P. McKenzie

University of Exeter
1985

First published 1985 by the University of Exeter
© Department of German, University of Exeter
ISBN 0 85989 251 4

Lc

Printed & bound in Great Britain by A. Wheaton & Co Ltd Exeter

CONTENTS — INHALTSVERZEICHNIS

ABBREVIATIONS —
ABKÜRZUNGSVERZEICHNIS

Wke.   Ferdinand Raimund, *Sämtliche Werke*. Historisch-kritische Säkularausgabe, hg. von Fritz Brukner und Eduard Castle, 7 Bde., Wien 1924–1934

WA   Franz Grillparzer, *Sämtliche Werke*. Historisch-kritische Gesamtausgabe, hg. von August Sauer und Reinhold Backmann, 42 Bde., Wien 1909–1948

SW   Johann Nestroy, *Sämtliche Werke*. Historisch-kritische Gesamtausgabe, hg. von Fritz Brukner und Otto Rommel, 15 Bde., Wien 1924–1930

GW   Johann Nestroy, *Gesammelte Werke*, hg. von Otto Rommel, 6 Bde., Wien 1948–1949

Briefe
Stücke 12
Stücke 13   Johann Nestroy, *Sämtliche Werke*. Historisch-kritische Ausgabe von Jürgen Hein und Johann Hüttner, Wien 1977 ff.
Stücke 14

GA   Ludwig Anzengruber, *Sämtliche Werke*. Kritische durchgesehene Gesamtausgabe, unter Mitwirkung von Karl Anzengruber hg. von Rudolf Latzke und Otto Rommel, 17 Bde., Wien 1920–1922

AWV   *Alt-Wiener Volkstheater*, hg. von Otto Rommel, 7 Bde., Wien — Teschen — Leipzig o.J. [1914]

DL   *Barocktradition im österreichisch-bayrischen Volkstheater*, hg. von Otto Rommel, 6 Bde., Leipzig 1935–1939 (*Deutsche Literatur in Entwicklungsreihen*, Reihe: Barock)

In quotations, spelling as in the sources is retained. *Sperrdruck* is reproduced in italics, except in the case of proper names.

Die Orthographie der Zitate entspricht grundsätzlich der der angegebenen Quellen. Sperrdruck wird *kursiv* wiedergegeben, außer bei Namen.

PREFACE

The essays included in this volume are based on papers given at a symposium on Viennese popular theatre held in London on 9-11 May 1984.

The major popular theatres of Vienna, which specialized in dialect comedy and spectacular drama, were essentially foundations of the late eighteenth century, though the playing of dialect comedy by established troupes goes back a hundred years before that, and its origins are even earlier. By the early nineteenth century it enjoyed a European reputation, and the dialect theatres as much as the opera house were inspected and admired by visitors to the city. If this international appreciation has not been maintained, so that the average theatre-goer in the English-speaking world nowadays has no knowledge of the Viennese popular theatre at all, that is no doubt partly due to the now unfamiliar conventions (in particular those of the *Zauberstück*) as well as to perennial difficulties of translation. Yet the phenomenon of the *Vorstadttheater* should be accessible. There are parallels elsewhere in European theatre, examples of flourishing traditions of comic drama played by established companies in major capital cities, from the Elizabethan comedy of Shakespeare's London to the vaudeville of nineteenth-century Paris, which was a rich source of material for Nestroy. Moreover, some of the principal features of the Viennese tradition follow a recognizable international pattern: the central comic figures; the fondness for spectacular visual effects (which had very close parallels in the nineteenth-century London theatre); the central importance of music; and the close relation that obtained between the theatres and their established audiences, with popular taste — as expressed partly in audience reaction, partly in reviews, partly in the dictates of the box-office — exercising a vital influence on the theatre repertoire.

Two further features of the Viennese popular theatre are perhaps particularly significant with regard to its character and importance in general. One is the interaction with court theatres: the interest in the popular stage taken by Burgtheater actors and serious dramatists; the irreverent or popularizing treatment on the popular stage of subjects featuring in the Burgtheater; and, no less important, the constant allusion in popular comedy to the principal grand operas of the time, including not least the musical allusions characteristic of the *Quodlibets*. The other point — and this is where the Viennese popular theatre scores over early nineteenth-century Paris or London — is that within the popular theatres dramatists of stature found their medium: significantly, as in Elizabethan London, actor-dramatists.

To devise a symposium to take account of all these features would hardly have been possible, though in the course of the three days many were touched on and some discussed in detail. But it seemed particularly important not to lose sight of the realities of live performance; and a highlight of the event was the performance of scenes from Raimund and Nestroy, on successive evenings, by the Viennese troupe *Team 65*. To Gottfried Riedl and his colleagues we owe our very sincere thanks for their lively performances, which met with keen appreciation in the audience that gathered in Tuke Hall, Bedford College.

The papers which formed the rest of the programme are, so far as possible, arranged more or less chronologically. They include contributions from two leading Viennese experts, Dr Johann Hüttner, one of the general editors of the new critical Nestroy edition, and Dr Walter Obermaier, director of the manuscript collection of the Wiener Stadt- und Landesbibliothek and the editor of the standard edition of Nestroy's letters. We are much indebted to them for their participation. The majority of the papers are the work of scholars working in Britain; and it is our hope that, together with the live performances given by *Team 65*, they will stimulate further interest in the Viennese popular theatre outside Austria, and that the publication of the papers will encourage further research in the field. What the volume contains amounts, indeed, to a representative range of approaches to the field. The first two papers consider traditional elements of language and style adopted in early nineteenth-century Viennese comedy. The next two present new documentary material. There then follow two that deal with the significance of theatrical conventions and contemporary taste for Nestroy's work. The seventh and eighth papers bear — in very different ways — on the question of the relation of comedy (principally in Nestroy) to aspects of social reality. The next two present strongly contrasted views on Nestroy's treatment of political material. And finally the work of Anzengruber is taken as the focal point for a discussion of the decline of the tradition.

One speaker who was due to come from Vienna, Dr Reinhard Urbach, to speak on the topic "Ferdinand Raimunds Harmonieversuche", was prevented at the last moment by illness. The fifth of the papers in this volume was given in place of Dr Urbach's; the substance of his argument will, however, be available in a study of Raimund being published by the Residenz-Verlag of Salzburg.

Our warm thanks are due to Bedford College, London, where most of the papers were given, and in particular to Professor W. E. Yuill who (together with Professor Yates) co-ordinated the programme and energetically shouldered a great deal of the administrative work. We would also thank no less warmly Dr Bernhard Stillfried, Director of the Austrian Institute in London, for his encouragement, initiative, and support; the relaxed atmosphere in which the symposium was held was due in no small measure to the generous hospitality provided by the Austrian Institute. Academically, the success of the occasion owed a great deal to the collaboration of scholars from all over Great Britain, who chaired the discussions after each paper. It was also most encouraging to the speakers and organizers to see a number of non-specialists from several different walks of life taking an active and informed part in the proceedings.

Finally we would like to express our thanks for generous financial support, which has made this publication possible, to the Austrian Institute, the International Nestroy Society, and the Modern Humanities Research Association; and to the Publications Committee of the University of Exeter for undertaking the publication, to our colleague Mr Jochen Rohlfs for his advice on many points of linguistic detail, and to Mrs Barbara Mennell for her help in seeing the volume through the press.

Exeter   W. E. Yates
                                        John R. P. McKenzie

VORWORT

Die in diesem Band veröffentlichten Aufsätze basieren auf Referaten, die am 9.–11. Mai 1984 in London bei einem Symposion über das Wiener Volkstheater vorgetragen wurden.

Komödien im wienerischen Dialekt wurden zwar schon seit der Zeit Stranitzkys, des ersten wienerischen Hanswursts, in der österreichischen Hauptstadt durch feste Schauspielertruppen aufgeführt, an die noch ältere Tradition der Wanderbühne anknüpfend. Die Geschichte der wichtigsten Wiener Vorstadttheater, wo vor allem Lokalpossen und Ausstattungs-dramen dargeboten wurden, geht aber auf das ausgehende 18. Jahrhundert zurück. Diese Wiener Volksbühnen waren schon in den ersten Jahren des 19. Jahrhunderts in ganz Europa berühmt. Vor allem das "Lachtheater" in der Leopoldstadt stand neben dem Opernhaus hoch in der Gunst der ausländischen Besucher. Wenn dieser internationale Ruf sich nicht bis in die Gegenwart erhalten hat, so daß nicht einmal die Namen Raimund und Nestroy dem Theaterbesucher in der angelsächsischen Welt heute ein Begriff sind, dürfte dies z.T. auf die fremden Konventionen (insbesondere die des Zauberstücks) sowie auf das grundsätzliche Problem der Übersetzung zurückzuführen sein. Dennoch sollte das Phänomen des Wiener Volkstheaters einem breiten Publikum zusagen, und zwar über den deutschen Sprachraum hinaus. Es lassen sich Parallelen zu anderen Blütezeiten des komischen Theaters in europäischen Hauptstädten ziehen, etwa zur elisabethanischen Komödie im London Shakespeares oder zur Pariser comédie-vaudeville, die Nestroy, besonders in den Jahren 1840–1845, mit dem Stoff zu mehreren Bearbeitungen versah. Viele der Grundelemente des Wiener Vorstadtdramas gehören zur internationalen Komödientradition: die komischen Zentralfiguren; die Vorliebe für großangelegte Ausstattungseffekte (zu der sich wiederum eine Parallele im Londoner Theater des 19. Jahrhunderts ziehen läßt); die wichtige Rolle der Musik; und nicht zuletzt das innige Verhältnis zwischen den Vorstadttheatern und ihrem Stammpublikum und der Einfluß des Zeitgeschmacks auf die Entwicklung des Repertoires, wie er sich z.T. in der Aufnahme der Premieren durch das Publikum und die Rezensenten, z.T. im finanziellen Erfolg oder Mißerfolg der jeweiligen Theaterdirektionen manifestierte.

Unter den weiteren Merkmalen, welche die Eigenart und die Bedeutung der Wiener Volkskomödie bestimmten, muß zunächst die Wechselwirkung zwischen den drei Vorstadttheatern und den beiden

xiii

Hoftheatern hervorgehoben werden. Die Burgtheaterschauspieler und
-dramatiker interessierten sich für das Repertoire der Vorstadttheater; auf
den Vorstadtbühnen wurden Stoffe des "höheren" Dramas travestierend-
popularisierend behandelt; auch auf die großen Opern der Zeit wurde,
namentlich in den parodistischen "Quodlibets", immer wieder angespielt.
Darüber hinaus wurde die Tradition der Wiener Volkskomödie — und
hierin liegt eine ihrer besonderen Stärken im Vergleich zum Pariser
oder Londoner Theater der Zeit — von bedeutenden Dramatikern (die
bezeichnenderweise auch Schauspieler waren) aufgegriffen und weiterent-
wickelt.

Daß bei einem dreitägigen Symposion nur eine Annäherung an diesen
theatergeschichtlichen Komplex angestrebt werden konnte, war zwar
von vornherein klar, dennoch wurden die meisten der oben erwähnten
Grundzüge in den Referaten und Diskussionen berücksichtigt. Es kam
den Veranstaltern besonders darauf an, dem Wesen der Wiener Komödie
als Bühnendrama gerecht zu werden, und einer der Höhepunkte des
Symposions bestand in der Aufführung von Szenenreihen aus den Werken
Raimunds und Nestroys durch die Wiener Truppe "Team 65". Herrn
Gottfried Riedl und den anderen Mitgliedern der Truppe gilt unser
herzlicher Dank für diese Darbietungen, die an beiden Abenden
vom Publikum am Bedford College mit lebhaftem Beifall aufgenommen
wurden.

Die Referate, die den Hauptteil des Symposions bildeten, sind im
vorliegenden Band in mehr oder weniger chronologischer Reihenfolge
abgedruckt. Zu den Autoren dieser Beiträge zählen zwei führende Wiener
Nestroyforscher, denen wir für ihre aktive Teilnahme am Symposion sehr
dankbar sind: Dr. Johann Hüttner, einer der Herausgeber der neuen
historisch-kritischen Nestroyausgabe, und Dr. Walter Obermaier, Leiter
der Handschriftensammlung der Wiener Stadt- und Landesbibliothek,
der den Briefband in dieser Ausgabe edierte. Die meisten Beiträge
stammen aber von Kollegen, die in Großbritannien tätig sind. Wir hoffen,
daß das Symposion, einschließlich der beiden Theaterabende, dazu bei-
getragen hat, das Wiener Volkstheater weiteren Kreisen auch außerhalb
Österreichs zu erschließen, und daß die Veröffentlichung der Referate zu
weiteren Forschungsarbeiten auf diesem Gebiet anregen wird. Der
Band gewährt Einsichten in ein durchaus repräsentatives Spektrum von
Forschungsthemen und -methoden. In den beiden ersten Aufsätzen geht
es um herkömmliche sprachliche Elemente, die in die Wiener Komödie
des frühen 19. Jahrhunderts aufgenommen wurden. Es folgen zwei
Berichte über neue dokumentarische Funde. Die nächsten zwei Aufsätze
befassen sich mit den Konventionen des Theaters, in dem Nestroy
arbeitete. Der siebte und der achte Aufsatz berühren — allerdings in
sehr verschiedener Weise — die Frage der Wirklichkeitsbezogenheit der

Komödie, insbesondere der satirischen Possen Nestroys. Es folgen zwei — methodische abermals stark unterschiedliche — Interpretationen von Nestroys Behandlung politischer Themen. Und schließlich bietet das Werk Ludwig Anzengrubers den Ansatz zu einem Überblick über den Untergang des Volksstücks.

Zu unserem großen Bedauern mußte ein weiterer Gast aus Wien, Dr. Reinhard Urbach, in letzter Minute wegen Krankheit absagen. Sein angekündigter Vortrag über "Ferdinand Raimunds Harmonieversuche" wurde beim Symposion durch den fünften der im folgenden abgedruckten Referate ersetzt, der Inhalt seiner Ausführungen ist aber im Wesentlichen in einer im Residenz-Verlag erscheinenden Raimund-Studie enthalten.

Die meisten Vorträge wurden, wie bei einer Reihe früherer Symposien über Themen zur österreichischen Literatur- und Kulturgeschichte, am Bedford College der Universität London abgehalten. Unser besonderer Dank gilt zunächst Professor W. E. Yuill, der in Zusammenarbeit mit Professor Yates das Symposion organisierte und der einen großen Teil der administrativen Arbeit energisch in die Hand nahm. Auch Dr. Bernhard Stillfried, dem Leiter des Österreichischen Kulturinstituts in London, von dem die Anregung zum Symposion kam und der das ganze Unternehmen mit Rat und Tat gefördert hat, danken wir aufs wärmste für sein großes persönliches Engagement; die gemütlich-zwanglose Atmosphäre des Symposions war nicht zuletzt auf die großzügige Gastfreundlichkeit des Österreichischen Kulturinstituts zurückzuführen. In wissenschaftlicher Hinsicht hing der Erfolg des Symposions weitgehend von der Mitarbeit jener Kollegen aus verschiedenen britischen Universitäten ab, unter deren Vorsitz die Diskussionen stattfanden; außerdem wirkte es besonders ermutigend sowohl auf die Referenten als auf die Organisatoren des Symposions, daß auch mehrere Nichtfachleute an den Diskussionen lebhaft teilnahmen.

Für die großzügige finanzielle Unterstützung, die die Veröffentlichung dieses Bands ermöglicht hat, gilt schließlich unser aufrichtiger Dank dem Österreichischen Kulturinstitut, der Internationalen Nestroy-Gesellschaft und der Modern Humanities Research Association. Ebenfalls haben wir der Universität Exeter zu danken, die den Band in ihr Verlagsprogramm aufgenommen hat, und insbesondere der Verlagslektorin Mrs. Barbara Mennell für ihre tatkräftige Hilfe bei der redaktionellen Arbeit und unserem Kollegen Mr. Jochen Rohlfs für viele sprachliche Ratschläge.

Exeter   W. E. Yates
                                                      John R. P. McKenzie

1

Margaret Jacobs

ASPECTS OF DIALOGUE IN VIENNESE COMEDY

Dialogue in drama mimes all kinds of verbal exchange between persons, for example polite and formal, relaxed, conversational and informal, dialectical, argumentative and aggressive, or simply exploratory, for the purposes of seeking or conveying information. Dramatic dialogue imitates a language of encounter which can give the appearance of these modes, that is, modes of exchange where characters' words interlock in patterns within a kind of tonality — polite and calm, emotional and passionate, aggressive, and so on. Further, patterns of dialogue can be established in drama which, at the same time as revealing an inter-personal relationship, approach stylization or abstraction. What this paper sets out to do is to outline how certain set devices and patterns of dialogue, internationally typical of the mechanics of comic drama, are adopted in eighteenth-century Austrian comedy and then developed and refined in the work of Raimund and Nestroy.

Particularly important in comedy is the kind of dialogue that simultaneously imitates a language of encounter and distances the speakers from each other or disrupts their fictional relationship in devices which have nothing at all to do with misunderstandings, argument, or quarrel. In comedy these dissociating devices — as opposed to interlocking patterns — set up a special relationship between actors and audience. The dialogue of comedy is much more likely than that of tragedy to break the rules of speech encounter. There is a taboo on what can be said in normal conversation, as Philinte instructs us in *Le Misanthrope*:

> Il est bien des endroits où la pleine franchise
> Deviendroit ridicule et seroit peu permise.
>
> (I, 1)

In flytings or quarrels we are outspoken. But transfer the business of being outspoken to a scene in which two characters meet for the first time in a calm atmosphere and lead us to expect formal openings, and the comic surprise is achieved by the rough tongue of the character who brushes aside all the formalities. Equally, comic surprise is achieved by the totally gratuitous insult, which the insulted character does not appear to notice or to which he does not respond. The instances of interruption, frustration of each other's speech, refusal to listen, deliberate misunderstanding, talking

1

past each other, short-circuiting of a sequence are more frequent in comedy than in tragedy. Beyond this, the rule of attending to each other in dialogue is manifestly not obeyed in the many examples of distancing which we find in comedy, from the simple aside "für sich" in the literal sense, to the aside spoken out to the audience either within the fictional role, or abandoning it in conscious awareness of role, using reflection and generalization. And even within the apparent exchange the distancing can be evident, as the individual speaker ironizes or parodies or reflects or generalizes away from the inter-personal encounter. So at the same time as imitating the language of encounter, comic dialogue can distance the speakers from each other or disrupt the fictional relationship in devices which need have nothing to do with the natural processes of alienation. (On the other hand, there is of course also a kind of distancing which is achieved by exaggerating the fictional *agon* instead of breaking out of it, since quarrelsome, testy, easily upset characters are a traditional ingredient in the comic dramatization of life.) In one way or other, the links in speech encounters are thus more likely to be broken in comedy. Modern black comedy, or indeed modern comedy in general, frequently uses such alienating and surprise effects already established in the tradition, transferring them to a serious or enigmatic or absurd mode in order to produce an estranged and grotesque presentation. Much of the impact of Expressionist drama derives from this source, with a skilful appropriation of the pattern of non-communicating voices.

The study of dialogue in drama has yielded the most interesting results when the text is ancient enough to be problematic, or when it is poetically fine, complex, or highly sophisticated.[1] The best study of dialogue in the field of Austrian comedy is Ansgar Hillach's *Die Dramatisierung des komischen Dialogs: Figur und Rolle bei Nestroy* (Munich 1967). The study of Nestroy's dialogue is rewarding because of its sophistication and the variety of his perspectives. But Nestroy too is aware of tradition, and it is interesting therefore to move further back and look at the factors governing the conduct of dialogue in some examples of the simpler, less sophisticated kind of Austrian comedy, in order to isolate certain conventions capable of being handed down and repeated with modifications in later developments.

The kind of comedy which is written for and around the Hanswurst figure (or the *komische Figur* or the *Lustigmacher*) is a string of proliferating situations, loosely connected with a simple *agon* (for example young lovers kept apart by a blocking character) — all this to give the *komische Figur* opportunities to manoeuvre, or to intrigue, or to disrupt and confuse, often involving swift changes of role and costume. This may not look very promising material for close analysis. It is questionable whether anyone would want to analyse in great detail the kind of dialogue one might meet in a Stranitzky comedy modelled on a *Haupt- und Staatsaktion* plot, such as the *Triumph römischer Tugend und Tapferkeit oder Gordianus der Große*, subtitled *Mit Hanswurst dem lächerlichen Liebes-Ambassadeur, curiösen Befehlshaber, vermeinten Toten, ungeschickten Mörder, gezwungenen Spion, und was noch mehr die Komödie selbst erklären wird*. Again, in the *Kasperliaden* the dialogue must have been invented to show off the specialities of the Kasperl figure within situations where he was helpless and endlessly teased by the magic spirit world, the opportunities created being only partly verbal as many of the *lazzi* would be extended in mime. However, a cardinal feature of such comedies is what can be called aerated dialogue, necessary for lightness and speed of exchange and essential for the skills of farce, especially for the handling of the *lazzi* of fear, mock death, and mock ghostly revival, not to speak of farcical exposition. The lively rhymed dialogue in short lines for the libretto of the comic opera *Der neue Krumme Teufel* takes three pages and 105 lines to exhaust the command of Arnoldus, Fiametta's guardian, to fetch Fiametta and the refusal of Bernardon to do so (DL I, 87–90). This is aerated dialogue indeed, with little literary content, but a great many words, as is necessary for comic libretto style. It is made up of repetition, repliques in a simple encounter between the commanding voice of a blocking character on the one hand, and on the other, the disobedient voice of a stumbling-block to the blocking character, relieved in the middle by contrasting arias. Such dialogue is designed for musical accompaniment. *Megära, die förchterliche Hexe* begins with a piece of stylized aerated dialogue on the theme of love:

LEANDER: Ach ich unglückseliger!
HANSWURST: Ach unglückseliges Malheur! ach malheureuses Unglück!
LEANDER: Ach! grausame Liebe, wie sehr quällest du deine Anhänger!
HANSWURST: Ach! bestialische Liebe, was machest du in der Residenz des hans-
wurstischen Herzen für Aufruhren?

(DL I, 135)

This introduces another important feature of such comedies, the pair of characters counterpointed against each other in verbal style. In the *Hanswurstiaden* this takes the form of a contrast between high and low style, the Hanswurst speaking for the "natural man" with a bluntness that defies the conventions, and a naive self-confidence ignorant of the effect it is having. So there is a nice counterpointing of Leander's high-flown letter asking for the hand of Angela and Hanswurst's letter asking for the hand of Colombina, both of them read out by Odoardo, Angela's father, giving the audience the two voices comically distanced in extended parallel.

The corresponding pair of female characters, Angela and Colombina, are also endowed with contrasting voices and styles, Angela referring to her love in the seventh scene in the following terms:

[. . .] es koste was es wolle, so muß ich Leandern besitzen; ohne ihm ist mir mein Leben zuwider, an ihm ganz allein finde ich alle jene Eigenschaften, die mein Herz vergnügen können [. . .]

and Colombina:

Sie sind so verliebt, wie eine Katze; haben sie ein wenig Geduld, ich werde trachten mit meinem allerliebsten Hanswurst zu reden; dieß ist ein Mensch zum fressen, und wenn ich mit ihm rede, so springt mein Herz vor lauter Freuden in die Höhe.

(DL I, 146–147)

These pairs with counter-voices are elaborated all through the history of Austrian comedy until in Nestroy we have complicated patterns of contrast and parody, as for example the play with the utterances of Hermann and Kilian Blau in *Der Färber und sein Zwillingsbruder*, or the attempted imitation of the sophisticated by the naive voice with Herr von Löwenschlucht and Peter in the same comedy. Nestroy can also use to great effect a pattern of two voices, one true to the fiction (e.g. Salome in *Der Talisman*), and one both inside the fiction and distancing it at the same time (Titus).[2]

The contrast of voices is sharpened in the stylizing device of dialogue in alternate lines (stichomythia in verse plays); this normally rational ordering and proportioning in sharp exchange, often lending itself to debate or angry encounter, and nearly always introduced at moments of high tension, is adapted in the early forms of comedy to the familiar contrast within parallel of high and low tone:

LEANDER: [. . .] Angebettete Angela! —
HANSWURST: Verfluchte Colombina! —
LEANDER: Weil ich in meinem Leben dich nicht besitzen kann —
HANSWURST: Ich wolt, daß ich dich in meinem Leben nicht gesehen hätt, aber weil ich dich gesehen hab —
LEANDER: So will ich aus Treue für dich, weil dich in eines anderen Armen zu sehen mir unmöglich ist —
HANSWURST: So muß ich schandenhalber mit meinem rasenden Herrn —
LEANDER: Meinen Geist aufgeben.
HANSWURST: Mein Geist erschiessen lassen.

(*Megära, die förchterliche Hexe* I, 11) (DL I, 154)

We can contrast Nestroy's use of this device in *Der Unbedeutende* for a stylized sending-up of Puffmann's womanizing habits, in which the aim is mockery rather than simple contrast or tension:

SEEWALD: Wo könnte er da sein?
ALTHOF: Beim Kaufmann —
MASSENGOLD: Der eine Cousine hat, die —
SEEWALD: Oder beim Stadtrichter —
MASSENGOLD: Der zwei Töchter hat —
LOCKERFELD: Oder beim Revisor —
MASSENGOLD: Der drei Frauen hat —
PACKENDORF: Drei Frauen?
MASSENGOLD: Das heißt, zwei tote und eine lebendige.
LOCKERFELD: Da kömmt er gerade wegen der lebendigen — ich gehe hin.
SEEWALD: Und ich geh' zum Stadtrichter.
ALTHOF: Und ich zum Kaufmann.
LOCKERFELD: Einer von uns muß ihn finden.

(I, 9) (GW IV, 526)

A dominant aspect in the dialogue of the early types of comedy is the contrast between the characters' two voices. The voice within the fictional situation allows of shading in individual speech (without necessarily any great psychological depth) or of characterizing speeches and songs as the characters don different masks or roles for the *lazzi* and practical jokes. On the other hand the characters are given a univocal voice in the moralizing sections, where there appears to be a break with the fiction and a distancing of the figure. This distancing is a step towards the more sophisticated forms of later comedy, for example Colombina's aside to the audience at the end of *Megära, die förchterliche Hexe*:

> Ach Frauenzimmer! seht doch mein Exempel an!
> Bleibt eurem Schatz getreu, sonst kriegt ihr keinen Mann.

(DL I, 204)

When we reach Nestroy, the univocal voice achieves a different, non-moralizing effect in *Der Talisman*:

> Wir sein nix als — wir sein nix als —
> Narren des Schicksals

and

> Mit ein' orndlichen Mag'n —
> Man kann alles ertrag'n,
> Kann man alles ertrag'n.

(III, 11) (GW III, 493–494)

In comedies where a world of magic and the realm of spirits is evoked, characters from the human world have to talk to supernatural beings, and supernatural beings have to make themselves understood to human creatures. This is a particularly engaging study in the *Besserungsstücke*, where spirits condescend to speak in familiar terms in order to be understood, resorting to their high-flown style at moments of solemnity or threat. Thus the entrance of the supernatural being is often marked by an aerated dialogue of recognition, the hero posing questions — Who are you? where do you come from? — and the spirit dawdling with enigmatic answers in a brief but well-intentioned cat-and-mouse game. So in Karl Meisl's *Der lustige Fritz* we have a rudimentary sketch for what is later developed with more skill and irony in Raimund's comedies:

FRITZ: Was ist das? wo ist mein Weib hingekommen? wer sind Sie? wie kommen Sie daher? Was wollen Sie? warum —
SATIRE: Ich bin deine Freundinn, die dich glücklich machen will.
FRITZ: Ist's möglich! (*für sich*.) Ein hübscher Kerl bin ich, sie hat sich in mich verliebt, das kann sich machen, ich kenn' mehrere junge Herren, die recht prächtig auf Kosten ihrer Geliebten leben. — Darf ich fragen um das, was ich nicht weiß?
SATIRE: Du wirst alles erfahren.
FRITZ: Das ist ein liebes Geschöpf, das! Kennen Sie mich denn schon lange?
SATIRE: Seit du existirst, hab' ich dich genau beobachtet.
FRITZ: Und im Stillen geliebt, da widersteh ein eisernes Herz, aber kein so weicher Patzen, wie das meinige ist!
SATIRE: So war es nicht gemeynt, auf eine andere Art will ich dich auf den Weg zu deinem Glücke führen, wenn deine Brust nicht von alltäglichen Zweifeln beengt ist; hast du Muth, mir zu folgen?
FRITZ: Wenn's zum Glück geht, wie der Alexander!

(II, 4) (DL IV, 58)

Gunther Wiltschko's remarks on "Das Erkennungsspiel"[3] show how Raimund varies and enlivens the "Fragespiel", for example by the coquettish answers of Hoffnung in *Der Diamant des Geisterkönigs*, by Wurzel's pretence of understanding what Jugend is referring to in the fine example of "Erkennungsspiel" in *Der Bauer als Millionär*, and by Lottchen's inability to take words except at their face value when Zufriedenheit addresses her in the same play. Even though the audience would probably recognize at a glance all these allegorical figures with their emblems, nonetheless Raimund loves and uses the old theatrical device, and the audience of course expects it, revelling in the delightful feeling of superior knowledge which the hero has to stumble after. Nestroy's mode is different. He exposes the mechanism of allegories and thus distances the scene from sentiment. An encounter in Meisl's *Der lustige Fritz* can be placed side by side with one from Nestroy's *Der konfuse Zauberer oder Treue und Flatterhaftigkeit* to reveal the difference:

ARMUTH: Da iß —
FRITZ: Abgenagte Beine soll ich essen, ich bin ja kein Hund.
ARMUTH: Ich nähre mich damit.
FRITZ: Wenn's nur gut anschlagt.

ARMUTH: So trink halt wenigstens!
FRITZ: Was soll ich denn trinken?
ARMUTH: Thränen!
FRITZ: Ich hab' keinen Durst; ich will mich an die andere Person wenden. Die tragt einen Voile nach der Mode, die wird g'wiß redseliger seyn. Sagen Sie mir, können Sie mir auch keine Auskunft geben?
SCHANDE: O ja — Seufzer!
FRITZ: Das ist zum tollwerden! Thränen und Seufzer, jetzt werd' ich's bald glauben, daß ich wieder auf der alten Welt bin, wo Seufzer und Thränen an der Tagesordnung sind.

(Der lustige Fritz II, 18) (DL IV, 74)

MELANCHOLIE: Du stehst nicht allein da.
SCHMAFU: Wer bist du?
MELANCHOLIE: Ich bin die Melancholie.
SCHMAFU: Was willst du?
MELANCHOLIE: Dich nach Hause begleiten.
SCHMAFU: Ha, Melancholie, du kommst nicht mehr von meiner Seiten.
MELANCHOLIE: Reich mir die Hand!
SCHMAFU: Da! (*Er gibt ihr die Hand und sagt plötzlich mit ganz herabgestimmtem Wesen.*) So! Jetzt bin ich ganz Melancholikus. (*Für sich.*) Das ist eine schöne Charge! (*Laut.*) Weil wir jetzt beisammen bleiben, wir zwei, so sag' mir, wie alt bist du?
MELANCHOLIE: Am selben Tage, wo die beiden Zwillingsbrüder Oh und Ach zur Welt kamen, wurde ich geboren.
SCHMAFU: Das find' ich in keinem Kalender. Von was lebst du?
MELANCHOLIE: Vom überspannten Gefühle des Unglücks.
SCHMAFU: Aha! Das hab' ich gleich gesehen, daß sie eine überspannte Person ist, denn sie ist weit über eine Spann' lang. — Was trinkst du?
MELANCHOLIE: Tränen.
SCHMAFU: Ein waßriges Zeug, da bringst du's 's ganze Jahr auf kein' Rausch. Und was ißt du?
MELANCHOLIE: Seufzer.
SCHMAFU: Das ist ein schönes Fressen, das ist noch über die spanischen Wind'.

(Der konfuse Zauberer I, 9) (GW I, 423–424)

As Austrian comedy develops, so these allegories tend to go into the language instead of appearing on stage, so that in *Der Alpenkönig und der Menschenfeind* only Astragalus communicates in person with human beings, and the old "Erkennungsspiel" has been replaced with a more sophisticated method of recognition. Raimund also introduces a special effect in his presentation of Longimanus and his court in *Der Diamant des Geisterkönigs* in the parodistic *Verwienerung* mode. He reverses the traditional contrast between high-flown spirit language and human speech by making Longimanus talk Viennese and giving him the good-humoured Hanswurst trick of cutting everybody down to size in the dialogue. This provides special comic reductive effects in the conduct of the dialogue.

Longimanus is guaranteed to lower the tone of his court, of Zephises, and of Eduard who has a penchant for romantic rhetoric, just as Florian is there to lower the tone or parody Eduard's rhetoric with equally ridiculous effect in his duologues with the hero. The traditional counterpoint in dialogue of high rhetoric and undercutting or parodying style is thus doubled by the *Verwienerung* of Longimanus.

Leander and the Hanswurst, Eduard and Florian are typical master-and-servant pairs whose dialogue as it were faces the same way. Masters and servants alternate in their repliques, boxing and coxing over against a third person, with the servant figure consciously or unconsciously reducing or parodying the words of his master. This can lead to wonderfully comic effects in the dialogue, as in the following scene from Nestroy's *Der Färber und sein Zwillingsbruder*:

LÖWENSCHLUCHT: Ich bin der Bruder des unglücklichen Fraüleins von Löwen-
schlucht.
KILIAN: Was geht mich der Fraülein ihr Unglück an?
LÖWENSCHLUCHT: Sehr viel, denn ich bin hier, es zu rächen. Sie haben ihr Herz
betört!
PETER (*dreinredend*): Die dreiunddreißigjährige Unschuld verblendet!
LÖWENSCHLUCHT (*fortfahrend*): Sie haben mit glatter Rede —
PETER (*wie oben*): Den Frieden der reinen Seele getrübt —
LÖWENSCHLUCHT (*sieht* PETER *scharf an*).
PETER (*dadurch etwas eingeschüchtert*): Und die Ruhe des Cherubs gemordet, hab'
ich noch sag'n wollen.

(II, 16) (SW x, 236–237)

This is based on the familiar deflating function of the Hanswurst, elaborated by a beautiful touch of "Unzulänglichkeitskomik".

In Nestroy's *Nur Ruhe!* a whole battery of effects is achieved by a grouping of characters who all face the same way in dialogue with a passive victim, Anton Schafgeist, who wants nothing more than peaceful retirement and is as it were attacked by hornets — the Hornissl family. This makes for a combination of dialogue with farcical mime, and at the same time gives Nestroy the opportunity to lampoon ridiculous speech habits. So, for example, two kinds of pretentious language vie with each other when the play-acting Leokadia, whose imitation of the widow Marloff in Lessing's play is heightened by her adoptive father's running commentary, shares a scene with the foppish Laffberger:

ROCHUS (*mit* LEOKADIA *zur Mitte eintretend*): Da sind wir schon! (*Zu* LEOKADIA).
Siehst, das ist der vortreffliche Herr!
LEOKADIA (*zu* SCHAFGEIST): Gnädiger Herr, ich konnte nicht umhin — ich bin
gekommen —
ROCHUS: Red', Leokadia, red', wenn dir auch 's G'fühl die Wort' erstickt, red' nur
zu!

LAFFBERGER (*sie lorgnettierend*): Eine nicht unhübsche Erscheinung!
LEOKADIA: Ich bin gekommen, den innigsten Dank auszusprechen, gnädiger
    Herr —
ROCHUS (*zu* SCHAFGEIST): Bemerken Sie, wie ihr die Stimme schwankt?
LEOKADIA: Für die zarte Schonung, für die großartige Milde —
SCHAFGEIST (*etwas freundlicher werdend*): Na, na, zu was denn das alles —
LEOKADIA (*fortfahrend*): Für die edle Nachsicht, mit welcher Sie meinem Ziehvater
    seinen Fehltritt verziehn —
ROCHUS (*zu* SCHAFGEIST): Hören Sie, wie ihr der Vortrag bebt?
LEOKADIA (*wie oben*): Sie haben sich ein Denkmal der Dankbarkeit in unserm
    Herzen erbaut —
SCHAFGEIST (*freundlicher*): Es ist schon gut, mein Kind!
LEOKADIA (*wie oben*): Auf welchem stets die Flamme lodern wird — welche — um
    nie zu verlöschen — es mögen Jahre in den Schoß der Ewigkeit —
ROCHUS (*zu* SCHAFGEIST): Hören Sie, wie die Schluchzer mit die Konstruktionen
    raufen, das is Gefühl! (*Sich die Augen trocknend.*) Es is ein gutes Kind!
LAFFBERGER: Kind, sagt er, sie ist eben nicht unjung, aber Kind — [. . .] Nicht
    unschlank, diese Taille, ihr Benehmen ist auch nicht ohne unlinkischem
    Wesen, aber zugleich nicht frei von Unnatur.
ROCHUS: Recht ein klares Urteil, das scheint kein Unaff' zu sein.
                                        (I, 14) (GW IV, 224–225)

All the examples of early Austrian comedies so far referred to make very sparing use of asides, and advances in technical accomplishment in this respect can best be illustrated by pointing to Raimund and Nestroy. Here they rain thick and fast, especially for instance in Raimund's *Der Alpenkönig und der Menschenfeind* and Nestroy's *Der Talisman*, for the obvious reason that the more complicated the intrigue, the more opportunity there is for comment on the way it is going, either from within the fiction, or in a fiction-breaking manner; within the fictional situation such comment has often to be "für sich" or "beiseite" because the characters cannot confide in each other (Titus is playing a lone game) or because disguise imposes secrecy (Rappelkopf/Silberkern). Fiction-breaking asides, on the other hand, are free-ranging and do not have to be established by a situation. Puffmann, the intriguer in *Der Unbedeutende*, speaks all his asides from within the situation and to himself, not out to the audience. The only one that comes near to breaking the fiction is to be found a few pages from the end of the play, where Puffman is trying to wangle his way verbally out of his difficulties:

MASSENGOLD (*mit Staunen und einiger Rührung*): Mein Puffmann wollte sich
    entleiben und ein entseelter Leichnam werden!? — Ja, aber warum? —
PUFFMANN: Warum? (*Verlegen und verwirrt für sich.*) Bankrottes Hirn, fallt dir gar
    nichts ein? (*Zu* MASSENGOLD.) Aus — aus Verzweiflung!
MASSENGOLD: Wie das?
PUFFMANN (*für sich*): Wegen was bin ich denn verzweifelt?
                                        (III, 34) (GW IV, 599)

But many examples of both kinds can be found in *Der Talisman*, and the coincidence of both is seen in *Eine Wohnung ist zu vermieten* when Gundlhuber ends a quarrel with his wife with an aside, "Jetzt muß ich's wieder gut machen", adding the distancing, "Länger als elf Minuten soll der eheliche Friede nicht gestört sein" (I, 8) (*Stücke 12*, 15). The ridiculously pedantic "elf Minuten" gives the edge to the free-ranging generalization.

There is a wonderfully flexible use of asides in *Der Alpenkönig und der Menschenfeind*. They highlight Rappelkopf's gratuitous insults in his first exchanges, showing him locked inside his own character, whereas Lischen's confident asides are of the kind that can be more pointedly directed to the audience. Habakuk's asides contrast most effectively with these in the frustrated or short-circuited exchanges with Rappelkopf, who constantly bites off Habakuk's sentences before he has finished them and ends them for him in a totally wrong direction so that the helpless servant has to resort to asides to vent his frustration. But the most skilful use of asides in this comedy is displayed in the mirror-image scenes where Astragalus/Rappelkopf imitates Rappelkopf, notching up his impossible behaviour even higher in parody form, and where Rappelkopf/Silberkern is made into observer. The asides do not even have to be stage-directed here, as Astragalus/Rappelkopf is totally impervious to Rappelkopf/Silberkern's reactions. Only when the two characters communicate directly are the asides noted in stage directions. And in the scenes with his family, with August and the servants, it is the asides that show the needle of Rappelkopf/Silberkern's emotions wavering now towards anger and distaste, now towards enlightenment and sympathy, until the incongruous gap between his persona and his real self is bridged.

These are but a few examples of the way in which stylizing and abstracting features in dialogue have been modified by the tradition. In a further study we need to consider the critical point that Nestroy, in creating the most highly developed sophisticated form of Austrian comedy, had three factors to accommodate: first, the residue of old techniques of stylization (seen for example in the aerated dialogue of Cajetan Balsam in *Eine Wohnung ist zu vermieten*), and old-established patterns of farce (*lazzi* such as Gabriel as baby in *Der alte Mann mit der jungen Frau*); secondly, the complex play of his perspectives (as in *Der Talisman*); and thirdly, the preservation of realistically conceived human relationships — what Hillach calls the "zwischenmenschlicher Bezug" — which is clearly evident in such a comedy as *Der Unbedeutende*. In spite of its excellence, Hillach's book on the comic dialogue in Nestroy's plays does not ask how these three factors relate to one another, whether there are visible joins (*Stilbruch*), whether they matter, and how comic dialogue can be made to move about easily in sophisticated, playful modern dress, while at the same time accommodating to realism in the theatre and occasionally letting its Hanswurst colours drop out of its sleeve.

Zusammenfassung

Die Dialogführung in der Komödie wird von ganz anderen herkömmlichen Regeln beherrscht als die in der Tragödie. Die besonderen Stilmittel bewirken, daß die Personen sich leichter von Handlung und Situation loslösen, statt an sie gebunden zu sein, wodurch die Regeln des Miteinanderredens und der zwischenmenschlichen Beziehungen durchbrochen werden. Ziel dieser Arbeit ist es, diese herkömmlichen Regeln anhand von Beispielen aus den früheren Formen der österreichischen Komödie darzulegen und aufzuzeigen, wie sie in späteren, komplizierteren Formen beibehalten und verändert werden. Die folgenden Stilmittel werden untersucht: "lockerer" Dialog; das Nebeneinander von gegensätzlichen Sprachebenen, die Hand in Hand gehen mit Gegensatzpaaren in der Handlung; Dialoge, in welchen einzeilige Äußerungen in schnellem Wechsel aufeinanderfolgen; der Unterschied zwischen dem situationsgebundenen Wort und der von der Situation losgelösten und verallgemeinernden Aussage; das traditionsgebundene Muster für die Begegnung des Menschen mit der Geisterwelt, einschließlich der Entwicklung des Erkennungsspiels; die parodistische Doppelwirkung der Äußerungen von Herr und Diener; die satirische Behandlung sprachlicher Angewohnheiten; und schließlich das Beiseitereden, wie es in den Komödien von Raimund und Nestroy äußerst geschickt verwendet und vervollkommnet wird. Die Auswirkung herkömmlicher Stilmittel auf den Dialog in Stücken mit realistischem und sozialkritischem Bezug, wie sie bei Nestroy vorkommen (und ob sie hier zu einem Stilbruch führen), könnte der Gegenstand einer weiteren Arbeit sein.

2

Ian F. Roe

RAIMUND'S "VIELE SCHÖNE WORTE"

After seeing a performance of Grillparzer's *Der Traum ein Leben*, Raimund asserted that in his own *Der Bauer als Millionär* he had treated essentially the same subject, but he concluded somewhat resignedly: "Nur die vielen schönen Worte habe ich nicht; die möchten s' do draußen a nit versteh'n. Es is ewig schad um mi'!"[1] By the time *Der Traum ein Leben* appeared, Raimund's own work after *Der Bauer als Millionär* had testified to his attempts to elevate or refine his language; the aim of this paper is to consider his conscious search for a more literary style, and in particular to inquire into the extent to which his adoption of this more literary idiom betrays a debt not only to the language but also to the ideals of the eighteenth century.

Raimund's comment that his *Vorstadt* public would not appreciate a more elevated style is undoubtedly a resigned assessment of the mixed or even hostile reception accorded to plays such as *Die gefesselte Phantasie* and *Die unheilbringende Zauberkrone*. When *Moisasurs Zauberfluch* was first produced, *Der Sammler* referred to it as Raimund's best work (*Wke.* v/i, 377), but on the whole critical opinion has rejected these three plays as misguided attempts to emulate the repertoire of the Burgtheater; Friedrich Sengle speaks of "der mißglückte Griff nach Burg-theaterehren", whilst according to Hans Weigel the defect of *Die gefesselte Phantasie* is that it contains all the "viele schöne Worte, die er [Raimund] nicht hatte und doch nicht lassen konnte".[2] While on the other hand few would agree with Bäuerle that Raimund's first two plays are his best (*Wke.* v/i, 514), there is an explicit or implicit belief that *Der Alpenkönig und der Menschenfeind* and *Der Verschwender* are Raimund's masterpieces because they reveal at least a partial return to the "boden-ständig" elements of his earlier work. Plays such as *Die gefesselte Phantasie*, by comparison, are seen as aberrations that prevented Raimund achieving his true potential: "Ferdinand Raimund wollte Schiller und Shakespeare sein, so konnte er nicht ganz Ferdinand Raimund werden", according to Weigel.[3]

Raimund himself, however, rejected any attempt to remove the serious or tragic elements in him, believing that without them he would no longer be Raimund.[4] The desire to be Schiller or Shakespeare should in turn be seen as part of "Raimund als Ganzes", without which he might well have been content to produce better-than-average *Zauberspiele* along the lines of his first two plays. Why, one might for example ask, was *Der Alpenkönig*

13

und der Menschenfeind so successful, not only in Vienna but also in other German lands and even in London? — Was this merely because of a return to traditional Viennese forms, or because of the philosophical framework in which the action is set?

Raimund's "viele schöne Worte" should not be dismissed so lightly, but the question remains: what are they? They are usually considered in somewhat general terms of high-flown language: poetic images, verse and metre, and the much greater use of High German. That is undoubtedly one aspect, but one that is not easily defined objectively: a line of intended or potential sublimity may be one man's pathos, another man's bathos. There is, however, another aspect of Raimund's intention that has received little or no critical attention: to what extent does he make use not so much of the style but of the ideas and philosophical terms of many of the plays performed at the court theatre in Vienna? Can one find evidence to support Urs Helmensdorfer's description of Raimund as "ein welt-fremder Priester des Wahren, Guten und Schönen"?[5] Do Raimund's plays reflect the themes of goodness and virtue, beauty, truth and nobility, and in particular the stress on humanity that is so central to the theatre of the Enlightenment and of Classicism, and which is also taken over by writers such as Grillparzer and H. J. Collin, by critics such as Schreyvogel, and incidentally by many of the contemporary critics of Raimund's plays?

As far as Raimund's first play is concerned, the answer to these questions is a simple "No". The few suggestions of literary or poetic language are immediately debunked, and Hassar's offer to express his subservience in verse is quickly refused (II, 1). The picture has not greatly changed in *Der Diamant des Geisterkönigs*. By contrast with *Der Barometer-macher auf der Zauberinsel*, there is at least a genuine quotation from Schiller, "Das ist das Los des Schönen auf der Erde", but this is introduced with an entirely comic effect in mind, and similarly the picture of "die Insel der Wahrheit und der Sittsamkeit" (II, 10) ruled over by Veritatius is a satirical one which seems to suggest that repeated talk of such virtues is a sign that they are in fact lacking. Amine and by implication also characters such as Eduard and Florian do possess both truthfulness and morals, but these clearly lie not in abstract ideals but "im Innersten des Herzens" (II, 16). Any serious element in the play, whether philosophical or didactic, is slight and entirely subordinate to the comedy and theatricality of the piece.

That is no longer the case in *Der Bauer als Millionär*. "Dieses neue Produkt ruht auf einem ernsteren Elemente" was the comment of the reviewer in the *Theaterzeitung* (*Wke.* v/i, 303). Certainly the personified vices and virtues may have been meant to add a certain philosophical weight to the proceedings, but such allegorical characters were not new to the popular stage, however much Raimund endows them with a greater degree of individualization than, for example, in Meisl's *Der lustige Fritz;* real depth of meaning is more obviously conveyed in Raimund's play in the character of Fortunatus Wurzel, who sings of the stages of human life as the courses of a meal and then himself visibly passes from youth to old age in a few brief moments. Overall, however, there is still no attempt to convey a deeper meaning through impressive vocabulary; the stress on peace and calm is common in the play as it was in the late eighteenth century, but by the time Raimund was writing it had long since become a cliché of the Viennese *Besserungsstück.* The greater degree of finely judged characterization, primarily in the figure of Wurzel, undoubtedly lifts the play above the level of Bäuerle, Gleich, and Meisl; but Wurzel is still very much the plaything of magical forces that grant and take away both physical and financial health, and it is difficult to equate his fate with the process of inner psychological development that we see in Rustan in *Der Traum ein Leben,* the play with which Raimund's has so often been compared. *Biedermeier* contentedness, personified on stage, does seem a universal panacea in *Der Bauer als Millionär,* rather than a very individual solution, as it is to Rustan's discovery of his own inadequacies.

Nevertheless, the première of *Der Bauer als Millionär* prompted one journal to write that Raimund "hat sich durch dieses Stück zum wirklichen Dichter gestempelt" (*Wke.* v/i, 321). Raimund may have had doubts as far as that particular play was concerned, but he set out subsequently to achieve his own ideals of "Dichtertum".[6] *Die gefesselte Phantasie* was already finished by the time of the première of *Der Bauer als Millionär,* but Raimund hesitated to have it performed. In the character of Nachtigall, Raimund presents a rejection of his own earlier work as coarse and rather vulgar. His new play was meant to reveal "Einfachheit" (*Wke.* IV, 371) and to be "ein unschuldiges Gedicht" (*Wke.* v/ii, 725). Most of the action, if that is the right word in the context, takes place on the island of poetry and features a Schillerian contrast between what is noble, beautiful, and aesthetic on the one hand and what is low and common on the other. Without the presence of poetic imagination, the world seems to Amphio to be one "in der das Edle trügt und nur Gemeines sich bewährt" (II, 8), it is a world of characters such as Nachtigall, who is not so much human as "Übergang vom Affen zu den Menschen" (II, 2), and who is later dismissed as "unempfindlich Tier" (II, 11). Poetic imagination, however, can produce "der höchsten Schönheit Bild" (I, 12). The iambic metre of Amphio's words and the Saxon genitives of Phantasie are symptomatic of the loftier style of certain sections of the play, although it is clear that Phantasie was not intended as a uniformly serious character of sublimity and pathos. In her first scenes she chats to the audience about her task as a match-maker, jokingly swears "bei Schillers Haupt, in dem ich stolz gethront" (I, 12), and speaks of her relief at having a day off from writing verse, as though she were one of the many craftsman figures of the Viennese stage — although whether her language can really be termed "ungezwungne Prosa" (I, 12) seems debatable. Raimund was no doubt aware of the need to compromise, and the play is not as "einfach" or "unschuldig" as he might have wished. There are certainly many Schillerian echoes,[7] but there is little use of Schiller's philosophical vocabulary apart from the few instances already noted.

At least in that respect, *Moisasurs Zauberfluch* is a much clearer departure from the earlier plays. Here Raimund is undoubtedly concerned with themes of good and evil, virtue and nobility, duty and morality, and with the theme of humanity in general. This last theme, briefly touched upon in *Die gefesselte Phantasie* in the character of Nachtigall, is much more fully employed in the context of Gluthahn, who thinks he is "ein guter Mensch", "ein edler Kerl" (I, 8), but who is exposed as "gemein", as "ein Unmensch", an animal without a human heart (I, 3; I, 6). This contrast provides a considerable amount of the play's comedy. Gluthahn's wife tells him, "du bist kein Mensch, du bist ein Krokodil" (I, 9); his treatment of Alzinde leads her to conclude "nicht Menschen hausen hier, Dämonen sind es" (I, 6), so that when Hans and Mirzel appear on the scene, Alzinde makes to run off with the horrified cry "Menschen!" (I, 7). Alzinde's own basic goodness is revealed when she resolves to assist the apparently sick Gluthahn: "er ist ein böser Mensch zwar — aber doch ein Mensch" (I, 9).

Clearly Raimund is here at least as much concerned with achieving a comic effect as with any deep philosophical investigation of the concept of humanity. Nevertheless he had previously found many ways of raising a laugh, whether by puns on Viennese street-names or by poking fun at serious ideas, as in *Der Diamant des Geisterkönigs*, so that what is important in *Moisasurs Zauberfluch* is that the moral content of a term such as "Mensch" is left unquestioned even if an essentially comic effect is the principal aim. Certainly the contrast between the coarseness and inhumanity of Gluthahn and the noble and virtuous humanity of Alzinde and Hoanghu is central to the play's meaning, and the treatment of the theme of "Tugend" is entirely serious. The concept is highlighted in the very first scene, set outside the temple of virtue which is adorned with the inscription, "Wer sich der Tugend weiht, hat nie des Bösen Macht zu scheuen". Alzinde constantly insists on her devotion to the cause of virtue, of "der Tugend reine Sitten" (I, 9), and after her somewhat undeserved fall into misery and suffering, her husband Hoanghu is presented as one whose virtue and selflessness will make him his wife's saviour and provide an example of "das Edle und Erhabene" (I, 12). The stress on virtue is most obvious in the words and very presence of "der Genius der Tugend", who speaks the play's final words in praise of Alzinde and Hoanghu and their great virtue:

> Heil der Tugend, die auf Erde
> Zählet solch erhabnes Paar,
> Das ein edles Herz bewährte
> In so schrecklicher Gefahr. [. . .]
> Groß kann nur der Nachruhm klingen,
> Wenn er sich durch Tugend krönt.
>
> (II, 10)

It is also the "Genius der Tugend" who spells out the philosophical framework of the play in the first act:

> Nur ein Kampfplatz ist die Welt
> Und das Böse hingestellt,
> Daß es mit dem Guten streite
> Und der Hölle werd zur Beute.
> Beide treten in die Schranken
> Dieser unruhvollen Welt.
> Tugend darf im Kampfe wanken,
> Eigne Schuld ists, wenn sie fällt.
>
> (I, 10)

According to one critic, "das könnte ebensogut bei Goethe stehen",[8] but that rather overlooks the essentially black-and-white contrast of good and evil, of virtue and vice, and the rather moralizing view that virtue should automatically triumph, all of which seems more in keeping with Enlightenment ideas than with Goethian Classicism. Alzinde is very mindful of her virtuousness, which she constantly insists on and to which she has sacrificed the joys of her youth:

> Ich hab alle Freuden meiner Jugend
> Aufgeopfert für den Ruhm der Tugend
> Und erwarte meinen Lohn
> Einst an deinem Himmelsthron
>
> (I, 6)

— sentiments that are more reminiscent of a character from one of Collin's plays than of Goethe's ideas of instinctive and natural virtue. Also, despite the insistence at the end that virtue has triumphed through the "edles Herz" of Alzinde and Hoanghu, it is difficult to agree with the claim that the problems within the play are solved by human volition, with the various spirits playing merely a supporting role.[9] For the present investigation such an approach is tempting, but it must be conceded that the action of the play remains to a considerable extent in the hands of supernatural forces who subject human beings to arbitrary tests of their virtue and use them as examples of behaviour for their fellow men. Here we are still in the realms of the Baroque or, to be more precise, in that rather strange mixture of Baroque and Enlightenment that is such a common feature of many products of the Viennese *Volkstheater*. The test of Alzinde's virtue is mechanically and arbitrarily engineered, and the spirits of virtue set out to defeat the evil forces represented by the devilish caricature Moisasur. Nevertheless, having been chosen by "der große Meister" to save Alzinde, the "Genius der Tugend" effectively hands over responsibility to Hoanghu, whose unselfish offer to die in Alzinde's stead prepares the way for the curse to be removed; and the real battle between good and evil is arguably fought out not between Moisasur and the "Genius der Tugend", but between Alzinde and Gluthahn, between "Mensch" and "Unmensch". If *Die gefesselte Phantasie* had seen something of a compromise between comic and serious, then in *Moisasurs Zauberfluch* there is one between a humanistic message of human independence and a more traditional treatment of man as subject to higher metaphysical forces.

Certainly, however, the philosophical content of *Moisasurs Zauberfluch* is more important than that in earlier plays, and this is only one of the ways in which it represents a further departure from Raimund's early work. In certain respects *Der Alpenkönig und der Menschenfeind* returns to the comic traditions of Raimund's first three plays, but without losing the more philosophical elements of *Die gefesselte Phantasie* and *Moisasurs Zauberfluch*. Futhermore the inconsistencies of the latter play have largely been overcome. The destiny of the human protagonists is now firmly in their own hands; we are now concerned not, as in Gleich's *Berggeist*, Bäuerle's *Wien, Paris, London und Constantinopel*, or to a slightly lesser extent in Raimund's own *Der Bauer als Millionär*, with a change of heart enforced by supernatural machinations, but with the inner process of awareness in the central character Rappelkopf. He is "ein Narr, der die Menschen verkennt" (II, 4), but his greatest guilt lies in his lack of self-awareness, which verges on schizophrenia. The theme of self-awareness, self-knowledge, was scarcely new on the Viennese stage, but Raimund's treatment of Rappelkopf's behaviour reveals extremes of self-hatred and "Zerrissenheit" that are far in excess of any hackneyed demand to "know thyself". In addition, the theme of development towards self-knowledge is couched very much in the terms of eighteenth-century idealism. Rappelkopf's behaviour in the first half of the play merits the descriptions "Halbmensch" and "Tier", he reveals "des Tieres unbarmherzige Roheit" (I, 21). He lacks both feeling and reason, and Astragalus admonishes him "du hast dich ausgeschlossen aus der Menschen Kreis" and warns him:

> Und wirst du liebend nicht dein Herz zur Menschheit wenden,
> So sollst du wildes Tier in Waldesnacht hier enden!
>
> (I, 21)

At the end of the play, Rappelkopf himself realizes, "ich war ein unvernünftig Tier" (III, 14).

A human being should be "mild" and "edel"; instead Rappelkopf is "wild" and "roh" — the standard Classical epithets for sub-human behaviour, as also in Grillparzer's later treatment of the theme in *Weh dem, der lügt!*.[10] In his failure to recognize humanity in himself and others, Rappelkopf sinks to the level of primitive nature: he sees only the woods as "noble" and flees human environment and society. To a certain extent, Rappelkopf reflects Raimund's own sentiments, as for instance in the poem "An Gutenstein" of 1827:

> Und edle Wahrheit thronet nur
> Im Herzen kräftiger Natur.
> (*Wke.* III, 236)

In the play, however, such an isolated existence in the midst of nature is seen as inferior; any suggestion that the world of nature is on a par with human existence is instantly dismissed, as when Malchen envies the freedom of the birds: "glückliches beneidenswertes Tier! Wer kann dir deine Freiheit rauben?" (I, 5) — at which point the bird is shot out of the sky by Astragalus. Rappelkopf's misanthropy has its origins in one unfortunate experience; his fault lies in seeing that experience as symptomatic of humanity as a whole, rather than recognizing that human life is a complex mixture of what Astragalus calls "bös und gut Gesinnte" (I, 3).

If such a recognition sounds rather Goethian, then it is important also to stress that Rappelkopf's understanding of what Grillparzer's Bishop Gregor was to call "die buntverworrne Welt" (WA I/5, 269) is a result of "freies Handeln" (II, 1), of his own insight and actions, even if these actions are carried out for the time being by his double, the personification of the hatred and violence within his character. "Von selbst schließt mit der Menschheit er dann neu den Frieden", insists Astragalus, who himself merely engineers a situation in which Rappelkopf's independent recognition of human goodness can take place. Similarly in Goethe's *Faust*, the intervention of Mephisto with the Lord's agreement produces a situation in which Faust can more readily shake off his negative view of life and through his own actions acquire a fuller and more positive attitude to the human condition.

Such a parallel should not of course be pursued too far: *Faust II* had not yet appeared, and the contrast in character and intention between Astragalus and Mephistopheles is obvious. Nevertheless, *Der Alpenkönig und der Menschenfeind* is the play by Raimund in which the use of eighteenth-century terminology is most successfully integrated into a unified dramatic whole. In *Die unheilbringende Zauberkrone* it is difficult to speak of any part as being particularly integrated; there are altogether too many settings, too many kings and princes, and too many ludicrous and impossible conditions to be fulfilled. Also, as far as our present line of inquiry is concerned, the realm of "Menschen" has been replaced by allegorical and two-dimensional characters. Despite the continuing use of "edel" and "wild" to describe Ewald and Kreon on the one hand, Phalarius on the other, the kind of vocabulary we have been examining is used less frequently and less consistently than in the previous two plays. Simplicius is himself incapable of "schöne Worte" and mocks those who use them, as when Ewald speaks of the nobility of mankind (II, 12). Simplicius, to whom Ewald refers as "ein Tier", is a more positive character than Gluthahn or Nachtigall, but it is unclear whether he is meant as a foil for or as an antidote to the more pompous language of the other characters. Raimund's reaction to the play's failure suggests that he had a high opinion of the language employed, although it is rather more empty than in *Moisasurs Zauberfluch*. If the role of Ewald, representing "echte Poesie" (I, 7), has undoubted significance, then Raimund, as in *Die gefesselte Phantasie*, has failed to make it a viable theatrical subject, and the compromise between serious and comic or between "edel" and "gemein" elements seems as uneasy and as unsatisfactory as in the earlier play. Also the character of Octavian, content in his limited realm of peaceful *Biedermeier* isolation, seems a retrograde step when compared to *Der Alpenkönig und der Menschenfeind*; he certainly should not be compared to the very active and humane emperor Rudolf in Grillparzer's *König Ottokars Glück und Ende*.[11] At the end of the play we are informed that virtue has been rewarded, but compared to the characters in *Moisasurs Zauberfluch*, which ends with a similar message, Kreon has done little to deserve his good fortune, which he owes entirely to the magical powers of Lucina, even though he professes his desire to earn the people's love and loyalty without the aid of magic in future.

In *Der Verschwender* we are back again on human soil. Flottwell is very much the master of his own fate, and Cheristane is reduced almost entirely to a spectator who can do no more than reduce the disastrous effect of Flottwell's behaviour:

> Kein Fatum herrsch auf seinen Lebenswegen,
> Er selber bring sich Unheil oder Segen.
> Er selbst vermag sich nur allein zu warnen,
> Mit Unglück kann er selbst sich nur umgarnen,
> Und da er frei von allen Schicksalsketten,
> Kann ihn sein Ich auch nur von Schmach erretten.
> (I, 10)

At the end Flottwell realizes, "ich hab mich selbst von diesem Thron gestürzt" (III, 10). Flottwell's guilt lies in his excesses, despite or even because of his positive qualities of generosity, warmth, and kindness. Unlike Wolf, whose view of man and the world is uniformly negative, Flotwell is "edel", "großmütig", but he is also significantly "wild", a man of violent passions, as he himself admits and as is seen in the frequent stage directions such as "wild und heftig" (I, 13), "immer heftiger" (II, 8). In a letter to Friedrich Ludwig Schmidt in 1835, Raimund summed up this contrast in speaking of Flottwell's "zwar edles, aber zu wild leidenschaftliches Herz", writing in the same letter of "seine nicht immer aus wahrer Tugend hervorgehende Großmuth" (*Wke.* IV, 440). Whatever the motives for Flottwell's generosity, it is certainly taken to extremes that are seen to flout both moral and social conventions. As in Lessing's *Minna von Barnhelm* and as in many of Grillparzer's plays, Flottwell's failing lies in an excess of something that is essentially positive: "die meisten Laster sind eigentlich nur der Exzeß guter Eigenschaften", to borrow a comment from Grillparzer's diaries (WA II/8, 83). At the beginning of Act Two, Valentin roundly praises his master and concludes with the words "er ist so wohltätig, so gut", to which Rosa replies: "Zu gut ist auch ein Fehler." With his wealth, Flottwell had the opportunity to help others to further what he himself calls "das Edle", he could have been "ein Arzt der Menschheit" (III, 10), but by his excesses he has wasted this opportunity, and Azur, in the guise of the beggar that Flottwell will one day be, calls on humanity to judge him: "Oh, hört es, Menschen alle. [. . .] Ich laß nicht ab, der Welt mein Leid zu klagen [. . .] und ruf die Menschheit zwischen uns zum Richter auf" (II, 18). Significantly it is humanity, not divinity or any other higher power, that is the measure and judge of Flottwell's guilt.

If excess of a positive quality is Flottwell's undoing, then one might ask whether the same is true of Valentin. Throughout he is the embodiment of "Dienertreue", but his at times blind obedience seems not simply comic but also excessive and above all humanly degrading when he is treated as an animal in the hunt. Like Grillparzer's "treuer Diener", Valentin allows himself to become a laughing-stock and is prepared to put loyalty to his master above family duties, so that one is tempted to recall the words of Bancbanus at the end of *Ein treuer Diener seines Herrn*:

> Laß dir den Menschen Mensch sein, und den Diener
> Acht als ein Spargut für die Zeit der Not.
> (vv. 2115–2116) (WA I/3, 314)

Undoubtedly, however, the concept of loyalty is less problematic and more positive in Raimund's play, although consideration of Valentin is complicated to some extent by the change in his role from the comic servant to the more serious craftsman of the final act. In Act One, Valentin is "gemein" and "roh" (I, 3), in Act Two he is "einfältig", and in Act

Three he is "ein rechtschaffener Mensch" (III, 4). By the end of the play
he has become a more fully developed character, decent and upright in his
modest surroundings, whilst Flottwell has descended to the level of a
beggar. The words of the famous "Hobellied" — "Das Schicksal setzt den
Hobel an / Und hobelt s' beide gleich" — are not, however, borne out by
the play's final scenes, in which social convention appears to dictate that
Flottwell must be allowed to find at least a modest fortune beneath the
rubble of his former home. The fact that the money is there at all is
admittedly due to Flottwell's quality of generosity, whilst Valentin's
outlook remains essentially limited; on the other hand one may feel that
Valentin has had a poor deal — but any question about the relative merits
of the two central figures appears subordinate to the rather stereotyped re-
establishment of the master-servant relationship.

It is perhaps dangerous to draw too many conclusions from the ending
of the play which, even more than in *Der Alpenkönig und der Menschenfeind*, descends into conventionality with the Baroque invocation of
"Traum" and "Wahrheit" and the final cliché of "zufrieden muß man
sein" (III, 10). Nevertheless, as also in the earlier play, it is the very human
qualities of Flottwell and Valentin that form the central issue of the play
and which contribute in no small way to the overall excellence of those two
plays. Certainly contemporary critics saw *Der Verschwender* in terms of
"Sittlichkeit", "das sittlich Gute", and "freie moralische Tätigkeit", and
when the play was performed in Hamburg in 1836, the journal *Thalia*
wrote: "dieser schöne reinmenschliche Glaube müßte allein hinreichen,
die Herzen zu gewinnen".[12] If such criteria are most clearly a product of
eighteenth-century philosophy, then there is no doubt that Raimund
makes increasing use in his plays of terms that were common in the works
of eighteenth-century writers. A purely statistical analysis would show a
gradual increase in the use of such terms to reach a peak in *Der Alpenkönig
und der Menschenfeind*, with *Moisasurs Zauberfluch* and *Der Verschwender*
close behind; statistics, however, are a dangerous commodity in literature,
and more important than arithmetical frequency is the significance
attached to certain terms in those three plays in particular.

I have no wish to question Raimund's place in specifically Austrian
traditions of literature in order to claim him as a latter-day Classicist.
Neither do I intend to suggest that he was a walking dictionary of
eighteenth-century vocabulary, which is, indeed, not remotely as promin-
ent in his work as it is, for example, in Grillparzer's, almost every one of
whose plays involves the treatment of one or more Classical themes; nor,
except to a certain extent in *Moisasurs Zauberfluch*, does Raimund rival
H. J. Collin's insistence on virtue, duty, and nobility, and in any case
Raimund's use of those themes lacks the harshness and moral rigour of
Collin. The political and moral vocabulary of laws, limitation, and

moderation, so frequent in the works of Goethe and Schiller, is almost entirely lacking in Raimund's plays, while the vocabulary of quiet contentment ("still", "sanft", "ruhig", "rein", "mild", etc.), which is frequently found in Raimund's plays and also very much in the poems, was, as I have already suggested, too much of a cliché of the Austrian *Biedermeier* to be a convincing indication of eighteenth-century influence. Equally the themes of humanity and virtue had been expressed on the suburban stage before, most notably in Schikaneder's *Die Zauberflöte*, but also elsewhere, as in Hensler's *Das Donauweibchen*, in which we are told that the man of noble heart who helps others "den Ehrennamen: Mensch! verdient" (III, 9) (DL II, 150). With the exception of *Die Zauberflöte*, however, the usage of such terms is much more frequent, and more central, in Raimund's work; above all, with Raimund it undoubtedly reflects a serious philosophical intent, which is also found in his correspondence, including the many letters that describe love in lofty terms of duty, virtue, and nobility, amongst the rather more conventional references to loyalty, hope, and eternal love. In one such letter of 1827 he wrote: "ich glaube ich habe es dir im Laufe meines Lebens stets bewiesen, daß ich das Schlechte verachte, und nur für das Edle entglühe" (*Wke.* IV, 277–278); two years later he wrote to assure her "daß es [mein Herz] mit unerschütterlicher Treue an Grundsätzen und Gegenständen hängt, die edler Gefühle würdig sind" (*Wke.* IV, 368–369). These "Grundsätze" are, as I have sought to show, principally reflected in his work in two ways. On the one hand Raimund saw his work as an artistic calling;[13] in his poems he makes reference to the truth and beauty of art, and he was increasingly concerned to stress the contrast between what is "edel" and what is "gemein" in art and poetry. However, the attempt to use such themes as a dramatic subject in *Die gefesselte Phantasie*, and to some extent also in *Die unheilbringende Zauberkrone*, resulted in what are arguably his two weakest plays.

On the other hand and much more successfully, three of his later plays are set clearly in the context of humanity and of human virtues and qualities, and these themes are increasingly expressed in terms of "Menschheit", "der Mensch", and the accompanying negative and positive epithets common to eighteenth-century writers. In Raimund's best works, this emphasis is not in any way "weltfremd" or openly moralizing, but is based on a clear presentation of the human character and of human foibles, good and bad. Even within the partially retained Baroque trappings of the Viennese stage, the independence of man and the judgement of human qualities by human criteria is an increasingly central theme in Raimund's work, and one that serves to distinguish him from the empty conventionality of his rivals.

Zusammenfassung

Der Versuch Raimunds, den Dichtern des Wiener Burgtheaters nach-
zueifern, wurde bisher immer als Irrweg bezeichnet; die "vielen schönen
Worte", deren Fehlen Raimund bedauerte und die er angeblich in seine
späteren Dramen verzweifelt einzubauen versuchte, wurden haupt-
sächlich im Sinne eines übertriebenen Pathos Schillerscher Art verstanden
und als Grund für den verhältnismäßig geringen Erfolg von Stücken wie
Die gefesselte Phantasie angeführt. Der Verfasser arbeitet einen anderen
Aspekt dieses Bestrebens Raimunds heraus: inwiefern weisen die Dramen
Raimunds den Einfluß des philosophischen Wortschatzes des achtzehnten
Jahrhunderts auf? In den ersten drei Dramen wird von Zitaten aus klassi-
schen Dramen sowie von philosophischem Gedankengut allenfalls aus
Gründen der Ironie Gebrauch gemacht, obwohl schon im *Bauer als
Millionär* die ersten Spuren philosophischer und psychologischer Tiefe
festzustellen sind. In den beiden darauffolgenden Dramen sollte eine
geschmackliche Verfeinerung und gedankliche Vertiefung vollzogen
werden. In der *Gefesselten Phantasie* handelt es sich um einen Vergleich
zwischen dem Edlen und Gemeinen, vor allem im Bereich der Poesie; in
Moisasurs Zauberfluch wird die Unmenschlichkeit Gluthahns der Tugend
und Menschlichkeit Alzindes und Hoanghus gegenübergestellt. Im ersten
dieser beiden Stücke, wie auch später in der *Unheilbringenden Zauberkrone,* ließ sich das philosophische Thema nicht völlig überzeugend in
dramatische Handlung umsetzen. In *Moisasurs Zauberfluch* gelang dies
Raimund zur Hälfte, doch bleibt die Haupthandlung allzusehr im Banne
des für die Volksbühne typischen Kampfes zwischen guten und bösen
Geistern. Erst im *Alpenkönig* gelingt es Raimund, eine in erster Linie
klassische Betonung des Menschlichen als Mittelpunkt und Leitgedanken
des dramatischen Geschehens überzeugend zum Ausdruck zu bringen.
Der edle Alpenkönig ermöglicht es dem rohen und wilden Rappelkopf,
den Weg zur Selbsterkenntnis zu finden; aus dem rohen, unvernünftigen
Tier wird ein milder und edler Mensch. Auch im *Verschwender,* in dem die
übermenschlichen Gestalten noch deutlicher zu Randfiguren geworden
sind, befaßt sich Raimund mit dem Menschen und dem Menschlichen:
Flottwell fällt seinen wilden Leidenschaften und seinem Mangel an
Mäßigung zum Opfer, während sich der treue Diener Valentin als
biederer und rechtschaffener Mensch entpuppt. Zwar werden solche
Themen vor allem in den zum Teil konventionellen barocken
Dramenschlüssen nicht immer konsequent behandelt, doch tragen sie
zum Erfolg und zum hohen Niveau dieser späteren Dramen nicht
unwesentlich bei.

3

Peter Branscombe

REFLECTIONS ON RAIMUND'S ARTISTIC RELATIONSHIPS WITH HIS CONTEMPORARIES

The expectations aroused by the title of this paper are potentially so extensive that we must begin with an outline of the ground actually to be covered. The subject matter — dictated, it must be admitted, more by serendipity than grand design — is concerned with Raimund's connexions with dramatists — one dead, the other already artistically moribund though destined to outlive Raimund by many years; with his theatrical aspirations and his relations with his fellow-actors in the *Volkstheater* and outside it; with the musicians who worked with him on his dramas; and I also offer some observations on Raimund's commercial acumen.

There is no cause for surprise in the fact that Raimund had quite close links with the plays of August von Kotzebue, especially in the early years of his career; in those days, virtually every actor did. Raimund's first role on the Viennese stage was the title part in Kotzebue's *Die Belagerung von Saragossa, oder Pachter Feldkümmels Hochzeitstag* (Theater in der Josefstadt, 13 April 1814), and he is known to have performed in other Kotzebue plays, or adaptations from Kotzebue, before and after that date.[1] In his adaptation from Herzenskron's *Die Heirat durch die Pferdekomödie*, which we normally think of as the model for Nestroy's *Der Zettelträger Papp*, and which was first performed for Raimund's benefit on 28 November 1822, Raimund in the role of Papp prides himself on his familiarity "mit Gelehrten und Dichtern": "Na, ich meins! Der Herr Goeth hat mich zur Firmung gführt — und der Schillerer, von dem die Kabbala und Lieb ist, die lesen mir all ihre Stück selber vor — und mit dem Kotzebueben war ich sehr gut, dem haben s' jetzt ein neuen Namen aufgebracht — [. . .]" (*Wke.* III, 54).

In his curtain-speech on the night before the première of *Der Barometermacher auf der Zauberinsel*, Raimund playfully alluded to Kotzebue's comedy *Armut und Edelsinn* (*Wke.* V, 221); in Act One of *Die unheilbringende Zauberkrone*, Simplizius Zitternadel fears that if he cannot pay his debt to his wine-merchant, "so heißt es: Marsch nach Kamschatka!" (I, 8) (*Wke.* II, 242). There are clearer references to the same Kotzebue play — *Graf Benjowsky, oder Die Verschwörung auf Kamtschatka* — in the letter which Raimund wrote to Adolf Bäuerle from Munich on 25 March 1830:

Mit meiner Gesundheit steht es wieder besser, ich habe, wie ich dir schrieb, meine
Reise ins Gebirg wirklich angetreten. Allein das hieße nach Kamtschacka reisen
um eine Molkenkur zu brauchen, auf meiner ganzen Reise, hat mich ein
immerwährendes Schneegestöber begleitet, ich kam also nur 6 Posten weit, gegen
die Grenze von Tirol, und machte rechts um, nach München zurück.

(*Wke.* IV, 381)

And towards the end of the same letter, still complaining about the vilely
cold weather, he says: "Ich komme mir hier vor wie der verbannte
Kozebue" (*Wke.* IV, 382), alluding to that author's experiences narrated in
his *Das merkwürdigste Jahr meines Lebens*.

Even as late as *Der Verschwender* Raimund has Valentin introduce his
youngest child, Pepi, to Flottwell as "Das jüngste Kind meiner Laune"
(III, 6) (*Wke.* II, 431) — surely a reference to Kotzebue's six-volume
collection of his works *Die jüngsten Kinder meiner Laune* (Leipzig, 1793-
97). It is also interesting to note that in his review of *Der Verschwender*
published in *Feierstunden für Freunde der Kunst, Wissenschaft und Literatur*
on 14 April 1834, Sigmund Schlesinger suggests that Raimund was
influenced by Kotzebue: "Kotzebues 'Deutsche Hausfrau' tritt, eine
Anekdote benützend, besonders in der Lösung des Knotens dem
'Verschwender' sehr nahe" (*Wke.* V/ii, 854).

There is little in these examples to suggest that Raimund had, or
needed, any specially close familiarity with Kotzebue's works, though it is
notable that all the references in his dramatic sketches and plays which
quote from, or refer to, that author, appear in Raimund's own roles. At
least it is now possible to say that Raimund had the opportunity to acquire
first-hand knowledge of Kotzebue's works at his leisure.

No detailed inventory of Raimund's possessions at the time of his death
seems to have survived. The official *Totenfallsaufnahme*, dated Vienna, 10
September 1836, contains the only indication I have been able to trace
that Raimund owned any books. To the printed question on the form,
"Ob Bücher und sonstige Censurgegenstände vorhanden, wann die
Anzeige an das k.k. Bücher-Revisionsamt geschehen sey", the information was inserted: "Einige Bücher, welche sich zu Guttenstein in dem erb-
lasserischen Hause befinden" (*Wke.* III, 405). There is no indication
whether Raimund also had books in his dwelling in Vienna, and I know of
no public or private library holdings of books that have any association
with him.

So much by way of preliminaries to the subject which I now want
to discuss. In the mid-1960s I ordered from a Viennese second-hand
bookseller's list one of two sets of Kotzebue's *Theater* which were offered
for sale. One set was offered complete; the other was lacking one of the
sixty volumes. In due course two bulky parcels arrived, and I unpacked
them to find myself the owner of an attractive but not-quite-complete set

of the edition of the *Theater / von / Kotzebue* that was printed in Prague between 1817 and 1824 ("gedruckt in der Sommerschen Buchdruckerei"), with frontispieces drawn mainly by Joseph Führich, and engraved by C. Pluth and others. What immediately caught my attention when I opened the volumes (and I infer from the lack of a descriptive note in the catalogue, and the modest price, that the bookseller had not bothered to inspect them very carefully) was that the title-page of each was stamped in black with the name "Ferdinand Raimund". Is it too much to hope that from the Plates and the description that follows, other books from Raimund's possession may come to light or be identified?

The 16mo volumes have a leaf size (trimmed) of 113 × 90 mm. They are bound in thin flexible boards covered with blue and brown marbled paper. It is not clear whether they were trimmed by the printer, but the fact that the bindings are sewn with the leaves (which are bound in gatherings of eight), and that the labels on the spine identifying author and volume-number (e.g. "Kotzebue / Theater / 45.") are likely to be as issued, makes it possible that the volumes are in their original condition, and the bindings at least are contemporary. Apart from the printed and glued spine-labels, there is in the top left-hand corner of the front of each volume a small blue and white octagonal oblong cartouche (24 × 17mm), similar to those that are often found in books of this period stuck inside the front cover of a volume with the binder's or bookseller's name printed in the centre of the blank space. These cartouches on Raimund's edition of Kotzebue contain an owner's simple library-numbering system; each volume contains, handwritten in black ink, the number (shelf-mark) "108" in the upper middle area of the label, with the volume-number from one to sixty (lacking, as I have indicated, volume 22) in smaller figures in the lower right-hand corner. The figures are quite clear, reasonably neat, but not written with particular care. There is no evidence whether the figures are in Raimund's hand, or even whether this numbering system dates from the time of Raimund's ownership of the edition.

There are few indications that any of the volumes have been much used, and there are no marginalia or other marks. Among the volumes that reveal signs of having been read more frequently than most of the others are volume 5 (which contains, significantly in view of what I have already said of Raimund's references to Kotzebue's works, *Graf Benjowsky, oder die Verschwörung auf Kamtschatka*, and *Die Spanier in Peru, oder Rollas Tod*); and volume 7 (which contains *Die Verleumder*, *Die Wittwe und das Reitpferd*, and *Der Wildfang*). The spine of volume 7 has cracked severely and has been amateurishly repaired with two blank cartouches very similar to those on which the shelf-marks are inscribed, cut lengthwise and stuck across the broken binding. One or two of the volumes reveal more

Ferdinand Raimund

Theater

von

Kotzebue.

Vierter Theil.

Bruder Moritz, der Sonderling.

Die edle Lüge.

Der Papagey.

Prag 1817,

gedruckt in der Sommerschen Buchdruckerei.

5 cm

Ferdinand Raimund

Theater

von

Kotzebue.

Fünfter Theil.

Graf Benjowsky, oder die Verschwörung auf Kamtschatka.
Die Spanier in Peru, oder Rollas Tod.

Prag 1817,

gedruckt in der Sommerschen Buchdruckerei.

5 cm

modern, and less clumsy, repairs; many of them are in a condition which would suggest the need for repair.

A feature of the application of the owner's name-stamp is the carelessness apparent in many of the volumes. The stamp itself, to judge from the impressions, was probably of metal; it seems to have been inked from some kind of pad, and the impression tends to grow progressively weaker through a series of four or five applications until the stamp was re-inked. The very first volume has the owner's name stamped upside-down, and then correctly aligned — a phenomenon familiar to wielders of individual name-stamps or date-stamps in our own day; one volume has the name only partially on the title-page (I am inclined to attribute this to the carelessness of the person applying the stamp rather than to an over-generous later trimming of the volumes). In one or two cases the owner seems to have tried to efface some of his over-liberal inking, and he has several times smudged, or over-printed, the name. I assume that the stamp was made of metal, rather than of wood or rubber, because of the way in which the lettering (and in one case the whole block on to which the lettering was mounted) has marked the verso of the title-page, or even bruised the following pages. Considerable pressure was clearly applied in some instances; indeed, the marks on the title-page of volume 4 enable one to estimate the size of the block itself to have been 80mm long, probably by about 20mm wide, simply because of the indentations in the paper which indicate an over-enthusiastic sweep of the owner's hand as he applied the stamp. The actual lettering measures 30 × 3mm, with raised initial capitals and lower case roman type for the remaining letters; impressions that were made with a superfluity of ink are very slightly larger than these average measurements, owing to the tendency of the ink to run on the rough, slightly absorbent paper.

Needless to say, I value these volumes of Kotzebue far above the few hundred Austrian schillings they cost me; I make no apology for having described them at some length, as I think they could well prove to be of considerable interest if, as seems likely, they shed light on a hitherto unrecorded aspect of Raimund's interests and possessions. As to the later history of these volumes, one can only speculate. They presumably passed with the rest of Raimund's estate to Toni Wagner, and were perhaps after her death in 1879 disposed of along with Raimund's manuscripts — many of them destroyed, others preserved largely through the good offices of Karl Glossy.[2]

We turn now to the matter of Raimund's relations with his Viennese contemporaries. Well before he himself turned to the writing of plays, Raimund was aware of the decline in standards of the dramatists of his day. "Mit unseren Dichtern geht es immer miserabler," he writes to Toni

Wagner in an undated letter of 1821, "sie betreiben ihre Kunst blos um Geld herauszulocken, nicht um Ehre zu ärnten, und es ist zum verzweifeln, was man für Schmierereyn lesen muß" (*Wke.* IV, 25). Four years later, by which time Raimund had established himself as a dramatist, his attitude towards his contemporaries — the emphasis here on actors and audience — is even more biting. Toni Wagner is again the recipient:

In den jetzigen Zeiten, wo die unpartheyische Meynung und das richtige Gefühl des Puplickums, durch Charletanerien wenigstens auf Augenblicke so sehr irre geleitet werden kann, daß manche Halbgenies ein ordentliches Handwerk mit diesen phantasmagorischen Trugbildern treiben, hat jeder Schauspieler der nicht den gänzlichen Reitz der Neuheit für sich hat, und der ohne Intrigue blos durch die Anwendung seines Talentes siegen will, es sehr nöthig alle Kräfte auf-zubiethen, wenn er gegen die Kabalen dieser theatralischen Buschklepper aufkommen, und stehen bleiben will.   (*Wke.* IV, 168–169)

There is something puzzling about Raimund's relationship with Adolf Bäuerle during the 1820s, and especially towards the end of the decade, when Bäuerle's career as a dramatist had reached a low point. Raimund and Bäuerle were on intimate terms — "Lieber Bruder!", they begin their letters to each other, using the "du" form. By 1825 Bäuerle was no longer able to supply Raimund with rewarding roles like Sandelholz in *Der verwunschene Prinz* (1818), Bims in *Aline* (1822), and to a lesser extent Schmieramperl in *Lindane* (1824). There seems to have been some tension between them in spring 1825, when Raimund was expected to create the leading role in Bäuerle's latest play, *Die Zauberschminke*, but seems to have used his poor health as a reason for postponing, and then finally refusing, the part. The *Theaterzeitung* reported on 10 May 1825:

Im Leopoldstädter Theater hätte noch im Monat Mai ein neues Zauberspiel zum Benefize der Dlle Ennökl[3] aufgeführt werden sollen: "Das Land der Erfindungen, oder: Die Zauberschminke", von Adolf Bäuerle, Musik von dem genialen Kanne. Da aber der geachtete Künstler Raimund, auf den die Hauptrolle berechnet ist, seine Gesundheit zu befestigen nächstens eine Reise in ein Bad machen dürfte, so unterbleibt die Produktion vorderhand.   (*Wke.* V/i, 282–283)

When the play was finally staged on 28 October 1825, it ran for only seven performances. That Raimund's failure to appear in it was not really due to his health is indicated by the fact that he played on ten nights in May, when the première should have taken place, and fifteen times in October and November, when *Die Zauberschminke* was actually in the repertoire.

The decline in Bäuerle's skill is unambiguously shown in the failure of his own benefit play, *Die Giraffe in Wien, oder Alles à la Giraffe*, on 9 May 1828. Wenzel Müller's diary entry states: "Fürchterlich gelacht und ausgezischt worden" (*Wke.* V/i, 426). And F. C. Weidmann in the

Theaterzeitung stated: "Am Schlusse der Darstellung suchte der geschätzte Direktor Hr. Raimund [. . .] in wohlgewählten Worten den Dichter zu entschuldigen, indem er auf die vieljährigen und oft erprobten Bestrebungen desselben, das Publikum zu unterhalten, hindeutete und seine Ansprüche auf dessen Nachsicht geltend machte" (*Wke.* v/i, 426–427).

So much by way of introduction to Bäuerle's next play, for which I want to argue a greater significance than has hitherto been accorded it. This was the "Original-Zauberspiel" *Der Mann*[4] *mit Millionen, schön, jung und doch nicht glücklich.*[5] It was first staged in the Theater in der Leopoldstadt on 10 January 1829, and it received twenty performances over the next three years. The previous autumn it had been the subject of two heated appeals by Bäuerle to the President of the *Polizeihofstelle*, ostensibly complaining that Rudolf Steinkeller, the owner of the theatre, was overriding the artistic decisions of Raimund, the director; but Bäuerle was actually concerned above all that Steinkeller was announcing *Der Mann mit Millionen* not only under Bäuerle's name, but with the name printed on the playbills in red lettering and larger-than-usual type. Bäuerle claimed that he had made the play available to "den verantwortlichen Direktor Raimund", and without a fee, only on the condition that it would be performed anonymously. In the end the Police President upheld Bäuerle's plea, and Steinkeller was prevented from naming Bäuerle on the bills when the play was finally given, without Raimund in the cast, on 10 January 1829.[6]

"Why all the fuss?", the reader may well be wondering. In the first place, Bäuerle presumably wanted to be spared another fiasco such as had attended *Die Giraffe in Wien*; secondly, there were clashes of personality; and thirdly, the question of literary influence arises. Let us take the personal difficulties first. Bäuerle was, along with Sartory, Schuster, Raimund, and Rainoldi, a member of the committee of five who at the beginning of October 1826 agreed to put up 2,000 gulden each and take over the Theater in der Leopoldstadt and thus prevent Karl Carl from securing it, and with it an absolute monopoly over the three suburban theatres (*Wke.* III, 353–358). However, on 3 January 1827, Rudolf Steinkeller, a twenty-two-year-old Pole, bought the theatre.[7] He was rich, but totally inexperienced in theatrical affairs, and the police insisted that the artistic direction should not be in his hands: initially Johann Sartory, and from 17 April 1828 Raimund, were responsible for artistic decisions. But, as we have already seen, Steinkeller interfered in artistic matters; a further instance may be found in Raimund's letter to Toni Wagner from Innsbruck, dated 17 July [1828], in which he laments bitterly that Steinkeller had dismissed around twenty actors and actresses as soon as Raimund had left for his vacation, thus implying that Raimund had been party to their dismissal (*Wke.* IV, 362). It seems to me more than possible that Bäuerle, on behalf of the committee of five, was satirizing Steinkeller in *Der Mann mit Millionen*. "Herr von Münzgraben aus Wien" (the play is ostensibly set in and near "Nordhart am Rhein") describes himself in Act I, scene 20, as "reich, gescheid, schön . . . soll ich auch noch rechtschaffen seyn? Das wär zu viel verlangt, ma foi!" Whether or not Bäuerle is here alluding to the new owner of the Theater in der Leopoldstadt, there is a specifically anti-Polish gibe in the last act. Münzgraben has been reduced by magic to a state of penury; his daughter, Linchen, still hopes that her loved one, Heinrich Walter, who has been transformed into a rich Polish nobleman, will help them: "Er war stets ein guter Mensch", she says, to which her step-mother replies: "Ja, so lang er ein deutsches Original war, jetzt hat er sich aber ins Polnische übersetzen lassen, und da weiß man ja, wie die Uibersetzer oft das beste Werk zu Grund richten" (III, 12). And just in case the anti-Polish comments have not yet made their mark, the eventual happy ending is briefly delayed when Frau von Münzgraben begs her husband's forgiveness for having been willing to compromise his daughter's happiness; he exclaims: "Ihnen soll das polnische Doñerwetter erschlagen!" (III, 14).

Der Mann mit Millionen, with its derivative *Freischütz*-like plot and superficial characterization, is an even worse play than this brief outline of its contents suggests; no wonder Bäuerle did not want to be named as author "des fraglichen Stücks", as the *Polizei Ober-Direktion* referred to it on 20 October 1828 (*Wke.* III, 369). Yet this same play, for which as director of the company Raimund was ultimately responsible, has a further claim on our attention. The setting for Act II, scenes 19–27, is "Ein schöner Garten, im Hintergrunde ein glänzendes Schloß [. . .] eine Treppe mit vergoldetem Geländer [führt] in den Garten [. . .]". This setting closely resembles that described for the opening of Act Three (and Act Two) of *Der Verschwender* (*Wke.* II, 419, 374). "Der alte Walter" enters with "eine arme Frau" (she reminds one of Zufriedenheit in *Das Mädchen aus der Feenwelt* III, 2–4; she too is in due course revealed as a tutelary spirit). They hope to see young Heinrich Walter, the "Mann mit Millionen", but before they can do so they are accosted by the gardener, Herrmann, a suspicious yet kindly man who talks about his phenomenally rich employer in unflattering terms, and agrees to help them see him. This scene-complex resembles in setting, mood, and content the opening to Act Three of *Der Verschwender*, in which Flottwell asks the gardener to help him gain access to the rich and usurping owner of the castle, "Herr von Wolf" — Flottwell's unscrupulous former valet. Indeed, in points of detail this resemblance is arguably more striking than that between *Der Verschwender* and the short story "Der junge Verschwender und seine Frau" which, as Richard Smekal has pointed out in claiming it as the model for Raimund's play,[8] was published in the *Taschenbuch des Theaters in der Leopoldstadt auf das Jahr 1829* — at very much the same time as Bäuerle's *Der Mann mit Millionen* was being squabbled over, and then performed. Raimund's originality is not here in question; like most creative artists, he adopted and adapted motifs from more than one source.

For the last word on the subject of the originality of Raimund's "Original-Zaubermärchen" we return to Bäuerle — his letter to Raimund of 12 March 1834:

> Lieber Bruder!
> Mit wahrer Aergerniß vernehme ich, daß irgend ein scheelsüchtiger Mensch dir hinterbracht hat, ich hätte mich geäußert, du hättest in deinem neuen Stücke "Der Verschwender" Ideen oder Worte aus meinen Stücken benützt. Ich habe dir mündlich erklärt, daß mir eine solche Gemeinheit nie in den Sinn gekommen, und daß ich derlei Unsinn gegen Niemand geäußert habe. — Ich bin nicht gewohnt, ausgezeichnete Talente zu verkleinern, noch Personen, die ich achte, zu verläumden, noch weniger aber sage ich Unwahrheiten und Unwahrheit der niedrigsten Art wäre es, deinem genialen Werke irgend ein Plagiat nachweisen zu wollen [. . .]. Schließlich gebe ich dir, was Verläumder auch noch jetzt vorbringen will, mein heiliges Ehrenwort, daß ich nur in den Enthusiasmus mit einstimmte, der deiner geistvollen Arbeit gebracht wird, und daß ich ein ganz gemeiner Kerl sein müßte, zu behaupten, du hättest auch nur *ein* Wort aus meinen Stücken benützt [. . .]   (*Wke.* IV, 489–490)

One must make what one will and can of this complex story. Perhaps there is something suspicious about Bäuerle's emphatic and repeated denial of the accusation that Raimund was guilty of plagiarism — does he protest too much? Or has he perhaps allowed *Der Mann mit Millionen* of nearly six years earlier to slip from his memory? Would Raimund for his part have remembered the source of a particular detail which he more or less unconsciously re-fashioned for a play of his own? — We are unlikely ever to know the answers to these questions.

A recurrent motif in Raimund's career is his desire for recognition at the highest level. August Ellrich speaks in his *Genre-Bilder aus Österreich und den verwandten Ländern* (Berlin, 1833) of the easy informality of Austrian aristocrats in artistic matters: "Es [hat] mir geschienen, daß [der hohe Adel] reich, prachtliebend, kunstsinnig und auch gegen Künstler sehr herablassend sein müsse, denn ich begegnete dem Schauspieler Raimund des Leopoldstädter Theaters, welcher mit dem Fürsten D—stein Arm in Arm ging" (*Wke.* V/i, 488). This was presumably Moritz Graf Dietrichstein, Director of the Burgtheater from 1821. Another reminiscence points up Raimund's reluctance to be associated with the popular theatre. A fortnight after Raimund's death his friend Costenoble, the Burgtheater actor, recorded in his diary:

Karoline Müller erzählte, daß sie einst mit Raimund in Gesellschaft diesem etwas Artiges habe sagen wollen, aber übel angekommen sei. "Es ist recht heilsam für die Kunst," — sagte Karoline — "daß Sie mit Ihren Schauspielen dem Volkstheater und der Localkomik eine höhere und edlere Richtung gegeben haben." — Raimund entgegnete mürrisch: "Localkomik? Volkstheater? — Ich will gar keine *Localstücke* schreiben und nichts wissen von *Volks*theater." — Das war Raimunds Krankheit.[9]

In the spring of 1834 there were rumours that Raimund was going to attain the Burgtheater. Costenoble's diary records for 26 March 1834:

> Es wurde viel in der Sitzung darüber gelacht, daß unser Publicum mit Gewißheit behauptet: Raimunds "Verschwender" werde auf Befehl des Kaisers auf dem Burgtheater erscheinen. Man weiß nicht, daß der Kaiser einen unbegreiflichen Widerwillen gegen Raimund hegt und dessen Namen ausgestrichen hat, als er und Ignaz Schuster auf der Wahlliste für den Congress in Troppau standen.
>
> (*Aus dem Burgtheater*, II, 189)

It was to be a further fifty-one years before *Der Verschwender* reached the Burgtheater. We may well wonder whether one reason why Raimund was drawn to make his famous series of guest appearances outside Austria was that in Germany and Bohemia he was appearing mainly in court and national theatres.

Raimund's sense of inferiority was not confined to his ambition to rise above the popular theatre. As early as 31 October 1819 he complained to Costenoble about the public's preference for Ignaz Schuster above himself, in terms both of "Vielseitigkeit" and of "Feinheit". Costenoble tried to reassure him:

> Ich verwies Raimund auf meine bedrängte Stellung am Burgtheater, wo ich doch weniger frei wirken könne, als er, der doch in seiner Sphäre die Volksdichter sich nach Bedarf ziehen und bilden könne, die obendrein froh sind, wenn er nur etwas von ihren Erzeugnissen acceptiert und zustutzt, ich hingegen müsse stets hoffen und harren, bis es einer hochmögenden Regie beliebe, mich mit einer Rolle zu betheilen, die irgendeinem Gewaltigen zu schlecht scheine.
>
> (*Aus dem Burgtheater*, I, 64–65)

But neither Costenoble's frequent and sincere expressions of Raimund's superiority to Schuster, nor his pleas to Raimund to write his own plays, were to bear fruit for some years. Raimund did ultimately come to terms with his jealousy of Schuster, but not until a few months after the latter's death, and only three months before his own:

> "Ach, der gute Schuster" — seufzte Raimund — "den[n] sein Andenken ehren die Wiener auch nicht nach Verdienst. Einen so ruhigen, wahren Komiker, wie Schuster war, hat Wien jetzt nicht mehr aufzuweisen. Scholz hätte das schönste Talent, aber der ist durch Carls Unnatur [. . .] angesteckt worden [. . .]. Würfel, Zweckerl und Staberl nach Schuster zu sein, hätte ich in meinem Leben

nicht gewagt. Der damalige Director Huber hat mir für jede Rolle, die ich nach Schuster spielen sollte, hundert Gulden W.W. geboten — damals eine große Summe für mich — ich hab' den Antrag wohlweislich abgelehnt."

(*Aus dem Burgtheater*, II, 285)

Raimund must have been in many ways a difficult colleague to work with. He set himself the highest standards, and he was not easily satisfied by the sometimes casual efforts of others. Castelli commented on the "unermüdeten Fleiß" with which Raimund worked to overcome his speech-impediment, and on the thoroughness of his preparation:

Raimund ließ sich nie einen Gedächtnisfehler zuschulden kommen [. . .]. Er hielt auch mit großer Strenge darauf, daß andere die Rollen in seinen Stücken aufs *Und* auswendig wußten. Korntheuer hat mir erzählt, daß er sich einmal wegen des einzigen kleinen Wörtchens "immer" fast mit ihm entzweit hätte. Er sprach nämlich als Geisterkönig: "Jetzt hab' ich die Agnes Bernauerin schon zwanzigmal gelesen und weiß halt noch nicht, warum sie ins Wasser gestürzt worden ist." Raimund wollte aber, er sollte sagen: ". . . und weiß halt noch *immer* nicht, warum usw." Korntheuer meinte, das sei ja gleichgültig. Raimund aber antwortete: "Nein, das ist nicht gleichgültig, das Wort immer verstärkt den Spaß", und da Korntheuer noch etwas dagegen einwendete, verließ er ihn zornig mit den Worten: "Meinetwegen, wenn du aber das "*immer*" ausläßt, so bleibst du immer ein dummer Kerl!"[10]

And it was about the première of this same play, *Der Diamant des Geisterkönigs*, that Costenoble recorded in his diary the general lack of appreciation for Raimund's marvellously subtle and natural Florian:

Stimmen hinter mir sagten ganz ohne Gêne und Scham: "Mir san nur wegen Korntheuer ins Theatta ganga!" — Korntheuer ist zwar ein sehr komischer Schauspieler; aber doch mehr ein manierirter Spassmacher. Am Schlusse wurde der Künstler und Dichter Raimund schwach gerufen — Korntheuer hingegen *lärmend* verlangt, der mit einiger Marktschreierei dankte, indem er sagte: "I bin a Wiener Kind" u.s.w.

(*Aus dem Burgtheater*, I, 333)

It was in the following year that Raimund finally broke with Korntheuer — whom, along with other men, he had suspected of making eyes at Toni. He tells her in an undated letter (1825) that he has determined to rid himself of his fair-weather friends: "Ich habe mir vorgenommen die falschen Steine aus dem Ring meiner Umgebungen auszubrechen und habe heute damit den Anfang gemacht, daß H. Korntheuer von morgen an nicht mehr bey mir speist" (*Wke.* IV, 172). Raimund says he has done this in the nicest possible way, but that he is no longer going to tolerate being addressed on stage by Korntheuer "als wenn er mit seinem Stiefelputzer sich über die gleichgültigsten Dinge konversirte".

On the other hand, when Raimund needed to fear no competition or jealousy, he could be superbly generous. We see this side of him time and again: in the way Joseph Krones turned to him for a loan when that talented family was in distress shortly before the death of Therese Krones at the end of 1830;[11] in the praise he bestowed on the stage-designer Michael Mayr at the time of the first performance in the Leopoldstadt of *Der Verschwender*, following the première in the Josefstadt (*Wke.* III, 280, 310–317); Raimund gladly released young Sophie Heurteur from her contract at her father's request so that she could appear at the Burgtheater in 1829 (*Wke.* IV, 468–469, 573), and sent Helmina von Chézy the tickets she had asked for during his Munich season in the spring of 1831 (*Wke.* IV, 396); he presumably managed to accede to Grillparzer's request for a ticket for the première of *Die unheilbringende Zauberkrone*, despite the short notice (*Wke.* IV, 469–470); and he allowed Charlotte Birch-Pfeiffer to use *Moisasurs Zauberfluch* for her benefit early in 1832, without a fee (*Wke.* III, 277), and in 1829 had similarly allowed an actor in Warsaw to use *Das Mädchen aus der Feenwelt* (*Wke.* IV, 378–379).

Despite these examples of Raimund's generosity (and they could easily have been multiplied), he was a cautious man where money was concerned. He did not want to have his plays published, as that would have opened the door to unauthorized, and unpaid, performance; he preferred to keep a firm hand on the distribution of manuscript copies, offering them to interested theatres as far apart as London and St Petersburg, Hamburg and Munich. Weimar could not afford Raimund's initial demands (*Wke.* IV, 388–389, 434, 471–472); theatres that obtained and used copies illegally were pursued by Raimund either directly or through the intervention of others: an unidentified correspondent in Magdeburg was asked to report to Raimund on the performance of *Das Mädchen aus der Feenwelt* in 1830 (*Wke.* IV, 383–384), L. F. Pauli in Dresden was asked in the same year to account for illegal performance of the same play (*Wke.* IV, 380), and on 28 September 1830 Raimund reported one Herr Gabriel Glass to the *k.k. Polizei Ober-Direktion* in Vienna for illegally offering the court theatre in Weimar a cut-price copy of *Der Alpenkönig und der Menschenfeind* (*Wke.* IV, 392–393, 471–472). Raimund's rights in his own works were frequently proclaimed in press advertisements as well as in letters.[12] Individuals who requested copies of his works from him were either ignored or politely turned down, whether it was Bäuerle requesting for the *Wiener Theaterzeitung* a copy of Raimund's "Wiederhohlungtexte" from Munich in March 1830 (*Wke.* IV, 380–381), or a complete stranger from Paris, a Frau Anna Gunz, writing to request copies of his "vortrefflichen, geistreichen Werke" (*Wke.* IV, 470–471, 390–391). Raimund's works, then, were not for dilettantes to read, but for theatres to perform. It was clearly quite a struggle for Raimund to secure his due honoraria, but he emerges from his business correspondence as a more decisive, positive campaigner for his rights than the reader of his letters to Toni might expect.

His relations with his collaborators confirm the picture of a man with considerable business acumen. When he sent the text of one of his plays to a prospective theatre director, he withheld copies of the music and the production notes until acceptance had been confirmed and payment received: see, for instance, his letter to the board of a theatre (Magdeburg?) dated 3 June 1825 (*recte* 1828) with the offer of *Der Diamant des Geisterkönigs* (*Wke.* IV, 345), and his letters of 18 September and 22 December 1830 to Karl Graf von Leutrum-Ertingen of the Royal Theatre, Stuttgart, concerning that theatre's request for copies of three of Raimund's plays on approval (*Wke.* IV, 391–392, 394).

Raimund's references to the composers who supplied the music for his works suggest a confident, almost dictatorial attitude rather than a collaboration between equals. An undated letter to Toni Wagner refers to preparations for the production of *Der Barometermacher auf der Zauberinsel* (première on 18 December 1823): "Ich habe jezt sehr viel Verdruß wegen meiner Einahme, und trotz aller meiner Bemühung wer weiß wie es ausfallen wird, nach meiner Einsicht sollte das Stück gefallen können, ich werde auch den Müller die Musickstücke aus meinem eigenen Kopf vorsingen" (*Wke.* IV, 103). The implication that Wenzel Müller had merely the task of transcribing and orchestrating Raimund's musical settings is borne out by numerous contemporary references to the dramatist's secondary function as composer.[13] Even clearer evidence is provided by the survival of musical manuscripts in Raimund's hand;[14] while at work on *Das Mädchen aus der Feenwelt* (première on 10 November 1826) he wrote to Toni in another undated letter: "Ich bin gestern den ganzen Tag gar nicht mehr ausgekommen und habe noch eine Arie in mein Stück componirt. In meinen Wagen habe ich den Drechsler abhohlen lassen, der bis Abends bey mir war" (*Wke.* IV, 264). The complaisant composer this time was Joseph Drechsler, Professor at St Anna's, Kapellmeister — and friend of Grillparzer, who was witness at his wedding nearly three years later (WA III/2, 54, 345).

The other principal source of evidence for Raimund's relationships with the composers who provided music for his plays is the *Notizen Buch* (*Wke.* IV, 443–445) in which, between 1830 and 1834, he kept a record of receipts and payments in connexion with rights in and performances of his plays. The entry covering outstanding transactions for 1829 ("Ausständiges 1829") includes: "*HE Weiß von Lemberg. 125 f Schein für den Barometermacher. HE M Gezahlt.*"[15] The second part of that entry presumably indicates that Raimund paid Wenzel Müller, composer of *Der Barometermacher auf der Zauberinsel*, his share of the honorarium. This interpretation is confirmed by the entry for 1830: "HE Pellet in Linz 80 f CM. zu bezahlen für die gefesselte Fantasie und Moisasur. Herr Müller und Riotti [i.e. the composers of these works] sind gezahlt." (*Wke.* IV, 444), and

especially by the series of entries suggesting that there was an agreement
between Raimund and Müller that the author would receive an honorarium from the composer for organizing a successful sale of their joint
work, and would pay the composer a smaller (and varying) sum in respect
of each such sale:

Capellmeister Müller hat an mich 100 f C Münze für den Verkauf des Alpenkönigs
zu bezahlen. [. . .] *Ich habe an ihn zu entrichten*
   30f Schein für die Musick der gefesselten Phantasie bey d. Aufführung in
Hamburg.
   50 f Schein für das Theater in Petersburg. Partitur des Alpenkönigs.
   30 f Schein für das Hoftheater in Braunschweig.
   30 f Schein für den Alpenkönig im Theater in der Josephstadt.
   30 f Schein für den Alpenkönig in Hanover.

(Wke. IV, 444)

Similar entries for 1834 indicate that Conradin Kreutzer received specified
sums from Raimund in respect of scores of *Der Verschwender*; in this case
the itemized copying-charge seems to have been repaid by Raimund:

An Herrn Kapellmeister Kreutzer
für d. Partitur des Verschwenders gezahlt

Im Theater d Josephstadt		50 f C Münze
Copiatur f. d. ⎞	den	
Leopoldstadt ⎬	15. Octobr	10 f 48 xr
Honorar ⎠	834	20 f CM
Fünf Partituren ⎞		München
⎬	Aufgeführt	Prag
vorausbezahlt ⎠		Hamburg

(Wke. IV, 445)

Raimund's letter to Anton Diabelli & Comp. of 16 September 1827 shows
the author selling "alle Lieder, Duetts, e cetera, welche sich in meinen
beyden Zauberspielen: Moisasurs Zauberfluch, und der gefesselten
Fantasie befinden", for 500 gulden (*Wke.* IV, 442); the songs were
published in Diabelli's *Neueste Sammlung komischer Theatergesänge*.

The contrast could hardly be more marked between Raimund the shrewd,
careful businessman, generous friend, and successful dramatic author on
the one hand, and the deeply insecure, jealous, and excitable individual on
the other — a man whom the stage-designer Michael Mayr could sum up
(admittedly on the basis of Raimund's eating and drinking habits, though
the phrase takes on a disturbingly prescient irony) as "Selbstmörder und
Martirer zugleich" (*Wke.* III, 319). Raimund himself found the most
appropriate phrase in a percipient piece of self-analysis in the letter to
Bäuerle which we have already discussed, referring to himself as

"Profeßor der Hipocondrie" (*Wke.* IV, 381). Yet fascinating as Raimund the man undoubtedly is, Raimund the artist is our proper concern. It is unlikely that we shall learn very much more about him as an actor; but the identification of books stamped with the name of Raimund as owner, and the discovery of evidence which throws fresh light on his relations with an influential contemporary, may remind us that there is perhaps still much to learn about Raimund's place in the history of the Viennese theatre.

Zusammenfassung

Der Beitrag untersucht Aspekte von Raimunds künstlerischen Beziehungen zu seinen Zeitgenossen. Seine Zitate aus, Erwähnungen von und Rollen in Kotzebues Stücken dürften im zeitgenössischen Kontext kaum überraschen, bis jetzt war es aber unbekannt, daß Raimund in seiner jetzt wahrscheinlich gänzlich zerstörten bzw. verstreuten Bibliothek die sechzig Bände umfassende Ausgabe des *Theaters / von / Kotzebue* (Prag, 1817–1824) besaß. Dieses Exemplar (59 der 60 Bände davon) ist im Besitz des Verfassers, der es Mitte der 60er Jahre von einem Wiener Antiquariat erwarb. Jeder Band trägt den (oft hastig, verkehrt oder zweimal gestempelten) Vermerk auf der Titelseite, "Ferdinand Raimund" (s. Abbildungen). An zweiter Stelle befaßt sich der Beitrag mit Raimunds Verhältnis zu Bäuerle, insbesondere während der 20er Jahre, als Bäuerles Laufbahn als Dramatiker schon ihrem Ende zuneigte. In Bäuerles "Original-Zauberspiel" *Der Mann mit Millionen, schön, jung und doch nicht glücklich* (1829) glaubt der Verfasser sowohl einen Stein des Anstoßes zwischen den zwei Dramatikern wie auch die Quelle zum ersten Auftritt im dritten Akt von Raimunds *Der Verschwender* gefunden zu haben. An dritter Stelle kommen Beispiele von Raimunds Abneigung, nur als Volksdramatiker und -schauspieler gewürdigt zu werden, und von seiner oft heiklen Zusammenarbeit mit seinen Kollegen. Schließlich läßt sich anhand einiger Beispiele von Raimunds Beziehungen zu den Musikern in seinem Kreise zeigen, daß seine Komplexe seinen geschäftlichen Scharfsinn nicht verhindert haben.

4

Walter Obermaier

NESTROY UND ERNST STAINHAUSER

Die Beschäftigung mit Ernst Stainhauser Ritter von Treuberg bedarf kaum einer näheren Begründung: weder was die Person selbst betrifft, noch hinsichtlich ihrer Beziehungen zu Johann Nestroy. Stainhauser war über vierzig Jahre in verschiedenen Funktionen beim Theater tätig, und was wir von ihm wissen bringt einiges an Informationen über das Theater — vor allem das Vorstadttheater — seit den Dreißigerjahren des 19. Jahrhunderts in Wien. Vollends aber ist von Interesse, daß Stainhauser im Laufe der Zeit zum Intimus von Johann Nestroy wurde und — neben dessen Gattin Marie Weiler — die Stütze Nestroys während seiner Direktionszeit am Carltheater von 1854 bis 1860 war. Ein Großteil aller erhalten gebliebenen Briefe Nestroys ist an Stainhauser gerichtet. Das Tagebuch Stainhausers aus dem Jahre 1835, das vor einigen Jahren für die Wiener Stadt- und Landesbibliothek erworben werden konnte, sowie erst kürzlich aufgefundenes Archivmaterial aus dem Jahre 1859 bieten zusätzliche Informationen.[1]

Tagebücher Stainhausers aus den Jahren 1844/45, 1847 bis 1851 sowie ein Theatermanuale von 1859/60 waren bereits früher bekannt.[2] Allerdings handelt es sich dabei nicht um Tagebücher im eigentlichen Sinn, sondern um Verzeichnisse der allabendlich aufgeführten Stücke im Theater an der Wien, bzw. im Theater in der Leopoldstadt, mit Angaben von Abendeinnahmen, Benefizien und fallweisen Eintragungen sonstiger Ereignisse — vor allem im Revolutionsjahr 1848. Ab 1850 fallen dann diese Eintragungen überhaupt weg. Das Tagebuch von 1835 hingegen — das einzige, das bisher aus dieser frühen Zeit bekanntgeworden ist — bringt täglich Notizen über Stainhausers Lebensführung, sein Privatleben, den Bekanntenkreis und die Familie und vor allem über Theaterereignisse. Wichtig ist die Zeichnung des Theaterlebens in Wien und in der Provinz aus der Sicht eines Beteiligten; zudem lernte Stainhauser in eben diesem Jahr 1835 Nestroy persönlich kennen.

Ernst Stainhauser Ritter von Treuberg wurde am 16. Dezember 1810 in Wien geboren.[3] Als Sohn aus gutem Hause besuchte er das Gymnasium, studierte dann durch einige Zeit Philosophie und Staatsrechnungswissenschaften und hat wohl auch einige Prüfungen abgelegt, das Studium aber nicht beendet. Schon damals hat er als Schauspieler dilettiert, denn als er 1835 seine Studienunterlagen verschenkte, betont er nicht nur seinen Fleiß als Student, sondern notiert auch: "Ich war in Wien quasi Student und quasi Schauspieler."[4] Wenn er nicht so lange studiert hätte, könnte er jetzt als Schauspieler schon weiter sein. Dem Theater konnte er sich wohl erst nach dem Tode seines Vaters völlig zuwenden — zumindest bemerkt er einmal, daß ihm sein Vater untersagt habe, als Knabe Klavier zu lernen, da er befürchtete, die dafür aufgewendete Zeit könne dem Lateinstudium abgehen.[5] Ein Mann mit solchen Grundsätzen hätte sicher gegen eine Theaterkarriere seines Sohnes einiges einzuwenden gehabt.

Im Frühjahr 1831 wurde Stainhauser nach Brünn engagiert. Die dortige Bühne gehörte zu den prominenteren Theatern der Habsburger-monarchie; sie hatte einen bedeutenden Klassikerspielplan, italienische, französische und deutsche Oper, und pflegte daneben natürlich auch das Lokalstück und das vaterländische Genre. Zur Zeit von Stainhausers Engagement — er wirkte zwei Jahre in Brünn, durchwegs in untergeordneten Rollen — stand das Repertoire allerdings auf keinem allzu hohen Niveau. Er selbst trat hier — wie auch bis Ende der Dreißigerjahre — unter dem Künstlernamen Ernst Ritter auf. 1833 wurde Stainhauser nach Agram (Zagreb) engagiert. Er debütierte hier am 2. Mai als Kunz von Laufenheim in Franz von Holbeins Stück *Das Turnier zu Kronstein*. Bäuerles *Theaterzeitung* rühmt ihm aus diesem Anlaß Talent und vielseitige Verwendungsmöglichkeit beim Theater nach.[6] In Agram wurde zu dieser Zeit — und zwar noch bis 1840 — ausschließlich deutsches Theater gespielt. Knapp vor der Eröffnung des neuen Agramer Schauspielhauses am 4. Oktober 1834 wechselte Stainhauser an das Theater von St. Pölten,[7] das damals unter der Direktion von August Seydler stand. Für Stainhauser war dieses Engagement wohl von allem Anfang an als Sprungbrett für Wien gedacht.

In St. Pölten stand er fast allabendlich auf der Bühne — nun auch in größeren Rollen, ja sogar Titelpartien. Kotzebue, Raupach, die Birch-Pfeiffer, Bäuerle, Angely und eine Fülle für den Tagesgebrauch geschriebener Stücke standen am Spielplan. In St. Pölten gehörte Stainhauser zu den besseren Schauspielern, distanzierte sich aber merklich von seinen Kollegen — zumindest verbal im Tagebuch: Er spricht vom "Komödianten Gesindel", den täglichen Streitigkeiten um Rollen und vor allem um Benefizvorstellungen, den häufigen Trinkgelagen, und dergleichen mehr. Und noch in Wien erinnert er sich an das "Gesindel in St. Pölten" und vermerkt:

Die üble Meinung von dem Schauspielerstande ist wahrhaftig kein Vorurtheil zu nennen, sondern auf vieljährige Erfahrungen u[nd] Beobachtungen gestütztes Urtheil. Kaum der hunderte Theil der Theaterleute ist solid, denn selbst jene, die den Schein der Solidität haben, sind mehr oder weniger Betrüger; Trinker, Spieler, Schuldenmacher, Vagabunden und Schlemmer sind sie fast durchgehends [. . .] Ob sie nun im k.k. Wiener Hoftheater mit 2000 f. Gage oder in einer Scheuer mit 20 f. Gehalt spielen, ihr innerer Gehalt bleibt sich meistens gleich.[8]

Er selbst schämt sich allerdings keineswegs Schauspieler, sondern nur Kollege solcher Schauspieler zu sein. Immer wieder stellt er klar, daß er etwas Besseres sei, wenn auch keiner von den "adeligen Lumpen, die Wohlgefallen an dem Schauspielerstande finden, um mit den Weibsbildern zu scherwenzeln".[9] Ob sein Gewissen tatsächlich so rein war, ist eine andere Frage. Immerhin warf ihm sein Bruder Erwin, der die militärische Laufbahn eingeschlagen hatte, brieflich einen üblen Lebenswandel vor.[10]

Nach einem einträglichen Benefiz am 29. Jänner — Stainhauser vermerkt stolz, daß die Einnahme vor allem durch die Honoratioren im Parterre und nicht durch den Pöbel zustande gekommen war — und einem dreitägigen Gastspiel in Krems verläßt er am 16. Februar St. Pölten.[11] Befriedigt notiert er, daß man versucht habe, ihn durch Gagenerhöhungen zum Bleiben zu bewegen, daß alle Abschiedsgeschenke gebracht hätten und man ihn sogar expressis verbis als "Augapfel der Schauspielfreunde" bezeichnet habe.[12] In Wien erwartete er sich aber eine ihm gemäßere Umgebung. "Hier bin ich abgesondert wegen Mangel an vernünftigem Umgange", schreibt er über St. Pölten, "da selbst ausgezeichneten Ranges die wenigsten auch ausgezeichneten Verstandes sind. In Wien hat ein Kellner mehr Witz und Kunstsinn als hier die Tonangeber."[13]

Sein erster Besuch nach dem Eintreffen in der Residenzstadt gilt dem Theateragenten Adalbert Prix, mit dem er bereits längere Zeit befreundet war und auch in brieflichem Kontakt stand.[14] Dieser sollte ihm den Weg zu einem Engagement im Theater an der Wien ebnen, das sich unter der Leitung Karl Carls eines hervorragenden Rufes erfreute. Prix war einer der wichtigsten und geschäftstüchtigsten Agenten Wiens, so daß sich Stainhauser von dieser Bekanntschaft mit Recht einiges erwarten durfte. Ungeachtet umlaufender Gerüchte, daß Prix' Methoden beim Erwerb von Theaterstücken nicht immer die solidesten seien, hält Stainhauser ihn für einen reellen und seelensguten Menschen. Prix hat auch die meisten Stücke Nestroys vertrieben. In eben diesem Jahr ist bereits vier Tage nach der erfolgreichen Uraufführung von *Zu ebener Erde und erster Stock* in der *Theaterzeitung* zu lesen, daß die Posse "auf rechtlichem Wege" nur durch das Theater-Geschäftsbüro des Adalbert Prix bezogen werden könne.[15] Bei diesem Manne — er hatte sein Büro gleich neben dem Theater an der Wien — verkehrte Stainhauser nun täglich, anfangs sogar mehrmals täglich. Erst im Laufe des Jahres — Stainhauser ist mittlerweile an Carls Bühne fix engagiert — läßt die Häufigkeit dieser Besuche nach, so daß Prix sogar einmal über das nunmehr seltenere Erscheinen Stainhausers Klage führt.

Der nächste, um dessen Gunst sich Stainhauser bemüht, ist der Theatersekretär am Theater an der Wien, Josef Franz. Am 18. Februar

sucht er ihn in der Theaterkanzlei auf, bleibt einige Tage später auf einem
Ball nur deswegen bis 5 Uhr morgens, um Franz heimbegleiten zu dürfen,
und erhält daraufhin prompt die erste Rolle auf Probe. In der Folge
studiert er verschiedene kleine Rollen ein, läßt sich von Franz auch die
Zufriedenheit Direktor Carls bestätigen, und steht endlich am 28. März in
Treuberts historischem Schauspiel *Die Belagerung von Antwerpen* in der
Chargenrolle eines spanischen Offiziers auf der Bühne. Doch ein fixes
Engagement läßt noch auf sich warten. Er ist aufgebracht über Franz und
bringt dies auch am 4. April zu Papier: "Dieser Jude führt mich bei der
Nase herum, u[nd] dehnt die Angelegenheit in beispiellose Länge." Er
erwartet nur geringe Gage und untergeordnete Beschäftigung und stellt
endlich resignierend fest: "Meine Rosen blühen an der Wien nicht."
Zwei Tage später wird ihm aber ein Vertrag auf vier Jahre offeriert, wobei
die monatliche Gage in den ersten vier Jahren von 16 über 24 und 33 zu 42
Gulden steigen soll. Über Anraten von Prix schreibt Stainhauser an Carl,
daß er nur einen Zweijahresvertrag, allerdings mit 24 Gulden monatlich,
wünsche. Franz beharrt auf seinem Offert, Prix aber bestärkt Stainhauser
und begleitet ihn schließlich zu Carl, wo er einen Vertrag auf 3 Jahre mit
einer Gage von 24, 28 und 33 Gulden aushandelt. Franz erhält für seine
Bemühungen — und wohl auch um ihn in Zukunft günstiger zu stimmen
— von Stainhauser 10 Gulden zum Geschenk.[16]
In Hinkunft ist Stainhauser weiter um die Freundschaft von Franz
bemüht, lädt ihn zum Essen und zu Festen ein, das Verhältnis scheint
aber nicht besonders ausgeglichen geworden zu sein, da Stainhauser
einerseits von Franz als niederträchtigem Menschen und von seiner
Dummheit und Schlechtigkeit spricht, andrerseits aber im November
1835 notiert:

Franz ist ein guter Mensch und weder falsch noch ungeschikt; doch hat er wie alle
Menschen seine Schwächen. Eine seiner zugänglichsten Seiten ist ein unendlicher
Drang nach Wichtigkeit. Seine Stellung bei unserem Theater ist wirklich von der
Art, daß er manchem Individuum schaden kann. Allein nützen kann er nicht
einem und hierin bleibt er nur bei dem Willen und der Sucht stehen, wichtig zu
sein oder zu scheinen. Er gäbe sich gar zu gerne eine Bedeutenheit.[17]

Bedeutendheit hätte sich auch Stainhauser gerne gegeben. Allein es bleibt
bei den kleinen Rollen, das Talent mag wohl zu bescheiden gewesen sein,
und der von St. Pölten verwöhnte Schauspieler bemerkt verwundert
anläßlich einer Aufführung von Schillers *Wilhelm Tell* — Wilhelm Kunst
gab ein Gastspiel am Theater an der Wien — "Sonderbar bleibt es, daß bei
einem so mittelmäßigen Personale und einer so großen Besetzung *ich* frei
geblieben bin."[18] Bis Ende 1839 ist Stainhauser (also Ernst Ritter) immer
wieder gegen Ende der Besetzungslisten zu finden, Rezensionen erwähnen
ihn praktisch nicht. Dann hängt er den Schauspielerberuf an den Nagel.
Er beginnt sich allerdings schon frühzeitig in der Theateradmini-

stration nützlich zu machen. So ordnet er Rollenbücher nach dem Alphabet, hilft mit, neu eingereichte Stücke zu lesen, schreibt im Auftrag von Franz Kontrakte, besucht auch fallweise dessen wöchentliches "Dichterkränzchen" (obwohl er sich dabei langweilt) und ist bereits Ende des Jahres so weit, daß es ihm zur Gewohnheit geworden ist, jeden Vormittag ins Theaterbüro zu gehen, um allfällige Arbeiten zu erledigen.[19] Das, was ihn später für Nestroy so unentbehrlich machte, das umsichtige Engagement in allem was mit dem Theater zusammenhängt, kristallisiert sich hier bereits heraus.

Für Direktor Carl hat Stainhauser die größte nur denkbare Hochachtung. Dieser ist für ihn "der umsichtige, einzige Direktor", der "verständige Carl", was nicht zuletzt darauf zurückzuführen ist, daß Carl Stainhausers Probenarbeit positiv beurteilt. Stainhauser bezeichnet Carl als "großen Meister der Schauspielkunst" wie überhaupt als "noblen feinen Weltmann", der "wenn man in keinem Geldanliegen zu ihm kommt, ein vorzüglich charmanter Mann" ist.[20] Und gleichsam als Zusammenfassung der Leistungen Carls als Regisseur und Schauspieler schreibt er:

Direktor Carl [ist] einer der ersten, wo nicht der erste Direktor und Regisseur Deutschlands. Als Arrangeur ist er unstreitig ein Meister ohne Gleichen und [. . .] bewundert. Er spielt jedes Fach, und ist der Mann, der jeden Ton und jede Miene rechtfertigen kann; alle Schauspieler sind seine Schüler, wenn sie nur auch alle Verstand genug hätten seine Andeutungen treffend zu benützen. Carl ist der Napoleon des Theaters.[21]

Ihm weiß sich Stainhauser zu allererst verpflichtet, jedes lobende Gespräch wird erwähnt, und als Prix einmal über Carl witzelt und dieser gerade in einem Nebenzimmer ist, findet dies ein sichtlich verängstigter Stainhauser ungehörig, traut sich aber nichts zu sagen.[22]

Stainhauser bemüht sich auch um das Wohlwollen von Wenzel Scholz, der damals bereits im Zenit seines Ruhmes stand. Er macht ihm Geschenke, "wofür mir der sonst unfreundlich rohe Mensch höchst verbindlich dankt".[23] Doch bald schon heißt es: Scholz ist "ungemein freundlich, und wird es immer mehr gegen mich werden, je mehr ich auf die Erlangung seiner Freundschaft spendire". Als Schauspieler und Mensch sei Scholz von vorzüglicher Bescheidenheit.[24]

Verglichen mit dem Enthusiasmus für Carl und dem Bemühen um Scholzens Freundschaft nehmen sich die ersten Kontakte zu Johann Nestroy eher bescheiden aus — was nicht zuletzt in dem wenig kontaktfrohen Wesen Nestroys begründet gewesen sein mag. Am 27. Februar 1835 sah Stainhauser Nestroy erstmals auf der Bühne: als Mosje Haxerl in Schickhs *Die Entführung vom Maskenball*, und er notiert: "Insonderheit ergötzlich war Hr. Scholz als Augustin und Nestroi als Haxel";

resignierend fügt er hinzu: "Ich fürchte mich beim bloßen Zusehen schon auf mein erstes Auftreten. Wenn ich mich blamirte!? Gott steh bei!". Tags darauf sah er Nestroys Parodie *Robert der Teuxel*: "Das Ganze ist sehr komisch u[nd] spritzig, und Nestroi zeigte sich als witzig satirischer Dichter wie als Darsteller ausgezeichnet." Und auch später noch konnte sich Stainhauser an der Parodie "herzlich lachend erheitern". Am 24. März wurde dann zum neunundneunzigsten Mal *Lumpazivagabundus* gegeben, ein Stück, das Stainhauser schon oft gesehen hatte, worüber er aber "auch heute noch von Herzen lachen" konnte. Bei der hundertsten Aufführung am 21. April spielte er selbst den Fludribus, und etwas später urteilt er:

> Dieses Stück ist ganz bestimmt die beste Dichtung Nestrois und die beste Leistung des Theaters an der Wien. Nach meiner Szene schaute ich in der 2. Gallerie zu, und ergötzte mich namenlos ungeachtet ich diese Lokal Zauber Posse schon unzählige male belacht habe. Jeder Witz in dem Munde Nestrois und Scholzs ist und wird neu.[25]

Am 27. März sieht Stainhauser Nestroys *Weder Lorbeerbaum noch Bettelstab*, äußert sich aber nicht näher. Am 10. April besucht er in Begleitung von Adalbert Prix Kringsteiners *Othellerl, der Mohr von Wien*, das "heute wirklich von bedeutendem Interesse war, da H. Nestroi die Rolle des als Othellerl unvergeßlichen Carl übernahm". Nestroy, der die Rolle übrigens schon 1830/31 während seines Preßburger Engagements gespielt hatte, konnte nach Stainhausers Dafürhalten Carl aber keineswegs ersetzen. Stainhauser machte diese Feststellung noch ein zweites Mal, als am 16. Juni Nestroy von Carl die Rolle des Fortunat in Lemberts *Fortunats Abenteuer* übernahm. Die Vorstellung sei insgesamt nicht exzellent gewesen, wozu noch kam, daß "überdieß H. Nestroi nicht an seinem Platze stand. Es ist sehr schwer dem Wiener Publikum sich in einer Rolle günstig zu presentiren, in welcher Karl ein so vortheilhaftes Andenken sich verdiente". Bei der Premiere von Nestroys *Eulenspiegel* am 22. April steht Stainhauser in der Rolle des Bedienten Johann auf der Bühne. Trotz der Bedeutungslosigkeit der Rolle "gefällt mir die Posse doch ungemein, und schien auch im Publikum sich ein großes Vorrecht gemacht zu haben; sie strotzt von Witz u[nd] komischen Einfällen", und an den der Premiere folgenden Abenden steigerte sich der Publikumsbeifall noch. Auch die Kritik nahm das Stück gut auf. Und Adalbert Prix saß über dem neu angekauften *Eulenspiegel* und hatte für nichts anderes Interesse.[26]

Auch im nächsten Nestroy-Stück, der überaus erfolgreichen Posse *Zu ebener Erde und erster Stock*, die am 24. September 1835 Premiere hatte, spielte Stainhauser mit: den Monsieur Bonbon. Anläßlich der Leseprobe am 18. September notierte er bereits:

Es ist ein äußerst gelungenes Werk, welches an Witz alles bisherige übertrifft, und meiner Meinung nach höher steht als sämtliche Produkte Raimunds. Eine moralische Tendenz, dramatische Handlung, ein gerechter Szenengang, Überraschung, Kürze, das sind Tugenden, die man bei wenig Stücken antrifft. Als einen besonderen Vorzug aber rühme ich, daß das ganze Lebensgemälde ohne allegorischen Personen seiner Entwicklung entgegengeht u[nd] doch mit einer schönen Moral schließt.

Und am Premierenabend kann Stainhauser feststellen:

Abends hielt unser Theater einen feierlichen Triumpf mit dem Nestroischen Stücke. Scholz u[nd] Nestroi wurden unzählige male gerufen, und Nestroi zwar mit einem: Vivat bewillkommt. Die Vorstellung war glänzend ausgestattet und ging sehr sicher studirt über die Szene. Der Beifall war beispiellos und Nestroi behauptete durch diese Arbeit allein schon den ersten Rang unter den Volksdichtern.

Zur eigenen Rolle sagte Stainhauser, daß er sie "größtentheils nach den Anleitungen des Direktors spiele. Leiste ich auch nichts Ausgezeichnetes in dieser nichts weniger als passenden Parthie für mich, so bin ich doch überzeugt, daß ich mir keine störende Einwirkung zu Schulden kommen lasse. Das Stück enthusiasmirt." Und das nicht nur in Wien; es wurde noch im gleichen Jahr auch in Graz, Prag, Pest und Brünn sowie in Hamburg und Leipzig gegeben, überall mit durchschlagendem Erfolg und war überdies "ein wahrer Goldfisch für die Direktion", wie sich die *Theaterzeitung* ausdrückte.[27]

Am 3. Oktober kam es allerdings abends im Theater zu einem Eklat. In der Zeitschrift *Der Sammler* war an eben jenem Tag ein negatives Feuilleton über Nestroys neues Stück aus der Feder von Franz Wiest erschienen. Nestroy revanchierte sich auf der Bühne durch das extemporierte Wortspiel, daß es ihn verwundere, daß ein so geistreiches Kartenspiel wie Whist ebenso heiße wie der dümmste Mensch von Wien. Stainhauser reagiert auf diesen Vorfall — der Nestroy übrigens eine Arreststrafe eintrug — zurückhaltend:

Abends ereignete sich ein merkwürdiges Skandal im Theater. Nestroi erfuhr während der Vorstellung, daß in einem Artikel der heutigen Nummer des Sammlers, worin der famose Schneiderssohn Wisth sein letztes Werk herabsetzt und selbst in eine Persönlichkeit ausartet, die zwar den Unwillen des gebildeten Lesers erregen mußte, ihm aber durchaus kein Recht [gibt] öffentlich auf der Bühne in seinem Zorne sich mit einem Extempore über besagten Rezensenten verlauten zu lassen.

Am 7. Oktober scheint sich ähnliches nochmals wiederholt zu haben, denn Stainhauser notiert: "Nestroi Wisth Historie".

Zu diesem Zeitpunkt war Stainhauser schon über den bloßen Bühnenkontakt hinaus mit Nestroy bekannt geworden. Am 14. September nämlich war er mit Scholz und einigen anderen nach Hetzendorf zu Nestroy gefahren, bei dem er zum Essen eingeladen war. Ins Tagebuch schreibt er darüber, daß "Nestroi [. . .] mit Dll. Weiler ein äußerst glückliches Leben zu führen scheint. Als Mutter und Hauswirthin dürfte man wenig Theaterdamen finden, welche ihr gleich kommen. Auch spricht sie sehr vernünftig, betragt sich recht modest u[nd] anständig, weit entfernt von abgeschmackter Ziererei." Stainhauser konnte nicht ahnen, daß es nicht zuletzt an ihm liegen würde, zwanzig Jahre später einen Sprung in diesem Eheglück zu kitten. — Am 1. Oktober verzeichnet er, daß er Nestroy im Bierhaus Keiner getroffen habe, "der tagtäglich dort frühstückt. Nestroi ist ein äußerst achtbarer Mann, den nebst vielen rühmenswerthen Eigenschaften besonders ein anspruchsloses Betragen auszeichnet". Bei Keiner sieht Stainhauser Nestroy noch öfters, begleitet ihn und die Weiler auch gelegentlich nach Hause und beklagt in den letzten Dezembertagen, daß es ihm aus Geldmangel nicht möglich sei nach Preßburg zu fahren, wo Nestroy, Scholz und Ignaz Stahl in Gastrollen auftraten.[28] Bei den gelegentlichen Einladungen, die Stainhauser gibt, finden wir zwar Scholz und den Theatersekretär Franz, nicht aber Nestroy unter den Gästen.

Wie sich das Verhältnis der beiden Männer in der Folgezeit entwickelte, läßt sich anfangs nur vermuten. Bis zu seinem Ausscheiden aus der aktiven Schauspielerlaufbahn Ende 1839 hob Stainhauser noch eine ganze Reihe kleinerer Nestroy-Rollen aus der Taufe: den Jäger Jackson in *Die beiden Nachtwandler* (6. Mai 1836), Glasermeister Flint in *Eine Wohnung ist zu vermieten* (17. Jänner 1837), Guido, den Sohn des Trüb, in *Das Haus der Temperamente* (16. September 1837), Bernhard Brand in *Glück, Mißbrauch und Rückkehr* (10. März 1838), Mr. Narciss und Pierre in *Gegen Torheit gibt es kein Mittel* (9. November 1838) und schließlich den Heinrich in *Die verhängnisvolle Faschingsnacht* (13. April 1839).

Der erste erhalten gebliebene Brief Nestroys an Stainhauser datiert vom 4. April 1839 und bezieht sich auf ein Walzer-Quodlibet, das Nestroy mit Stainhausers Hilfe zusammenstellen möchte (*Briefe*, 43). Zu diesem Zeitpunkt haben die beiden bereits das Du-Wort gewechselt. Es scheint hier aber noch angebracht, ein Wort zu dem, was man die "musische Persönlichkeit" Stainhausers nennen könnte, einzuflechten. Stainhauser liebte es, im geselligen Kreise Lieder zu singen, und hatte auch auf der Bühne hie und da kleine Gesangsrollen inne. Er hatte sich als Autodidakt in Brünn Notenlesen und Gesangsvortrag beigebracht und bezeichnet die häufigen Gesangsnachmittage als "für den wahrhaft Kunstgeweihten die angenehmsten Genüße".[29] Vor allem die Lieder des damals hochgeschätzten Siegismund Thalberg — "wahrhaft deutsche Gesänge"[30] — haben es ihm angetan, und er hofft, daß auch seine eigenen Gedichte von

Thalberg vertont werden würden. In ganz besonderem Maße aber schätzt
er Schubert: "Schubert war und ist der Lieder-Gott."[31] Dies gilt ganz
besonders für den Zyklus *Die Winterreise,* bei dem "Dichtung und
Komposition [. . .] Hand in Hand mit höchster Phantasie einher"[32]
schreiten. Auch der *Erlkönig* gefällt ihm, nicht so sehr das eben aus dem
Nachlaß edierte — übrigens bereits Jänner 1828 entstandene — Lied *Der
Winterabend* (D.938). Stainhausers Tagebucheintragung vom 30. Mai
1835 — die Erstausgabe des Liedes wurde erst am 9. Oktober ange-
kündigt, es scheint demnach aber schon früher vorgelegen zu sein — ist
interessant:

Der Winterabend von Schubert gefällt mir nicht so unbedingt als seine
Winterreise, welche an Gemüthlichkeit und Kunst alles bisherige in den
Hintergrund setzt. Auch ist jenes Lied aus dem Nachlasse des verewigten
Schubert. Ich aber halte auf solche nachgelassene Werke nicht viel, denn theils
sind es Kompositionen der Freunde des Verstorbenen, oder Spekulationen der
Kunsthändler, oder von Tondichtern nicht beendigte und von fremder Hand
ausgeführte Gedanken, oder Schöpfungen, welche der Verfasser der öffentlichen
Herausgabe noch nicht würdigte, und einer sorgfältigeren Ausfeilung unterwerfen
wollte.

Im konkreten Fall traf allerdings dies alles nicht zu.

Stainhauser sang aber nicht nur, er dichtete auch. Vornehmlich Lyrik,
meist an Anlässe gebunden, die sich jedoch nirgends über die Dutzend-
produktion der Zeit erhob. Im privaten Kreise trug er die Kinder seiner
Muse auch vor, einige seiner Gedichte wurden sogar vertont. Er schrieb
auch auf Bestellung Gedichte für Prix, Franz oder Privatpersonen und
vermerkt stolz, daß er sich am 16. März 1835 erstmals mit seiner
Dichtkunst Geld verdient habe. Die poetische Produktion begleitete ihn
durch sein ganzes Leben, 1848 erschienen seine *Lieder der Nationalgarde*
und ein Zwiegespräch zwischen einem Studenten und einem National-
gardisten mit dem Titel *Man sagt!* sogar im Druck; das Zwiegespräch
wurde überdies am 11. September 1848 im Carltheater gesprochen. Auch
ein patriotisches Festgedicht anläßlich der Vermählung Kaiser Franz
Josephs I. mit Elisabeth von Bayern 1854, mit Musik aus Haydns *Die
Jahreszeiten* unterlegt, wurde gedruckt und ebenso 1876 ein Gedicht zum
fünfundzwanzigjährigen Jubiläum von Josef Hellmesberger als Direktor
der Gesellschaft der Musikfreunde in Wien. Dazwischen gab es Gedichte
in der *Theaterzeitung,* in Almanachen und Stammbüchern oder einfach für
den Abend geschrieben, wie der Festprolog im Carltheater anläßlich der
Geburt von Erzherzogin Gisela 1856, der Stainhauser ein gesondertes
Honorar von 10 Dukaten eintrug, und zwar — wie Nestroy schreibt —
weil "der Freund Stainhauser und der Dichter Stainhauser sind zwey
verschiedene Individualitäten, aus dem Grunde schon, weil Deine
Freundschaft zu mir kein Gedicht ist" (*Briefe*, 133).[33] Stainhauser dürfte

diese lyrische Tätigkeit hoch geschätzt haben, und nach seinem Tode
äußert sich sein Sohn brieflich zu einem Bekannten über die nachgelassene
Lyrik, die er als kostbares Vermächtnis empfindet.[34]

In seinem ersten Jahr am Theater an der Wien versuchte sich
Stainhauser — wenn auch letztlich erfolglos — im dramatischen Genre.
Am 28. April 1835 schreibt er in sein Tagebuch: "Gestern Nachts fing ich
an ein Schauspiel zu kritzeln, wovon ich die ersten vier Szenen heute
schon der Mutter vorlas." Dabei hatte er aber große Vorbehalte gegen als
Stückeschreiber dilettierende Schauspieler, die er "witz- u[nd] sinnlose
Ignoranten, welche sich Komödien zu schreiben erkühnen" nennt, was
ihn auch abhält, sich "über eine ähnliche Leistung zu wagen".[35] Aber wie
er selbst bei anderer Gelegenheit so treffend feststellt: Es "fühlen sich am
allerschwersten derlei Schwächen selbst, die einem anderen ins Auge
stechend sind".[36] Fast täglich arbeitet er nun an seinem Stück und am 9.
August bringt er das fertige Werk zu Scholz, der es Carl für sein Benefiz
überreichen soll. Die positive Aufnahme durch Carl ermutigt ihn, schon
wenige Tage später mit einer Zauberposse zu beginnen: Carl

ließ sich in viele Lobeserhebungen über mein Stück ein, munterte sehr
schmeichelhaft mein Talent auf, und weissagte mir von diesem Versuche eine sehr
günstige Aufnahme. Er bemerkte mir die nöthigen Abänderungen selbst, lobte
besonders die Lieder u[nd] Karakterzeichnungen, und will in dieser Posse sogar
einen eigenen eingeschlagenen Weg, eine populäre Poesie, entdeckt haben.[37]

Nach einigen Schwierigkeiten mit der Zensur und Verschiebungen des
Aufführungstermines wird die Premiere endlich für den 25. November
festgesetzt. Mittlerweile hat Stainhauser auch das Zauberspiel bei Carl
eingereicht und arbeitet an drei selbständig-zusammenhängenden Einak-
tern, von denen er sich eine originelle Überraschung für das Publikum
erwartet.[38] Der völlige Mißerfolg seines Erstlings *Die Mißverständnisse* —
das Stück erlebte nur eine einzige Wiederholung vor leerem Haus —
dämpfte zwar Stainhausers dramatische Begeisterung, hielt ihn aber von
weiteren Versuchen nicht ab.[39] Nestroy war bei diesem verunglückten
Theaterabend seines späteren Freundes unter den leidtragenden Mit-
wirkenden gewesen.[40]

Für die unmittelbar folgenden Jahre läßt sich nur wenig zu Stainhauser
und Nestroy sagen. In den rudimentären Tagebuchaufzeichnungen der
Jahre 1847 bis 1851 wird Nestroy nur ein einziges Mal erwähnt, und zwar
anläßlich einer Absage der Vorstellung von *Glück, Mißbrauch und
Rückkehr* am 25. November 1848 "eingetretener Hindernisse wegen", und
in Klammer ist vermerkt: "Nestroi Heiserkeit".[41] Ansonsten findet sich
nur einiges zum Umbau des Leopoldstädter Theaters 1847 und zur
Revolution des Jahres 1848.[42] Als Taufpaten für seinen Sohn bittet Stainhauser — seit 1846 als Kassier und dann als Kassenkontrollor und

Ökonomieverwalter am Carltheater beschäftigt — mit Erfolg Direktor Carl und nicht Nestroy.[43] Zu diesen Zeiten vermittelt er auch in finanziellen und Theaterangelegenheiten für Nestroy bei Carl, wie sich aus den erhaltenen Briefen ablesen läßt. 1848 kam es — laut einem Polizeibericht aus dem Jahre 1859[44] — zu einem vorübergehenden Zerwürfnis zwischen Stainhauser und Carl, das indes bald wieder beigelegt wurde. Unter Nestroys Direktion 1854 bis 1860 — vollends aber nachdem 1855 der damalige Hauptkassier Aaron Jeiteles wegen Defraudation in Untersuchung genommen worden war — war Stainhauser "als verantwortlicher Leiter für die ganze Ökonomie und Cassagebarung der Theater-Unternehmung angestellt".[45] Während dieser Zeit — dies geht vor allem aus den Briefen Nestroys an ihn ganz deutlich hervor — ist er die Seele des Carltheaters. Er ist, wie es ein Zeitgenosse formuliert, "Nestroys intimster Freund und Vertrauensmann"[46] aus den späten Jahren. Abgesehen von einer kleinen Verstimmung im Jahre 1855, bei der Stainhauser Nestroy vergeblich um die Auflösung seines Vertrages ersuchte (*Briefe*, 118), ist Stainhauser der zuverlässige Vertraute in allen Theater- und Privatangelegenheiten Nestroys. Und auch nachdem Nestroy Stainhausers Vertrag 1859 gelöst hatte, um ihm ein Überwechseln in die Ökonomieverwaltung der Hofoper zu ermöglichen, betreibt Stainhauser Nestroys Theatergeschäfte weiter, so daß man ohne Übertreibung sagen kann, daß während Nestroys Direktionszeit vor allem Stainhauser und die Weiler das Carltheater geleitet hatten. Besonders das Geldwesen wird von Stainhauser penibel geregelt, und die bereits erwähnten Aufzeichnungen von 1847 bis 1851 sowie 1859/60 zeigen seine Genauigkeit beim Verzeichnen der Einnahmen und in allen Verrechnungsangelegenheiten. Der bereits zitierte Polizeibericht aus dem Jahre 1859 unterstreicht dies, wenn es heißt: "Steinhauser genießt das volle Vertrauen des Direktors Nestroy, ist bei demselben wegen seiner Geschäftüchtigkeit und Verläßlichkeit ebenso wie bei den Angestellten des Theaters wegen seines humanen Benehmens beliebt, und erfreut sich allenthalben des Rufes eines ehrenhaften und anständigen Wandels".

Aber auch im privaten Bereich ist Stainhauser Nestroys Vertrauter schlechthin. Sei es, daß er den immerwährenden Geldbedarf Nestroys — vor allem durch häufige Verluste im Kartenspiel bedingt — auf diskrete, d.h. der Weiler nicht auffallende Weise deckt, sei es aber auch, daß er der bewährte und verschwiegene Mittelsmann bei Nestroys amourösen Abenteuern ist. Nicht nur bei der bekannten Liaison Nestroys mit Karoline Köfer (*Briefe*, 131–136, 140–144), bei der Stainhauser der Hauptvermittler zu der mit Recht schwer gekränkten Marie Weiler war, sondern auch bei der Ehekrise 1858, deren Ursache nicht genau zu erkennen ist, die aber sicher wieder in Nestroys Eskapaden vom häuslichen Herd zu suchen sein wird (s. *Briefe*, 169–171). Und auch bei

einer wahrscheinlich in die Mitte der Fünfzigerjahre zu datierenden
Bekanntschaft Nestroys mit einer Mathilde K. ist es Stainhauser, der das
Ende der Beziehung regelt und Nestroy weitere Behelligungen erspart.
Ein erhalten gebliebener, undatierter Brief dieser Mathilde, in dem sie —
aus Ödenburg nach Wien gekommen — Stainhauser mitteilt, sie "harre
mit Ungeduld und Sehnsucht meines Retters, ihres Freundes N[estroy].
Ich muß ihn sehen!",[47] usw., wird kurz abgewehrt:

> Als ich mich das letzte Mal meines Auftrages an Sie entledigte, geschah es mit der
> ausdrücklichen Bemerkung, daß jede fernere Anmeldung zu unterbleiben habe
> u[nd] daher alle obwaltenden Angelegenheiten als abgeschlossen zu betrachten
> sind. Mich auf jene unzweideutige Darlegung berufend bin ich ausser Stande
> gesetzt irgendwie als Mittelsm[ann] aufzutreten.[48]

Nestroy wußte, was er an seinem Freund Stainhauser hatte: immer wieder
betont er dies auch. Stainhauser habe in der Affäre Köfer als "wahrer
Freund" gehandelt, er ersucht ihn um völlige Offenheit der Ansichten,
auch "wenn sie mit den meinigen nicht harmonisieren sollten", er
versichert ihn — vor allem der Weiler gegenüber — gegenseitiger
Diskretion und weiß überhaupt Stainhausers "wahre Freundschaft zu
meiner Person, treue Anhänglichkeit an meine Sache" (*Briefe*, 169) zu
schätzen. Aus manchem Brief klingt an, daß Stainhauser sich bewußt oder
unbewußt darum bemüht hat, Nestroy und wahrscheinlich auch der
Weiler nach dem Munde zu reden. Auch andere Zeugnisse zeigen, daß
Stainhauser seiner ganzen Natur nach ein treuer Diener seines jeweiligen
Herrn war und immer die Freundschaft und Anhänglichkeit zu einem
zweiten, bedeutenderen Menschen brauchte. Dabei stellt er selbst sich
ganz zurück, weil er eben seine eigene Stellung vor allem aus der seiner
Freunde herleitet. Ein Brief Stainhausers an die Weiler ist diesbezüglich
sehr aufschlußreich. Er, der einst permanent das Lob des Direktors Carl
gesungen hatte, erinnert nun an die schlechten Zeiten unter Carl und
daran, daß alle — auch Scholz und Nestroy — Opfer gebracht hätten, und
er fügt hinzu: "Wahrhaftig, einige Worte Lobes meines Vorgesetzten sind
mir lieber und wertvoller als alle Gagen der Welt, und ein noch so
winziges Zeichen der Huld läßt sich mit Geld nicht aufwiegen."[49] Und
ähnliche Lobesworte hat er später für Karl Treumann bereit, als dieser
sich 1866 von der Direktion des Kaitheaters zurückzieht.[50] Stainhauser
ist der klassische Zweite.

Von Interesse ist auch noch die Übereinstimmung Stainhausers und
Nestroys in politischen Fragen. Man kann dies nicht nur einem Brief
entnehmen, in dem Nestroy von ihrer "Übereinstimmung in politischen
Ansichten über Völker und Volk" spricht (*Briefe*, 218), sondern auch den
wenigen Sätzen, die Stainhauser zur Revolution des Jahres 1848 notiert.[51]
Hier zeigt er sich als vorsichtig konstitutionell, kaisertreu und von einer

gewissen Skepsis den Arbeitern gegenüber. Und auch der Polizeibericht von 1859 betont:

Bezüglich seiner politischen Haltung ist nie eine Wahrnehmung gemacht worden, welche zu einem Bedenken gegen ihn in dieser Richtung einen Anlaß hätte geben können, vielmehr sind die von ihm verfaßten theatralischen Gelegenheitsgedichte des wärmsten Patriotismus und inniger Anhänglichkeit an das a[ller]h[öchste] Kaiserhaus durchdrungen so, daß mit Grund seine Gesinnungstüchtigkeit in politischer Beziehung vorausgesetzt werden kann.

Dieser Polizeibericht ist Bestandteil eines Aktes, den die Hoftheaterintendanz anläßlich der Übernahme Stainhausers in den Dienst der Hofoper 1859 anlegen ließ. Mit Stainhauser wurde die neugeschaffene Stelle eines Ökonomie-Kontrollors der Wiener Hofoper besetzt. Der Akte liegt nicht nur der Brief Nestroys vom 19. Jänner 1859 bei, in dem dieser Stainhauser "zur Gründung seines Lebensglückes" aus dem Vertrag des Carltheaters entläßt, um ihm den Antritt des neuen Postens zu ermöglichen (*Briefe*, 183–184), sondern auch eine etwas umständliche Beschreibung Stainhausers über seine Agenden als Ökonomieverwalter am Carltheater. De facto führte Stainhauser neben seinen Agenden an der Hofoper Nestroys wichtigste Geschäfte bis zum Auslaufen von dessen Direktionszeit am 31. Oktober 1860 weiter. 1869 wurde Stainhauser — ungeachtet einer 1867 gegen ihn vorgebrachten Beschwerde wegen angeblicher Unzukömmlichkeiten bei den Dekorationsmalereien (Stainhauser wurde glänzend rehabilitiert) — Kanzleivorstand an der Hofoper und trat als solcher mit 31. Dezember 1883 in den Ruhestand. Am 23. Februar 1893 ist er betagt in Wien gestorben.[52]

. Die solideste Basis der Freundschaft zwischen Stainhauser und Nestroy, die bis zu Nestroys Tod 1862 bestand — auch mit Marie Weiler blieb Stainhauser bis zu deren Tode 1864 in Verbindung — war die unerschütterliche Ergebenheit und Anhänglichkeit Stainhausers an Nestroy, die diesem die Möglichkeit gab, sein Innerstes einem Menschen aufzuschließen, dem er vertrauen konnte und der in diesem Vertrauen einen hinlänglichen Lohn für seine Dienste und seine Freundschaft erblickte.

Summary

The diary of Ernst Stainhauser Ritter von Treuberg (1810–93) for the year 1835, recently acquired by the Wiener Stadt- und Landesbibliothek, and newly discovered archival material dating from 1859 add to our knowledge of this close friend of Nestroy's, to whom most of the dramatist's extant letters were written. The diary for 1835 is of importance for evidence it provides about the theatrical life not only of Vienna but also of the provinces: since October 1834, following engagements in Brünn and Agram (Zagreb), Stainhauser had been acting in St. Pölten, under his professional name Ernst Ritter, and it was only in February 1835 that he returned to his native Vienna. There he cultivated the influential agent Adalbert Prix and also Josef Franz, the secretary of the Theater an der Wien, on the stage of which he appeared for the first time in March 1835. He played small parts, including small singing parts (he had taken singing lessons in Brünn and was particularly fond of Schubert's songs), acted in small roles in a number of Nestroy's plays, and quickly involved himself in tasks to do with the administrative side of the theatre. He was also an occasional poet, and he tried his hand at writing several plays in the mid-to-late thirties, though these enjoyed little success.

It was in 1835 that he first made Nestroy's acquaintance, their contacts growing by the time of Nestroy's notorious extempore against the critic Franz Wiest in October. The first surviving letter from Nestroy to Stainhauser dates from 1839; he became Nestroy's closest friend in later years, sharing his political views and abetting him loyally in his private affairs. When Nestroy became the director of the Carltheater in 1854 — and especially after the retirement of the chief cashier, Aaron Jeiteles, in 1855 — Stainhauser was in control of the finances of the theatre, and indeed it was he and Marie Weiler who in effect jointly managed it. He continued to look after Nestroy's most important financial business after his appointment in 1859 as finance officer to the Opera House, where he continued to work, eventually as *Kanzleivorstand*, until his retirement in 1883.

5

W. E. Yates

DAS WERDEN EINES NESTROYSTÜCKS

Die Betrachtungen im folgenden Referat ergeben sich aus meiner
Mitarbeit an der neuen, von Jürgen Hein und Johann Hüttner
herausgegebenen historisch-kritischen Nestroy-Ausgabe.[1] Indem ich
mich mit der Entstehungsgeschichte der fünf von mir edierten Stücke, die
alle in den Jahren 1837–1838 im Theater an der Wien uraufgeführt
wurden, befaßte, gelangte ich zur Erkenntnis, daß gerade die editorische
Beschäftigung mit Nestroys Werk — sowohl mit den überlieferten
Manuskripten als auch mit der Rezeption der Premieren — besonders
aufschlußreiche Einblicke in die Eigenart der Alt-Wiener Posse im
allgemeinen gewährt. Es handelt sich also im folgenden nicht um die neue
Nestroy-Ausgabe, die wohl keiner Reklame mehr bedarf, sondern eher
um die Entstehung der Werke nicht nur Nestroys, sondern auch jener
anderen zeitgenössischen Stückeschreiber minderen Ranges, die sich
ebenfalls der Tradition der Lokalposse anschlossen.

Es sei gleich vorausgeschickt, daß der Uneingeweihte, der Nestroy nur
oberflächlich kennt und flüchtig liest, gerade durch seinen Gebrauch der
Gattungsbezeichnung "Posse" dazu verleitet werden kann, sein Werk als
trivial abzutun. Der Terminus "Posse mit Gesang", mit dem er die
Mehrzahl seiner Stücke bezeichnete, dient aber zum Teil dazu, seine
Verbundenheit mit seinen Vorgängern auf der Wiener Vorstadtbühne zu
verkünden, und zwar insbesondere mit Karl Meisl und Adolf Bäuerle, die
beide bis in die fünfziger Jahre hinein lebten. (Namentlich zu Bäuerle,
den er 1842 als sein glänzendes "Vorbield in dem Genre dramatischer
Dichtung" lobte, in dem er sich selber bewege (*Briefe*, 57), hatte er trotz
vereinzelter ärgerlicher Kritiken, die in der von Bäuerle herausgegebenen
Theaterzeitung erschienen, ein sehr gutes Verhältnis.) Darüber hinaus ist
schon zu seinen Lebzeiten eine gewisse Unklarheit in der Nestroy-
Rezeption zu bemerken, die damit zusammenhängt, daß er nicht nur als
Dramatiker berühmt war, sondern auch als Schauspieler. Dreißig Jahre
lang blieb er einer der großen Lieblinge des Wiener Vorstadtpublikums,
und wie bissig und kontrovers sich die Kritiker der Tages- und
Wochenblätter auch immer über manche seiner Stücke ausdrückten, seine
schauspielerische Leistung (und insbesondere seine Zusammenarbeit mit
dem beleibten und gutmütigen Wenzel Scholz) wurde immer wieder
rückhaltlos gelobt. In seiner vierzigjährigen Tätigkeit hat er beinahe
neunhundert Rollen gespielt, und für seine Zeitgenossen bedeutete der

Name Nestroy in erster Linie den Komiker, dessen Soloszenen — die witzigen Monologe und Couplets, mit denen er nicht nur in seinen eigenen Stücken, sondern auch in denen aller anderen Possenschreiber der Zeit versehen wurde — Höhepunkte der Unterhaltung bildeten.

Nestroy hat über achtzig Theaterstücke geschrieben, wovon rund neunzig Prozent erhalten sind. Daß er an Fruchtbarkeit etwa seinem Zeitgenossen und Rivalen Friedrich Kaiser nachstand, erklärt sich wohl zum Teil aus seiner Tätigkeit als Schauspieler: Wer allabendlich auf der Bühne steht und Hauptrollen spielt, hat ja alle Hände voll zu tun. Und dennoch schrieb er in den dreißiger und vierziger Jahren durchschnittlich drei Stücke pro Jahr. Mitten in dieser Zeit, in den Jahren 1838 und 1840, wurden Friedrich Kaiser und Karl Haffner, der später einer der Librettisten der *Fledermaus* werden sollte, zum ersten Mal vom Direktor Karl Carl als "Theaterdichter" angestellt. Carl verwendete für die Verträge ein gedrucktes Formular: seinen berüchtigten "Korsarenbrief", der die Verpflichtungen der Hausdramatiker festsetzte. Kaiser und Haffner wurden dazu verpflichtet, pro Jahr sechs bzw. acht abend-füllende Stücke in bestimmten Zeiträumen abzuliefern, alle von Carl angegebenen Änderungen vorzunehmen und jedes Stück, das entweder von Carl zurückgewiesen oder von der Zensur nicht bewilligt wurde, durch ein neues zu ersetzen. Alle diese Stücke mußten "genau für das zur Zeit der Ablieferung des Stückes bei dem Theater an der Wien angestellte Kunstpersonale berechnet sein".[2]

Es ist bekannt, daß das volkstümliche Unterhaltungstheater im Laufe des neunzehnten Jahrhunderts einer zunehmenden Kommerzialisierung ausgesetzt war. Die Fruchtbarkeit Nestroys und seiner Zeitgenossen — Friedrich Kaiser hat etwa hundertfünfzig Stücke geschrieben — war aber ein Phänomen, zu dem es viele Parallelen in der früheren Geschichte der Wiener Vorstadtbühne gibt. So verfaßte zum Beispiel Karl Friedrich Hensler, der Autor des *Donauweibchens*, zwischen 1786 und 1803 etwa achtzig Stücke für das Theater in der Leopoldstadt; und zwischen 1813 und 1828 wurde dasselbe Theater von Meisl, Bäuerle und Joseph Alois Gleich, dem Schwiegervater Raimunds, insgesamt mit durchschnittlich zweiundzwanzig Stücken pro Jahr versehen. Genau wie solche Kollegen und Vorläufer mußte auch Nestroy bühnenwirksame Stücke liefern, die auf bestimmte Schauspieler zugeschnitten waren und sich im Spielplan zu bewähren hatten. An Begabung war er zwar alles andere als ein typischer Volksdramatiker; aber die Arbeitsbedingungen, unter denen sein Werk vollbracht wurde, waren im großen und ganzen durchaus bezeichnend für das Vorstadttheater in der ersten Hälfte des neunzehnten Jahrhunderts.

Denn auch Nestroy hatte einen Kontrakt als Theaterdichter, der ihn allerdings ab 1847 nur dazu verpflichtete, "*zwei* neue Stücke in jedem Kontraktjahr zu schreiben" (SW xv, 563). Die erste Anregung zur Wahl eines neuen Stoffs ging in der Regel von der Lektüre aus: In irgendeinem populären Roman oder Theaterstück stieß er auf eine Handlung, die sich in einer Posse verwenden ließ, und er notierte die Hauptmotive und -rollen. Ein Brief aus seinem letzten Lebensjahr zeigt nicht nur, daß er immer auf der Suche nach brauchbaren Vorlagen war, die sich ohne große Schwierigkeiten für das Wiener Vorstadttheater bearbeiten ließen, sondern auch, wie sorgfältig er eine solche Vorlage auf die Möglichkeit der Umgestaltung hin untersuchte. — In diesem Fall kam er zum Schluß, es könne ihm nicht gelingen, aus einem französischen Operettentext "etwas den Anforderungen des deutschen Publicums Entsprechendes" zu machen: Es türme sich "eine Masse von Schwierigkeiten" auf, die Zensur müsse berücksichtigt werden, und darüber hinaus müßten "für gänzlich motivlose Momente Motive gefunden werden". "Es ist damit nicht gesagt," fügt er allerdings hinzu, "daß das Stück durchaus unmöglich ist, denn beym Theater giebt es ja eigentlich keine Unmöglichkeit" (*Briefe*, 226–227) — er entschied sich dennoch gegen das Projekt.

Zeit seines Lebens wurde Nestroy immer wieder des Plagiats beschuldigt. Noch 1847 konnte ein Rezensent feststellen, er besitze "eine Armuth im Erfinden".[3] In Wirklichkeit folgte er durchaus der internationalen Theatertradition, indem er einen fremden Stoff in eine Lokalposse verwandelte, die dankbare Rollen für das Komikerensemble Karl Carls deckte. In diesem Schaffensprozeß lieferte er nicht nur schablonenhaftes Theatermaterial, sondern er formte, wenn er im besten Zug war, die jeweilige Vorlage dichterisch zur selbständigen Komödie um. Sein Werk ist eines der Beispiele, die Egon Friedell für seine These anführt, daß es "im Wesen gerade der fruchtbarsten Dichter" liege, daß sie "ganz unbedenklich fremdes Gut verwerten". Das "vollblütige Genie ist," so fährt Friedell fort, "im sichern Bewußtsein, daß alles sein Eigentum ist, von hemmungsloser Gefräßigkeit."[4] Daß Nestroy aber Vorlagen besonderer Art benötigte, wurde schon zu seinen Lebzeiten von einigen Kritikern erkannt. Gerade diese Einsicht kommt z.B. — allerdings abschätzig formuliert — in einer sehr kritischen Rezension der Posse *Der Schützling* zum Ausdruck:

[. . .] Überhaupt tritt es in diesem Stücke neuerdings wieder ganz deutlich hervor, daß Nestroy in der Charakterzeichnung und szenischen Behandlung seiner Stücke nur so lange klar war, als er einfache und unbedeutende Stoffe behandelt, wie er an eine komplicirtere Erfindung kömmt, kann er sie nicht mehr bewältigen.[5]

Tatsächlich ergaben sich für Nestroy im Grunde zwei Möglichkeiten: Er mußte entweder eine an sich skizzenhafte Vorlage verwerten, die er schöpferisch erweitern konnte, oder aber ein rein schablonenhaftes Rohmaterial, das sich satirisch-parodistisch verwienern ließ. Gerade deshalb entnahm er seine Dramenstoffe vorwiegend Werken der Trivial-literatur. Wählte er als Vorlage ein selbständiges Kunstwerk, dann kam der Bearbeitungsprozeß über die bloße Imitation — also einen schlechthin unschöpferischen Prozeß — nicht hinaus. Diese verschiedenen Möglichkeiten sind an drei Werken aus den vierziger Jahren, die alle auf englische Vorlagen zurückgehen, mit besonderer Deutlichkeit nachweisbar.[6] In der fünfaktigen Posse *Die Anverwandten* merkt man, wie Nestroy sich bei der Bearbeitung seiner Vorlage, des großangelegten komischen Romans *Martin Chuzzlewit* von Charles Dickens, darauf beschränken mußte, Hauptszenen zu dramatisieren, wobei — mit Ausnahme der mit politischen Anspielungen gewürzten Monologe Edelscheins — sogar der Dialog großenteils nicht frei erfunden ist, sondern den Dialog der Vorlage resümiert und übersetzt. Das Ergebnis dieses offenbar nichtschöpferischen Verfahrens war, wie der Rezensent im *Humoristen* erkannte, daß "der vortreffliche Roman [. . .] zu einer entsetzlich langweiligen Posse" wurde (SW v, 609), — und daß das Stück durchfiel. Die Posse *Liebesgeschichten und Heiratssachen* hingegen ist ein Beispiel dafür, wie Nestroy nur das Handlungsgerüste einer fremden Komödie (*Patrician and Parvenu* von John Poole) übernahm, dem Dialog der Vorlage aber höchstens einzelne Anregungen verdankte, indem er die Vorlage zu einem vollkommen eigenständigen Werk verwandelte, wobei die konventionellkomödienhafte Dienerfigur Moonshine zum scharfzüngig-geistreichen Zyniker Nebel umgeformt wurde; und in *Einen Jux will er sich machen* gestaltete er einen kurzen und etwas farblosen Schwank (John Oxenfords Einakter *A Day Well Spent*) zu einer abendfüllenden Posse aus, in der sich ein breites Gesellschaftspanorama um die beiden komischen Hauptfiguren Weinberl und den eigens für Wenzel Scholz erfundenen Melchior entfaltet.

Aufgrund der geborgten Handlung entwarf Nestroy zunächst ein Szenarium, wobei er auch einzelne Einfälle aufzeichnete. Es folgten dann größere Entwürfe, und er formulierte einzelne Dialoge, in denen die größeren Rollen bereits bestimmten Schauspielern zugeteilt sind. Erst dann machte er sich an die erste Ausarbeitung der einzelnen Akte. Dieser typische Schaffensprozeß mit den verschiedenen Phasen der Vorarbeit ist am ausführlichsten von Helmut Herles am Beispiel vom *Talisman* dargelegt worden, und zwar in einer Studie, die sämtliche Entwürfe zum *Talisman* untersucht und die beweist, welch guten Einblick in seine Schaffensweise der Nachlaß Nestroys gewährt.[7]

Nestroy schrieb, wie es der Schauspieler Franz Wallner ausdrückte, "mit reißender Schnelligkeit",[8] und zwar meistens mit Bleistift. In die ersten Entwürfe trug er oft Änderungen und Verbesserungen ein, die häufig aus Platzmangel quergeschrieben wurden, und zwar in kleiner und sehr gedrängter Schrift, mit vielen Abkürzungen. Schließlich schrieb er eine Reinschrift, die dann von einem Kopisten abgeschrieben wurde. Es ist bisher, so viel ich weiß, kein Vertrag veröffentlicht worden, aus dem zu ersehen wäre, wie gut oder schlecht bezahlt die Kopisten waren. Die Hauptfigur in Nestroys Posse *Glück, Mißbrauch und Rückkehr*, Blasius Rohr, ist ein Kopist — allerdings nicht an einem Theater, sondern in einer Rechtsanwaltskanzlei. Sein stolzes Losungswort lautet: "Was ich abschreibe, das bleibt abgeschrieben" (*Stücke 14*, 12), die anderen Figuren erkennen aber eindeutig, daß er nur "ein hungriger Schreiber" ist. Es dürften die Verhältnisse im Theater nicht wesentlich anders gewesen sein; die Kopisten dürften zum Beispiel noch weniger verdient haben als die Dramatiker, und wir wissen, daß das Gehalt Friedrich Kaisers und Karl Haffners viel niedriger war als das der führenden Schauspieler — obwohl es irreführend wäre, eine bestimmte Summe anzugeben, da es sich nicht nur um ein Jahresgehalt handelte, sondern auch (was ebenfalls für den Kapellmeister gilt) um ein Honorar für jedes Stück, das es zu einer bestimmten Zahl Aufführungen brachte.

Man muß sich vergegenwärtigen, inwieweit die Überlieferung eines Texts von der Arbeit der "hungrigen Schreiber" abhängen kann. Man denke etwa an Nestroys Gelegenheitsposse *Moppels Abenteuer*, die bei der Premiere von der Kritik ziemlich einstimmig abgelehnt wurde, die sich aber auf der Bühne bewährte und bis in die fünfziger Jahre hinein im Spielplan blieb. Die Originalhandschrift ist verschollen. (Dies kommt natürlich sehr häufig im Theater vor und ist ein Problem, mit dem zum Beispiel die Forscher des Londoner Theaters des ausgehenden sechzehnten Jahrhunderts — mit dem das Wiener Theater der Biedermeierzeit auffallende kulturgeschichtliche Ähnlichkeiten hat[9] — vertraut sind.) Es sind aber vier Manuskripte von fremder Hand erhalten. Eines trägt das Datum des Entstehungsjahrs 1837, die drei anderen, die aus dem Archiv des Carltheaters stammen, sind vermutlich erst in den fünfziger Jahren entstanden. In dem am frühesten entstandenen Manuskript, das im Band *Stücke 12* der neuen Ausgabe als T_1 bezeichnet ist, sind die zwei Akte von verschiedener Hand, woraus mehrere auffallende Diskrepanzen in der Schreibung resultieren. Diese Diskrepanzen sind im Grunde genommen ziemlich unbedeutend; daraus aber, daß sie auch in zwei der anderen Manuskripte vorkommen, ist zu schließen, daß auch diese späteren Manuskripte mehr oder weniger unmittelbar auf T_1 zurückgehen. Nicht nur die Tatsache, daß das Stück überhaupt erhalten ist, sondern auch die Überlieferung des Texts bis in kleine Einzelheiten hinein hängt also von der Arbeit der Kopisten ab.

Daß die Stücke Nestroys und der anderen Vorstadtdramatiker alle als Spieltexte verfaßt wurden, bedeutet, daß es — im Gegensatz zu dem vom Dichter für den Druck vorbereiteten und sorgfältig durchgesehenen Text, mit dem die Literaturwissenschaft es gewöhnlich zu tun hat — grundsätzlich keine definitive Fassung ihrer Werke gibt. Es gibt eine Urfassung, die vom Autor stammt, sobald er aber das Manuskript dieser Urfassung dem Theaterdirektor überreicht, treten Änderungen ein — um Unebenheiten der Dialogführung oder der Szenenfolge zu bessern, um neue Witze (oder auch alte Witze) und musikalische Einlagen einzufügen, um den Einwendungen des Zensors entgegenzukommen. Dieses Verfahren setzt schon vor den Proben ein, indem der Komponist den Wortlaut der Lieder variiert, um den Text seiner Musik anzupassen. Der Text des Quodlibets scheint oft erst in der Zusammenarbeit von Autor und Komponist entstanden zu sein: In die Partituren zu den Possen *Die beiden Nachtwandler* und *Der Kobold*[10] ist der Text des Quodlibets z.t. von Nestroy selbst eingetragen, z.T. von Adolf Müller, dem begabten und sehr fruchtbaren Kapellmeister des Theaters an der Wien, der ihn mit den Partituren für etwa die Hälfte seiner Stücke versah. (Die sorgfältig geschriebenen Originalpartituren Müllers sind großenteils in der Musiksammlung der Wiener Stadt- und Landesbibliothek erhalten.)

Weitere Änderungen erfolgten im Laufe der ersten Aufführungen, um der Reaktion des Publikums und der Rezensenten Rechnung zu tragen. So heißt es z.B. in einer der ersten Kritiken über Nestroys Zauberposse *Der Kobold*: "Einige Kürzungen, insoweit die Ökonomie des Stückes sie gestattet, würden dem Ganzen sehr dienlich sein, und es steht zu erwarten, daß dieselben vorgenommen werden" (*Stücke 14*, 266). Schon drei Tage später konnte ein anderer Rezensent im selben Blatt berichten, das Werk gewinne "durch die seit der ersten Aufführung vorgenommenen zweckmäßigen Abkürzungen [. . .] immer mehr Leben und Beifall" (*Stücke 14*, 273). Auf dem Theaterzettel der Premiere war dieses Stück als eine "parodirende Zauberposse mit Gesang in 3 Aufzügen" angeschlagen worden (sowohl der erste Akt als auch der zweite waren in je zwei Abteilungen, so daß es also insgesamt fünf Abteilungen hatte); der erhaltene Text ist in vier Akten, was dem Kürzungsprozeß genau entspricht. Und sollte sich ein Stück jahrelang im Spielplan behaupten, wie z.B. bei *Der böse Geist Lumpazivagabundus* der Fall war, kamen im Laufe der Jahre weitere Änderungen und Zusätze hinzu, die Nestroy auf Einzelblättern und -zetteln dem vollendeten Text mit Stecknadeln anheftete.

Es handelt sich also bei dieser Theaterarbeit um etwas grundsätzlich Wandelbares, welchem man viel näher kommt, indem man die Theatermanuskripte mit allen ihren Schreibfehlern, ihren Zusätzen und Streichungen behandelt, als wenn man den Text als geschlossenes Ganzes betrachtet — als ob es sich tatsächlich um eine Ausgabe letzter Hand handelte. In diesem Zusammenhang verdient auch ein weiterer Umstand erwähnt zu werden. Da ein neues, für ein bestimmtes Theater geschriebenes Stück auf anderen Bühnen nachgespielt werden konnte, sobald es im Druck vorlag, wurden Stücke oft erst dann gedruckt, wenn sie nicht mehr als zugkräftige Repertoirestücke wirken konnten. Der Erstdruck eines solchen Stücks wie *Glück, Mißbrauch und Rückkehr* trägt allerdings auf dem Titelblatt die Mahnung, es sei *"für Wien* ausschließendes Eigenthum der unter der Leitung des Herrn Directors Carl stehenden Bühnen", und die meisten Stücke Friedrich Kaisers erschienen unter ähnlichen einschränkenden Bedingungen: viele wurden in das "Wiener Theater-Repertoir" aufgenommen — eine Reihe, die bei dem aufs Theater spezialisierten Wiener Verlag Wallishausser erschien, und in der jeder Band "den Bühnen gegenüber als Manuscript gedruckt" wurde. Ob ein Stück überhaupt veröffentlicht wurde, hing jedoch oft von der Berechnung ab, ob mehr Geld durch den öffentlichen Verkauf des gedruckten Texts zu machen war oder durch die Unterdrückung des Texts (mit Ausnahme der Gesangsnummern, die mit Klavierbegleitung in Einzelheften verkauft werden konnten), solange das Stück im Spielplan blieb. Daher kommt es, daß viel weniger Nestroy-Stücke zu seinen Lebzeiten gedruckt wurden, als Stücke eines Friedrich Kaiser. In den einzelnen Heften des "Wiener Theater-Repertoirs" begegnet man noch bis in die fünfziger und sechziger Jahre hinein der Angabe, daß "sämtliche Theater" verschiedener Autoren bei Wallishausser erschienen seien, von Nestroy aber nur ein Dutzend Stücke. Daher kommt es auch, daß etwa *Glück, Mißbrauch und Rückkehr*, einer seiner größten Erfolge, erst 1845 — sieben Jahre nach der Wiener Uraufführung — bei Wallishausser im Druck erschien. (Ähnlich ging es nebenbei dem größten Zugstück Grillparzers, dem Märchen *Der Traum ein Leben*, das 1834 uraufgeführt wurde, aber erst gegen Ende 1839 in Buchform erschien, während das Lustspiel *Weh dem, der lügt!*, das vier Tage vor der Premiere von *Glück, Mißbrauch und Rückkehr* durchgefallen war, schon im nächsten Jahr [1839] in den Buchhandlungen zu haben war.) Nestroy führte ein sorgfältiges Verzeichnis aller von ihm gespielten Rollen und bewahrte die Reinschriften seiner Stücke ebenfalls sorgfältig auf; da aber die Drucke für die eigentliche Aufgabe des Theaters, die Aufführung, ohne Belang waren, gab er sich mit deren Vorbereitung nicht ab, und sie sind schlampig gedruckt, mit vielen Druckfehlern.

So sind wir beispielsweise für die zuverlässige Überlieferung des Texts von *Glück, Mißbrauch und Rückkehr* eher auf drei Theatermanuskripte, die alle viele Gebrauchsspuren aufzeigen, angewiesen, als auf den nachlässig hergestellten, 1845 erschienenen Erstdruck, dessen Text eine bearbeitete, am Schluß der mittleren Akte etwas gekürzte Fassung darstellt. Es befindet sich außerdem unter den anderen erhaltenen Manuskripten ein sogenanntes Rollenheft, eine Abschrift der Lieder, die von der Hauptfigur gesungen werden. In dieses Rollenheft hat Nestroy selber nicht nur einzelne Verbesserungen, sondern auch den Text einer ganzen Strophe eingetragen.

In den Partituren sind oft vor den einzelnen Nummern einige Worte mit Bleistift notiert, die offensichtlich als Stichworte — Hinweise für den Kapellmeister — dienen sollten. Im Falle eines Stücks, dessen Text nicht handschriftlich gesichert ist, können solche Aufzeichnungen, obwohl sie flüchtig und skizzenhaft geschrieben wurden, nicht nur die Authentizität der Überlieferung durch die von Vinzenz Chiavacci und Ludwig Ganghofer herausgegebenen *Gesammelten Werke* von 1890/91 zum Teil bestätigen, sondern zugleich einen Einblick in den Text gewähren, wie er zur Zeit der letzten Proben bestand. An einer Stelle im gedruckten Text von *Eine Wohnung ist zu vermieten* ruft z.B. eine der jungen Damen, von einem Liebhaber umworben, aus: "Gott, warum brachte ich jetzt nicht die einzige kleine Silbe 'Nein' heraus?" (*Stücke 12*, 44). In der Partitur wurde diese Rede, auf die ein Chor folgt, zunächst in etwas gekürzter Form notiert: "Warum bracht ich nicht die einzige Sylbe Nein heraus", diese Worte wurden dann gestrichen und durch eine andere Fassung ersetzt: "Gott in welcher peinlichen Lage befinde ich mich jetzt" (*Stücke 12*, 170). In diese Rede ist im ursprünglichen Kontext gar keine indezente Zweideutigkeit hineinzulesen; es drängt sich immerhin die Vermutung auf, daß es sich hier um eine Änderung handelt, die aus einer Einwendung des Zensors hervorging. Diese Vermutung hängt mit einem der großen Rätsel der zeitgenössischen Nestroy-Rezeption zusammen, nämlich mit der Frage, warum diese durchaus lebenskräftige Posse 1837 durchfiel. (Sie wurde vom Theaterpublikum schroff abgelehnt und ärgerlich ausgezischt und erlebte nur drei Aufführungen.) Weil sich der Mißerfolg der Premiere nicht — oder nicht allein — mit der Einstellung des Publikums zur Satire begründen läßt,[11] erhebt sich die Frage, ob die Wirkung des Stücks durch die Eingriffe der Zensur entkräftet wurde — ob der Aufführung ein verstümmelter Text zugrundelag. Dies läßt sich freilich nicht mehr nachweisen, da das Zensurmanuskript (das heißt, das von einem Kopisten abgeschriebene Manuskript, das dem Zensor vorgelegt wurde und seine Streichungen zeigt sowie alle Änderungen, die infolge seiner Einwendungen vorgenommen wurden) nicht erhalten ist. Es ist aber von großem Interesse, daß die in die Partitur eingetragene Änderung die Möglichkeit bestätigt, die Zensur habe ihre Hand im Spiel gehabt.

Der Zensor beanstandete allerlei Wendungen, die er aus politischen, religiösen und gesellschaftlichen Gründen für fragwürdig hielt — bekanntermaßen war es gesetzlich verboten, nicht nur "geistliche Personen", höhere Staatsbeamte und das Militär, sondern auch "Stände der bürgerlichen Gesellschaft", "wäre es auch nur durch eine entfernte Hindeutung", ins Lächerliche zu ziehen[12] — , und er verfuhr besonders streng mit allen Stellen, die als zotenhafte Zweideutigkeiten aufgefaßt werden konnten, oder die als sexuelle Anspielungen hätten erscheinen können, wenn sie mit ausdrucksvollen Gebärden begleitet worden wären.

Er strich solche Stellen mit schwarzem Bleistift durch. Zwei Stellen im ersten Akt vom *Haus der Temperamente* sind für die Kriterien der Zensur bezeichnend.[13] In der 13. Szene drückt der junge Sanguiniker Felix seinen Gefallen an der schönen Isabella aus: "Papa, Sie haben immer hübsche Stubenmädln gehabt, aber die ist das Capo" (*Stücke 13*, 49). Der Zensor hat offensichtlich die Möglichkeit einer indezenten Nebenbedeutung gewittert: Die Worte "Sie haben immer gehabt" sowie die letzten fünf Worte der Rede sind beanstandet worden, so daß die Rede auf den farblosen Wortlaut "Papa, das ist ein hübsches Stubenmädl" reduziert werden mußte. In der 22. Szene überlegt sich Herr von Fad die Implikationen eines an seine Tochter adressierten Briefs: " 's Madl kann ja unschuldig seyn" (*Stücke 13*, 76). Auch hier hat der Zensor eingegriffen, und bei der Premiere lautete die Rede: " 's Madl kann vielleicht nichts davon wissen." Es kommt sehr oft vor, daß man die Zweideutigkeit solcher Stellen erst deswegen bemerkt, weil der Zensor gewisse Worte durchgestrichen hat. Als ein weiteres Beispiel mag eine Stelle in der 3. Szene angeführt werden, wo Herr von Froh freudig ausruft: "In wenig Tagen ist Hochzeit, und dann wird's gehen!" (*Stücke 13*, 17). Ständig auf der Suche nach Anzüglichkeiten, strich der Zensor das Wort "gehen", worauf die Rede harmloser formuliert wurde: "In wenig Tagen ist Hochzeit, und dann wird getanzt." Noch erstaunlicher wirkt die Wachsamkeit des Zensors bei einem Dialog im zweiten Akt, wo der verliebte Herr von Froh dem Friseur Schlankel seine Absicht anvertraut, sich um eine gewisse Witwe zu bewerben, worauf Schlankel fragt: "Kann ich da vielleicht in was dienen? Sie ist Kundschaft von mir" (*Stücke 13*, 102). Hier strich der Zensor das eine Wort "da", was wohl nur daraus zu erklären ist, daß Nestroy, der selber die Rolle des Schlankel spielte, für die ausdrucksvolle Kraft seiner Gebärden bekannt war.

Es wird selten darauf hingewiesen, wie schnell die von der Zensur verlangten Änderungen durchgeführt werden mußten. Aus dem Zensurvermerk auf dem Manuskript vom *Haus der Temperamente* ist zu ersehen, daß die Aufführung erst fünf Tage vor der Premiere behördlich bewilligt wurde. Da aber die Einwendungen des Zensors sich zum Teil voraussehen ließen, wurde im Vorstadttheater eine Art provisorischer Vorzensur ausgeübt. Nestroy selbst bearbeitete regelmäßig seinen handschriftlichen Text, und zwar meistens in seiner eigenen Reinschrift, indem er möglicherweise angreifbare Stellen nicht — wie bei gewöhnlichen Verbesserungen — mit geraden Linien strich, sondern sie spiralenartig durchstrich und weniger bedenkliche Wendungen darüber eintrug. Daß es sich nicht um definitive Änderungen und Besserungen handelt, ist daraus zu entnehmen, daß die angestrichenen Stellen manchmal in den Theatermanuskripten und Erstdrucken ungekürzt wiederkehren, was beweist, daß sie dem Zensor entgangen sind.[14] Im ersten Akt der Zauberposse *Der*

Kobold sagt z.B. der "Beherrscher des unterirdischen Feuerreiches", Brennroth: "Der Spruch des Schicksals is ergangen, und gegen das Schicksal seyn wir mächtige Wesen alle nur arme Narren" (*Stucke 14*, 115). Offensichtlich ist es dem Autor oder dem Regisseur, vielleicht im Laufe der Proben, aufgefallen, daß diese Stelle als eine politische Anspielung gedeutet werden könnte; die Worte "mächtige Wesen" sind im erhaltenen fragmentarischen, auf dem Einband als "Souflierbuch" bezeichneten Theatermanuskript provisorisch "überringelt", und als Alternative ist das Wort "Geister" eingetragen worden (*Stucke 14*, 284) — übervorsichtigerweise, wie es sich herausstellt, denn die Stelle kehrt unverändert im vollständigen, auf einem nicht mehr erhaltenen Manuskript beruhenden Text wieder, der in den *Gesammelten Werken* von 1890/91 wiedergegeben ist.

Daß die Änderungen, denen der Text in letzter Minute infolge der meist kleinlichen — oft willkürlich erscheinenden — Eingriffe des Zensors unterzogen werden mußte, den Erfolg der Aufführung beeinträchtigen konnten, braucht wohl nicht weiter dargelegt zu werden. Die Aufnahme ist aber auch in anderer Hinsicht von Bedeutung, denn aus den Kritiken ist nicht nur zu ersehen, wie die Rezensenten und das Publikum auf ein Stück reagierten, sondern sie belegen auch die kritischen Erwartungen, die einer Novität entgegengebracht wurden. Sie sind also nicht nur als Dokumente der Wirkungsgeschichte zu betrachten, die vom Erfolg oder Mißerfolg einer Aufführung berichten, sondern sie bringen zugleich jene Kriterien zum Ausdruck, die, insofern die Rezensenten die öffentliche Meinung vertraten oder bildeten, für den Geschmack des Publikums — einen der wichtigsten konstitutiven Faktoren des Volkstheaters — maßgeblich waren.[15]

Kann man etwa daran zweifeln, daß Nestroy, nachdem er die ganze Handlung von *Eine Wohnung ist zu vermieten* konsequent in Wien und der Umgebung Wiens lokalisiert hatte, gerade durch den Mißerfolg dieses Stücks beim Publikum dazu verleitet wurde, im *Haus der Temperamente* einen virtuosen Sprung ins Spielerisch-Unrealistische zu machen? Kann man daran zweifeln, daß jene Besprechungen, die "lustspielhafte" Elemente im *Haus der Temperamente* lobend hervorhoben, der Entscheidung zugrundelagen, sein nächstes Stück, *Glück, Mißbrauch und Rückkehr*, auf dem Theaterzettel als ein "Lustspiel" zu bezeichnen (einem Wagnis, das allerdings auf scharfe Kritik stieß)? Kann man daran zweifeln, daß die freundliche Aufnahme der Tanzeinlage im dritten Akt von *Glück, Mißbrauch und Rückkehr*, in der Nestroy und seine Partnerin Marie Weiler das Ballett satirisch nachahmten, bei Nestroys Entschluß, in seinem nächsten Stück ein romantisches Ballett zu parodieren, maßgebend war?

Die Vielfalt der kritischen Urteile, die in den Besprechungen der

Premieren zum Ausdruck kamen, gehört aber zur schöpferischen Atmosphäre, in welcher ein Text für das Vorstadttheater entworfen und bearbeitet wurde. Es ist z.B. unmöglich, den ästhetischen Voraussetzungen, von denen Nestroy und seine Zeitgenossen ausgingen, gerecht zu werden, ohne sich des schon in den dreißiger Jahren immer wieder zum Ausdruck gebrachten Begriffs des erbaulichen, im Volksleben wurzelnden "Volksstücks" bewußt zu sein. Diesem Geschmack, der mit der Forderung nach einer "gesunden Moral" verbunden war und gegen den Nestroy sich auflehnte, kam Friedrich Kaiser 1840 mit dem sogenannten "Lebensbild" *Wer wird Amtmann?* entgegen, um von Nestroy noch im selben Jahr in der Salonszene im *Talisman* satirisch angegriffen zu werden (obwohl Nestroy selber die Hauptfigur spielte, deren Name Florian Baumlang eine Anspielung auf seinen eigenen Wuchs war).

Genau wie alle die Vorstadtdramatiker Stoffe und sogar einzelne Witze von anderen Dramatikern übernahmen, so mußten sie ebenfalls nicht nur die Aufnahme ihrer eigenen Stücke, sondern auch die Einstellung der Kritiker und des Publikums im allgemeinen und deren Urteil über die Stücke anderer Dramatiker berücksichtigen. Gerade die entstehungsgeschichtlichen Zusammenhänge werden dadurch differenziert und erhellt, daß man die einzelnen Stufen des Schaffensprozesses vom editorischen Gesichtspunkt aus verfolgt: die ersten Entwürfe, die Reinschrift, die Partitur, die Herstellung von Theatermanuskripten durch die Kopisten, die provisorische Vorzensur, die Zensur durch die Behörde, die Aufführung, die Aufnahme durch das Publikum und die Rezensenten, die wiederum die Konzeption des nächsten Stückes beeinflussen konnte. Das einzelne Theaterstück erweist sich schließlich nicht nur als etwas Wandelbares, es entsteht mitten im Kontinuum der Theaterpraxis, und wer ihm gerecht sein will, muß es im Kontext dieses Kontinuums, im Kontext seiner Entstehung betrachten.

Summary

Editorial work on the transmission and reception of Nestroy's plays vouchsafes helpful insights into the typical genesis of a comedy in the Viennese popular theatre. Like other dramatists working for Karl Carl, Nestroy was contractually committed to providing a certain number of acceptable plays a year, written specifically for the members of the theatre company — the quantity of plays being limited in Nestroy's case by his exceptionally heavy workload as an actor. He started by choosing a source that lent itself to adaptation as a *Posse*; ideally, as his adaptations of English originals illustrate, he would take as his source either a thin and trivial work that he could creatively expand or else a stiffly conventional piece that he could in effect parody. After sketching a scenario and drafting his first notes he would proceed rapidly to complete a first manuscript and then make a fair copy, which would subsequently form the basis of copies made for submission to the censor and for work in the theatre. These manuscripts produced by hack copyists can be of vital importance for the transmission and even survival of a text, and are certainly often of greater authenticity than the published versions, which in Nestroy's case were carelessly produced. For there was no such thing as a finished text in the popular theatre. As soon as the dramatist's fair copy was submitted it was subject to alteration: the words of the songs might be varied by the composer, the dialogue changed either in rehearsal or — as in *Das Haus der Temperamente* — at the hand of the censor (or in the precautionary "pre-censorship" widely practised in the popular theatre), or again later in response to audience reaction and to criticisms in reviews, or as new ideas were added over the years. The plays of the years 1837–1838 provide a clear example of how the reception of Nestroy's plays could influence his selection of the form and manner of his next work, and so underline the importance of viewing his works in the context of the continuum of the theatre for which they were composed.

6

Johann Hüttner

DER ERNSTE NESTROY

Nestroys Stellung als Satiriker, als Sozialkritiker, als Meister des Worts sowie als Komiker ist unumstritten — er bildet eine der am meisten durchforschten Schlüsselfiguren zum Verständnis des Alt-Wiener Volkstheaters.

Dem Leser des Nestroywerks wird aber nicht entgangen sein, daß — wenn auch nicht der größte Teil — dennoch ein merkbar umfangreicher Teil des überlieferten Werks mit den uns bekannten Elementen der Alt-Wiener Volks*komödie* nicht gut zusammenpaßt (da weder komisch noch dialektbezogen noch das Volk thematisierend).

Man wird in diesem Zusammenhang Ferdinand Raimund erwähnen, dessen ernste Elemente in mehreren seiner Stücke mitunter als individuelle Versuche gewertet wurden, Raimunds unzureichende Bildung zu kompensieren oder seine Burgtheaterfähigkeit unter Beweis stellen zu wollen.

Wie dem auch sei, Vorstadtschauspieler konnten sehr wohl ans Hoftheater engagiert werden oder hätten es werden können (z.B. die vergeblichen Versuche um Wenzel Scholz[1]), aber das Repertoire hatte frei von Lokalanspielungen und den anderen "Niederungen" in Possenpersonal und -inhalt zu sein. Raimund hätte keine Chance gehabt, als Autor ans Burgtheater zu kommen; sogar Grillparzers *Der Traum ein Leben* wurde als nicht gerade geziemend fürs Burgtheater gehalten, vor allem, was das Sujet und die notwendige fürs Burgtheater unübliche dekorative Pracht- und Kostenentfaltung betrifft;[2] das Werk entpuppte sich allerdings als einer der größten Geschäftserfolge des Burgtheaters der damaligen Zeit (die Zahl der Leser muß jedoch aufgrund der Verkaufszahlen seines Texts zu Lebzeiten sehr, sehr klein gewesen sein).[3]

Bei Friedrich Kaiser, an den man im "ernsten" Kontext nach Raimund wahrscheinlich am ehesten denkt, wird man ebensowenig den versuchten Sprung in die Hohe Literatur vermuten wie bei den ernsteren Stücken Nestroys oder besser: seinen Stücken mit ausgeprägteren ernsten Stellen. Mit Anzengruber tut man sich, je nach Sichtweise, schon schwer, ihn in das richtige Schächtelchen innerhalb des Alt-Wiener Volkstheaters zu stellen — seine ernsten Theaterstücke werden da schon lieber einer neuen Epoche und neuen Theatern zugeordnet, was unter anderem im Kontext des Nationalitätenstreits gesehen werden kann.

Bei Nestroy muß die partielle Abkehr von der Possenkomik andere Gründe gehabt haben.

Vieles, was wir über das Alt-Wiener Volkstheater wissen, ist uns durch
die Forschungen Otto Rommels klargeworden. Andererseits muß aber
gesagt werden, daß das Erkenntnisinteresse und damit die Richtung der
Forschung (auch die von Rommels vielen Nacheiferern und -ahmern)
durch die Einschränkung auf Alt-Wiener Volks*komödie* und durch die
eindeutige Höherbewertung folkloristischer, bodenständiger Stränge
eingeengt worden war.

Das wirkt sich negativ aus auf Versuche, die Wiener Entwicklungen in
einen internationalen Kontext zu stellen, um dadurch mehr über
traditionsbildende Erscheinungsformen und mehr über das, was Volkstheater im weiteren Sinne sein kann, zu erfahren, und negativ auf Frage-
stellungen, die sich um anderes als um Aspekte der Komik, der Satire, der
Lokalanspielungen etc. kümmern — so z.B. auch auf die Frage nach dem
ernsten Nestroy.

Es sei hier nicht auf sein historisch-romantisches Drama *Prinz
Friedrich*, in dem er nicht mitwirkte, eingegangen, sondern es sollen bei-
spielhaft einige von seinen anderen Stücken mit größerem Anteil des
Ernsten im Rahmen eines Komikertheaters herangezogen werden:
Bezeichnenderweise sind in der oft überlappenden und problematischen
Einteilung der Stücke Nestroys durch Rommel in den "Volksstück"-
Bänden am ehesten solche mit ernsten Elementen zu finden, aber nicht
nur: *Der Erbschleicher* und *Die beiden Herren Söhne* sind Possen, und *Prinz
Friedrich* schien ja bekanntlich in der Rommelschen Nestroyausgabe nicht
auf. Wieso gerade das "dramatische Gemälde" *Der Treulose oder Saat und
Ernte* zu den Volksstücken gezählt wurde? wohl, weil es woanders schon
gar nicht hingepaßt hätte.

Ich beziehe mich im besonderen nicht auf jene Stücke, in denen
Repräsentanten aus dem Volk im Vordergrund stehen, wie gerade bei
den späten Volksstücken in Rommels Einteilung, sondern auf jene
ernsten, weniger populär gewordenen (dennoch damals nicht unbedingt
alle als Versager eingestuften) Produkte, in denen der Anteil des
(Komiker-)Lachtheaters am wenigsten ausgeprägt ist: Und ich denke hier
besonders an das "dramatische Gemälde" *Der Treulose* von 1836 und *Der
Erbschleicher* von 1840; aber auch das "lustige Trauerspiel" *Gegen Torheit
gibt es kein Mittel* (1838) und *Die beiden Herren Söhne* (1845) hätten
vielleicht dankbare Objekte abgeben können.

Beim "ernsten Nestroy" geht es nun nicht um die Ernsthaftigkeit seiner
Aussage — hier ist es ja anerkannt, nach einem langen Weg, nicht immer
von der Forschung angeführt, daß im Kleid der Posse viele ernste,
Betroffenheit auslösende Anliegen formuliert, problematisiert wurden, oft
auch in *der* Form, daß auf einer zweiten Ebene Aussagen an der Ober-
fläche relativiert wurden, getarnt wurden könnte man vielleicht auch
sagen.

Wie sieht das nun beim ernsten Nestroy aus, ernst im Sinne von Stücken und Passagen, in denen Komik und Satire zumindest vordergründig nicht Platz greifen? Überliest man das wenige, das in der Bewertung von der Forschung gesagt wurde, kommt man zu dem Schluß: All das, was wir beim heiteren Nestroy an Ernsthaftigkeit finden, vermissen wir beim ernsten Nestroy.

Rio Preisner hilft nicht wesentlich weiter; er meint allerdings, *Gegen Torheit gibt es kein Mittel* zum Beispiel sei in unserer Einschätzung unterbewertet[4] — es handelt sich dabei um eines der vorhin genannten Werke, mit denen die zeitgenössische Kritik am wenigsten anfangen konnte. Franz H. Mautner schreibt 1974: *Gegen Torheit gibt es kein Mittel* war

weder ein Trauerspiel, noch als Text lustig [. . .] Es war ein übler, an Geschmacklosigkeit streifender Einfall, einen unwahrscheinlich törichten und außerdem dummen Menschen, Simplicius Berg, zum Helden eines lustigen "Trauerspiels" zu machen, ihn darin in drei "Abteilungen", den drei Stadien seines Lebens, nicht nur sein Vermögen verlieren, sondern auch, am Schluß, sein Glück zerstören und darüber strahlend triumphieren zu lassen, ein Ende, das zu albern ist, um tragikomisch genannt zu werden. Die "Lustigkeit" soll durch das mitleidlose Amusement über seine Dummheit und durch eine Anzahl von Scherzen erzeugt werden [. . .], die zumeist so krud sind, als wäre das ganze "Trauerspiel" für ein Publikum von Dummköpfen bestimmt.[5]

Er spricht von einem "ärgerlichen Text", einer unabsichtlich absurden Handlung, und findet die Summe aller dieser erstrebten disparaten Effekte bejammernswert. Mautner sieht offenbar so wenig wie die kritikenschreibenden Zeitgenossen Nestroys das Wesen der Dummheit, das mir wohl darin zu bestehen scheint, sich wider besseres Wissen nicht überzeugen zu lassen (manchmal, wie es scheint, heute als politische Tugend gepriesen).

Über den *Erbschleicher* weiß Mautner wenig zu sagen, außer daß er ein Zwitterprodukt sei mit vorwiegend ernster Handlung,[6] während Preisner das Doppelgängermotiv ortet,[7] ohne zu sehen, daß es hier als Teil einer Intrige als Verkleidung eingesetzt ist und für die Betrachtung des Stückgehalts nur von peripherem Interesse sein kann. Zum *Treulosen* lohnt es sich mit Ausnahme zweier oder dreier Szenen nach Mautner nicht "dieses endlos lange 'Gemälde' [. . .] um ästhetischen Vergnügens willen zu lesen";[8] er hat vielleicht recht, wenn er weiter sagt: "Auch scheint dem Nestroy-Leser in den ersten beiden Akten das bilderreiche *ernste* Pathos und die sentimentale Schwermut der Mädchen manchmal an Parodie zu grenzen, im dritten aber kann kein Zweifel mehr darüber bestehen, daß die papierene Redeweise des edlen Freundes und wahrhaft treuen Gatten Herrn von Solwig [*sic*] ernst gemeint ist."[9]

Man wird der Annahme, daß wir die Ernsthaftigkeit des heiteren Nestroy beim ernsten Nestroy vermissen, vorerst einmal rechtgeben

müssen, wenngleich sich die Frage stellt, ob wir nicht beim ernsten
Nestroy — mangels bisheriger eingehender ernster Beschäftigung damit
durch die Forschung — in einer ähnlichen Lage sein könnten wie wir mit
dem heiteren Nestroy waren, sagen wir vor 1912?
Aus meiner Sicht möchte ich am ausführlichsten auf den *Treulosen*
eingehen.
Der Treulose oder Saat und Ernte, ein "dramatisches Gemälde", in
welchem sich Nestroy eine ernste Hauptrolle zudachte, fand am 5. März
1836 seine Uraufführung.

Herr von Falsch, ein reicher, junger Rouè, hat Liebeshändel mit der ganzen
Mädchenwelt; jede neue Bekanntschaft macht ihn der früheren treulos; bei der
neuesten wird er in einem Rendezvous mit Ernestinen von einigen früheren
Geliebten und den Eltern des Mädchens überrascht. Um sich aus der Verlegenheit
zu ziehen heiratet er Ernestinen. Sehr bald ist er ihrer überdrüssig, setzt seine
Liebesintrigen fort, kränkt seine Frau durch Kälte und Starrsinn, und wird
überdies von ihr auf seinen Schleichwegen attappirt, was zu einer ihm
erwünschten Trennung der Ehe führt, wobei sich Falsch ohne alle Theilnahme, ja
wie ein schlechter Mensch benimmt. Fünfundzwanzig Jahre sind vorüber; die
entfernte Ernestine längst todt, Falsch, alt und sehr stark berührt von der Hand
der Zeit, sieht sich mit dem Gefühle der Reue in der Welt allein stehen, ein
Spielball fremder Launen, von Freunden betrogen, von Verwandten um der
Erbschaft willen ins Grab gewünscht, auf ein unstetes Leben angewiesen, um
durch diesen Wechsel seine innere Stimme zu übertäuben. Es treibt ihn in die
Welt hinaus, weil er nirgends Theilnahme findet, noch finden will. Ihm zur Seite
wandeln im Stücke, als Bilder des Contrastes, Solming, der die redlich Treue aus
Uiberzeugung repräsentirt, und für sein ganzes Leben in häuslichem Glück und
Frieden seinen Lohn findet; Treuhold, sein Bedienter, ein Repräsentant der Treue
aus Dummheit, die sich weiterhin ihr Glück durch selbstgeschaffene Qualen
vergällt.[10]

Glaubt man den Rezensionen, dann war das Haus bei der Premiere über-
füllt, und die Präsentation (Nestroy als Herr von Falsch, Scholz als dessen
komischer Diener Treuhold) kann durchaus als Erfolg gelten. Im Jahr der
Uraufführung wurde das Werk in Wien zwar nur siebenmal (praktisch en
suite) gespielt — also kein Vergleich mit den Aufführungszahlen von *Zu
ebener Erde und erster Stock* vorher und *Die beiden Nachtwandler* nach-
her —, doch nahm Nestroy das "dramatische Gemälde" auch anläßlich
seiner Gastspiele nach Graz (1836) und Pest (1837) mit, und es erlebte
auch Aufführungen ohne ihn, wie etwa in der Arena in Preßburg als
Ausstattungsstück unter der Direktion Franz Pokorny.[11]
Am 25. April 1840 wurde *Der Treulose* wieder in Wien, als Benefizvor-
stellung, mit Nestroy in einer kleiner Nebenrolle,[12] gespielt, und zuletzt
kam es 1854 in drei Vorstellungen im Carltheater (Nestroy als Treuhold,
Treumann als Herr von Falsch) heraus. Man kann also annehmen,

daß dieses Werk für Nestroy insoweit ein Anliegen war, als er es trotz des zahlenmäßig geringen Erfolgs nicht der Theatervergessenheit überließ.

Handlungsmäßig könnte man von Nestroy vieles (allerdings beispielsweise *nicht* den *Treulosen*) in die Nähe der Gattung (aus heutiger Sicht) des Kriminalstücks rücken, in dem sich die Übeltäter durch zu viel Briefeschreiben oder zu viel Reden vor ihrer krönenden Missetat auszeichnen und verraten und letztlich ihre erschlichenen Erbschaften doch noch an den Richtigen abtreten müssen. (So gesehen sind sicherlich auch viele heitere Nestroy-Possen Kriminalstücke, z.B. *Das Mädl aus der Vorstadt*, *Einen Jux will er sich machen*.) Es ist dies sicherlich *eine* Form des populären Theaters, wenngleich nicht im Sinne von dialektbezogenem, satirisch-kritischem Volksstück — und bezeichnenderweise fallen relativ viele solcher Werke Nestroys bei Rommel unter "Volksstücke". (Auch hier ist anzumerken, daß gerade *Der Treulose* wenig von einem Volksstück, vom Personal her gesehen, an sich hat.)

Wie kann es aber sein, daß einundderselbe Dramatiker, auf seine ganze Schaffenszeit bezogen, uns im einen Fach so zu begeistern vermag und in einem anderen völlig außerhalb unserer Wertschätzung und damit außerhalb unseres Erkenntnisinteresses liegt? Daß es sich nicht um zwei voneinander getrennte unabhängige Welten handelt, mögen einige Beispiele veranschaulichen.

Wir wollen dabei in Erinnerung rufen, daß komische und melodramatische Wirkungen (vermeiden wir das Wort "tragisch" als Gegensatz zu "komisch") durchaus nach ein und demselben Rezept zubereitet werden können — sowie, daß ein und dieselbe Wirkung verschiedene Ursachen haben mag, ebenso natürlich wie gleiche Symptome gleiche Ursachen haben können. Ich sage dies deshalb, weil uns Einteilungsversuche ihrer selbst willen nicht viel weiterbringen würden, doch soll auf die Verzahnung ernst und heiter hingewiesen werden. Vielleicht könnte auch unsere Kenntnis des heiteren Nestroy uns beim Erkennen des ernsten Nestroy weiterhelfen.

Ein Beispiel aus *Gegen Torheit gibt es kein Mittel* (1838): Dieses "lustige Trauerspiel" beginnt damit, daß der törichte Simplicius Berg in der Putzwarenhandlung der Madame Foulard für seine ihn ausnützende "Braut" alles mögliche auswählt. In diesem Moment flüchtet sich Schnapp, ein von zwei Kommis verfolgter Ladendieb, in das Geschäft und gibt vor, etwas auszusuchen; in die Enge getrieben, wird er schließlich von Simplicius gerettet, indem dieser den Gegenwert des gestohlenen Atlasstoffs für Schnapp bezahlt. Wenn auch heiter gezeichnet, so wird doch die Auffassung des Simplicius: "Lernen Sie daraus, meine Herrn, daß man nie nach dem Scheine urteilen soll" (I, 4) (GW III, 256) ironisiert. Die Uneinsichtigkeit und Dummheit jener Torheit, gegen die es kein

Mittel gibt, hat für diese Stelle Aussagekraft, nicht so sehr der Wunsch, eine Situationskomik auszuspielen.

Wie sieht das in *Einen Jux will er sich machen* aus? Weinberl und Christopherl sind ebenfalls auf der Flucht, sie stürzen ins Gewölb der Madame Knorr (II, 4 ff.), sind gezwungen ein Motiv für ihr Kommen zu finden, und da sie mit wenig Geld ausgestattet sind, erkundigen sie sich bloß nach der Rechnung einer Kundin, deren Namen Weinberl aufs Geratewohl erfindet. Die Folgen kennen wir.

Dennoch besteht ein Unterschied. In *Gegen Torheit gibt es kein Mittel* dient die Szene als Illustration der Torheit der Hauptgestalt Simplicius; in *Einen Jux will er sich machen* wird zwar eine extrem heitere Flucht, aber tatsächlich eine Flucht nicht nur vor dem auf der Straße befindlichen Prinzipal, sondern vor der Realität des Biedermeiers, ja der eigenen Identität vorgeführt.

Im *Treulosen* bestellt der treulose (in dem Sinne, daß er keiner Frau die Treue halten kann) Herr von Falsch seine Amouren zu verschiedenen Zeiten in den Pavillon, um sich mit ihnen zu treffen; da die Termine durch Hilfe seines Dieners Treuhold durcheinandergebracht werden, endet das Ganze mit einem Eklat. An sich ist diese Situation eine wie sie sich später auf jeder besseren Boulevardbühne findet. Man könnte sagen, eine archetypische Situation für Slapstick-Komödie, hier aber in der Form melodramatischer Traurigkeit eingesetzt. Ähnliche Slapstick-Situationen *verhindern* will offenbar Nestroys Briefwechsel mit Karoline Köfer, was Anbahnung und Abwicklung des Liebesverhältnisses mit ihr betrifft, oder Nestroys Testament, worin festgelegt ist, wie das Lebendigbegraben-werden unterbunden werden sollte — die Angst vor dem Scheintod ist sicherlich in der damaligen Zeit als eine Form der Massenhysterie zu bewerten —: man male sich nur einmal die possenhaften Situationen aus!

Blicken wir auf den *Treulosen*, finden wir Situationen, die wir in anderer Gewichtung vielleicht schon aus anderen Meisterwerken Nestroys kennen: Don Juan-Falsch lernt seine zukünftige Frau Ernestine, die er dann unglücklich machen und ins frühe Grab bringen wird, folgender-maßen kennen:

HERR VON FALSCH: [. . .] (*Man hört in der Szene links in einiger Entfernung einen Schrei von zwei weiblichen Stimmen, er sieht nach der Gegend.*) Was ist das? Der Wagen — (*Eilt pfeilschnell links ab. Man hört von innen links Peitschenknall, Herrn von Walters und eines Kutschers Stimme verworren untereinander, nach einer kleinen Pause treten folgende Personen auf.*)

(I, 31) (SW VI, 184)

Und dann (I, 32) erscheinen die Geretteten, unter denen sich auch Ernestine befindet:

HERR VON WALTER: Wenn Sie nicht im rechten Augenblick die Zügel fassen, so liegen wir jetzt alle drei zerschmettert[13] im Graben.

(I, 32)(SW VI, 185)

Ernestine und ihre Familie hätten genausogut auf konventionellere Weise die Bühne betreten können oder einen konventionelleren Anlaß bieten können, miteinander bekannt zu werden, zumal diese Episode später im Stück in keiner Weise wiederaufgegriffen wird. Darin das Zeigenwollen einer Schicksalhaftigkeit zu sehen, liegt nahe, wenn wir diesen Vorfall mit dem *Talisman* vergleichen: Das Paradies dar falschen Werte hinter der Gartenmauer, das dem Titus Feuerfuchs verschlossen war, öffnet sich, sobald der Friseur Marquis, dessen Verkehrsunfall mit dem Fuhrwerk wir in Mauerschau durch Salome miterleben (I, 9), den Talisman (=Perücke) als Dank zurückläßt, für einen, der sich und seinesgleichen als Narren des Schicksals empfinden muß.

Eine andere Situation im *Treulosen* hat eine gewisse Entsprechung im *Zerrissenen*: Als Freund von Solming seine Absicht zu heiraten erklärt, findet Falsch, er könne das auch tun: "Ich hab' alles auf der Welt mitgemacht, nur geheirat't hab' ich noch nicht [. . .]. Das Ungenierte in meinen jetzigen Amouren macht die Geschichte alltäglich, mit der Zeit langweilig, wenn ich aber verheiratet bin, da heißt's dann: Verbotne Frucht schmeckt süß! Da werden aus den öffentlichen Liebschaften heimliche, aus den uninteressanten interessante — ich heirat' auch, es ist beschlossen, ich heirat'!" (I, 9) (SW VI, 157).[14] Er hat also gar nicht vor, den Moralbegriffen besser zu entsprechen, vielmehr soll seine Ehe den Höhepunkt der "Treulosigkeit" bilden. Im *Zerrissenen* (I, 6) finden wir eine ähnliche Situation. Herr von Lips ist nicht so sehr zerrissen, sondern viel eher fadisiert; bei ihm geht es um den Reiz des Neuen, weniger was die Ehe betrifft als die Originalität der Wahl.

Wir haben es also mit Situationen zu tun, die in verschiedenen Intentionen (Lachen, Ernst) auftreten, aber wegen ihrer Wiederkehr besteht die Möglichkeit einer Abhängigkeit zueinander.

Wir haben uns aber angewöhnt, davon auszugehen, daß es nicht die Handlung ist und daß es nicht die Situationen sind, an denen sich Nestroys Stärke und Selbständigkeit am klarsten zeigt, sondern daß sein Metier die sprachliche Durchdringung ist. (Besonders die nonverbalen, theatralen Aspekte und die Möglichkeit, sie zur Stützung oder Ironisierung des Dargebotenen zu verwenden, also die Perspektive zu verändern etc., lassen es gefährlich erscheinen, sprachliche Formulierungen als einziges Zeichen zum Verstehen des Werks und seiner Wirkung zu nehmen.) Gerade in den ernsten Passagen wird man die wenigsten Stellen finden, die sich in Nestroy-Schatzkästlein finden oder im Zitatenwortschatz der wissenschaftlichen Literatur über Nestroy gelesen werden können.

Voranzustellen ist, daß viele ernste, sprachlich nichtssagende Formulierungen an Wert gewinnen, wenn man sie vom Dramaturgisch-Technischen betrachtet: Das Theaterstück wird vom unnötigen Ballast, das Wie, Was und Warum ausführlich zeigen zu müssen, befreit, etwa durch die höheren Wesen wie Rübezahl in *Müller, Kohlenbrenner und Sesseltrager* von 1834, die als eine Form der Informationsvergabe fungieren.

Ein sprachliches Beispiel aus *Höllenangst* (1849), das folgendermaßen beginnt, möge dies illustrieren:

> (Es ist Nacht. REICHTHAL *tritt mit Vorsicht von Seite links auf, er ist in einen grauen Mantel gehüllt und hat eine Reisemütze tief in die Augen gedrückt.*)
> REICHTHAL: Ich bin am rechten Orte. Nur die Eile, die Ungeduld und hundert schmerzliche Erinnerungen, die meine Sinne fast verwirren, ließen mich nach kaum zweijähriger Abwesenheit die wohlbekannten Häuser und Straßen nicht sogleich erkennen. (*Nach dem großen Hause im Prospekte zeigend.*) Hier steh' ich vor dem Palais Reichthal, dem einstigen Wohnsitz meiner teuren Schwester, die so schnell ihrem Gatten in jene Welt gefolgt. Ohne Zweifel hat des verstorbenen Strombergs habsüchtiger Bruder, so wie die Güter, auch diesen Stammsitz an sich gerissen, jener Bösewicht, der mich durch seinen Genossen Arnstedt einer Verschwörung verdächtigen und ins Gefängnis werfen ließ. Was mag aus Adelen geworden sein? Hat sie den Tod ihrer Mutter überlebt? Ist sie in ihres bösen Oheims Gewalt? Nur eine Person kann und wird mir auf diese Fragen Antwort geben, die Amme meiner Nichte Adele! In diesem Häuschen wohnt sie. (*Zeigt nach dem obbeschriebenen kleinen Hause im Vordergrunde rechts.*) Die gute Frau wird mich auch einige Zeit verbergen; als Flüchtling, von mächtigen Feinden bedroht und aller Hilfe entblößt, wüßte ich mir keinen anderen Zufluchtsort. Ich habe zu vorschnell auf die Nachricht von der lebensgefährlichen Krankheit des Ministers das gastfreie England verlassen. (*Hat sich der Haustür des kleinen Häuschens genähert und ergreift den Türklopfer.*) Soll ich — ? (*Sich umsehend.*) Doch nein — noch ist es zu früh — der Lärm zu dieser ungewöhnlichen Zeit könnte die Nachbarn aufwecken. — Ich will lieber noch ein paar Stunden die Straßen auf und nieder gehen und den Anbruch des Tages erwarten. (*Hüllt sich fester in seinen Mantel und geht links durch den Hintergrund ab.*)
>
> (GW v, 255–256)

Er kam her, um nichts zu tun, geht wieder weg — aber gibt es eine prägnantere Form, für den komplizierten Sachverhalt eine Exposition zu liefern? Hier wäre zum Beispiel eine dramaturgische Funktion, die sich die Bühnenkonventionen zunutze macht und sie auch als solche aufzeigt, als Erklärung anzusetzen — in dieser Intention ähnlich den vielen Onkeln und Tanten, die sterben müssen, nur damit alles gut ausgehen kann (*Einen Jux will er sich machen* IV, 10) (GW III, 700).

Auch Sprachbilder, wie wir sie bei Nestroy in anderer Umgebung bereits kennen, finden sich: Wenn z.B. im *Treulosen* Herr von Falsch im Gespräch mit seinem Freund von Solming sagt

Eine Sonnenaufganglandschaft ist am schönsten nach einer durchschwärmten Nacht. Wenn man so halb in Schlafdusel noch etwas glüht im Gesicht und die kühle Frühluft weht einen an, wenn man mit halb zufallenden Augen hinaussieht in die Natur, der halbe Geist gehört der Erinnerung der Nacht, die andere Hälfte dem Anblick des Morgens —, o, das ist ganz etwas Eigenes! So wie eine Schöne leicht verschleiert am schönsten ist, so ist auch eine Gegend am reizendsten, wenn man sie durch diesen gewissen übernächtigen Schleier anblickt. Das ist das wahre mezza voce im Naturgenuß — o Freund, du weißt nicht, was schön ist!

(I, 9) (SW VI, 154–155)

so erkennen wir diese Stimmung in *Einen Jux will er sich machen* wieder, allerdings aus einer anderen Perspektive, als Wunschbild eines, der auch einmal den Tag sehen will, aber durch seine Arbeitszeit im Gewölbe keine persönliche Erfahrung hat:

WEINBERL: Der Kommis hat auch Stunden, wo er sich auf ein Zuckerfaß lehnt und in süße Träumereien versinkt [. . .]. Wenn man nur aus unkompletten Makulaturbüchern etwas vom Weltleben weiß, wenn man den Sonnenaufgang nur vom Bodenfensterl, die Abendröte nur aus Erzählungen der Kundschaften kennt, da bleibt eine Leere im Innern, die alle Ölfässer des Südens, alle Heringfässer des Nordens nicht ausfüllen, eine Abgeschmacktheit, die alle Muskatblüt' Indiens nicht würzen kann.

(*Einen Jux will er sich machen* I, 13) (GW III, 621)

Die vielen wohlbekannten, oft sarkastischen Nestroy-Aussprüche finden sich in den ernsten Passagen spärlicher; überhaupt ist besonders in den ernsten Stellen das Spiel mit der Sprache und das Ringen um den treffenden Ausdruck — und damit auch der neue, ungewohnte Zugang kaum festzustellen.

Im *Treulosen* erwidert Herr von Falsch dem für seine Begriffe zu spießerischen von Solming: "Mit dem Wort Grundsatz verschone mich. Ich habe nur einen Grundsatz, und das ist der, gar keinen Grundsatz zu haben. Grundsätze sind enge Kleidungsstücke, die einen bei jeder freien Bewegung genieren" (I, 9) (SW VI, 155).[15] Wir erkennen darin einen Charakterzug, ähnlich jenen Figuren wie der des Johann in *Zu ebener Erde und erster Stock*, dem Emilie ins Gesicht sagt, er hätte keine Grundsätze (II, 19), was er relativiert, indem er von schlechten Grundsätzen, die für einen Bedienten gut genug seien, spricht (GW II, 491). Johanns Rezept lautet: "Man nehme Keckheit, Devotion, Impertinenz, Pfiffigkeit, Egoismus, fünf lange Finger, zwei große Säck' und ein kleines Gewissen, wickle das alles in eine Livree, so gibt das in zehn Jahren einen ganzen Haufen Dukaten" (1, 3) (GW II, 437–438). Strick in *Die beiden Nachtwandler* I, 16 denkt wohl ähnlich, wenn er von allen Leuten das schlechteste glaubt, auch von sich selbst (GW II, 570).

In der oben angeführten Situation wendet sich Herr von Falsch gegen die Ansicht des von Solmig, befindet sich also sozusagen im Angriff.

Schwerer tut man sich mit Passagen, die offenbar ernst gemeint sind und zum Nennwert zu nehmen sind. *Der Treulose* eignet sich als Anschauungsobjekt dafür aus mehreren Gründen: die Nestroy-Rolle, im Gegensatz zu allen anderen Nestroy-Rollen seiner Possen und dgl., ist keine heitere, auch nicht satirisch und parodistisch — zumindest soll dies vorläufig unterstellt werden, da sie sich aus der Lektüre als ernst-gemeint anbietet und die damalige Kritik der Aufführungen besonders den Realismus von Nestroys Spiel lobend hervorhob. Herr von Falsch (=Nestroy) ist wohl als Hauptrolle aufzufassen, doch ist diese Figur manchmal dennoch nur als Stichwortbringer zu sehen (I, 20) und hat auch kein Couplet zu singen. Die komische Wirkung ist auf Wenzel Scholz als Treuhold konzentriert, wie überhaupt der Eindruck besteht, daß in den ernsteren Stücken das komische Gewicht der Scholz-Rolle wuchs.

Als Belege für Klischees (auch die der Sprache) im *Treulosen* seien von Solming und Marie herangezogen (I, 25–27) (SW VI, 176–179):

VON SOLMING: Noch nie fühlt' ich beim Anblick eines Mädchens mein Herz so süß bewegt. Sie ist ein Engel! — Ein Engel, gewiß, wenn ihre Seele so schön ist, wie ihr Gesicht — wenn die edle Weiblichkeit, die auf ihrer Stirne thront, ein Widerschein ist von jenem unschätzbaren Edelstein, den sie im Busen birgt, wenn — o, ich sage immer "wenn" und "wenn" — 's ist ein fatales Wort, das "wenn", denn wenn das alles nicht so ist, dann ist sie ja kein Engel, dann gehört sie unter die zahllose Zahl jener galanten Lärvchen, die da herum-schwärmen, im bunten Schmuck ihr inneres Nichts verhüllen, die eine Promenade göttlich, eine Kinderstube unerträglich, schale Courmacherei amüsant, wahrhaft liebende Huldigung langweilig finden, die in Modewaren und Ballgeschichten vollkommen bewandert, in stiller Häuslichkeit aber so fremd sind wie in den Dörfern des Mondes. Nein, bei ihr kann das nicht der Fall sein; es gibt eine Sprache im Auge, die noch keine Lügnerin nachgeäfft, die das größte mimisch-kokette Talent nicht erlernen kann. [. . .]

(I, 25)

Die Tugendideale von Marie und von Solming manifestieren sich zum Beispiel, als die kleine Kathi der Marie um den Hals fällt und ihr dabei "das ganze Chemisett verdruckt":

MARIE: Was tut das? Die ungezwungene Zuneigung[16] des Kindes freut mich mehr als die abgezirkelte Form meiner Pelerine. Komm her, Kleine, umarme mich noch einmal!
VON SOLMING: Es ist beschlossen, diese oder keine. Die Liebkosungen eines Kindes[17] sind ihr lieber als ein Putz, die wird ein herrliches Weib, eine treffliche Mutter sein.

(I, 26)

Nachdem sich von Solming vorgestellt hat, will er ihr noch "drei Worte" sagen:

VON SOLMING: Gleich bei Ihrem ersten Anblick, mein Fräulein, ward mein Herz wundersam ergriffen, ich mußte hinsehn auf Sie unverwandt mit Blicken, die Sie nicht bemerkten, die Ihre himmlische Gestalt umflogen;[18] nun hat ein schöner, wahrhaft edler[19] Zug mir verraten, daß diese schöne Hülle ein noch schöneres Herz verbirgt, und seit diesem Augenblicke ist meine Seele nur ein Gedanke, nur ein Entschluß, und der heißt: Sie oder keine!

(I, 27)

Diese Klischees, die er mit seiner Zukünftigen austauscht, sind auf den ersten Blick vom Autor anscheinend in keiner Weise in Frage gestellt.

Ähnliche Beispiele finden wir bei Herrn von Falsch und Ernestine (wobei Falsch natürlich falsch sein darf und dadurch das Klischee in Frage stellen mag).[20] Beim *Treulosen* läßt sich bis zu einem gewissen Grad noch die Vermutung anstellen, daß gerade von Solming und Marie und gerade Ernestine, so gute und rechtschaffene Personen sie auch seien, dennoch Spießbürger repräsentieren; daher hat Herr von Falsch — tendenziell zumindest — Möglichkeiten, sich von diesen abzusetzen, und Nestroy vielleicht die versteckte Möglichkeit, diese Tugendapostel bewußt extrem pathosbeladen und klischeehaft in ihrer Sprache zu zeigen.[21]

In anderen "ernsten" Stücken, in denen Nestroy mitwirkte, bleibt er als Schauspieler im heiteren Fach, z.B. im *Erbschleicher*, aber eher in der nicht so recht erwarteten Rolle des einfältigen Bauernburschen Simon Dappel, während Wenzel Scholz hier eine sehr wichtige heitere Intrigantenrolle des Wirts Gregorius Tost innehat: "[. . .] ich bin das geheime Triebrad aller Umtriebe, die da droben auf dem Schlosse getrieben werden, ich bin der, der in unsern Herrschaftsangelegenheiten das politische Kraut fett macht" (III, 3) (SW X, 335).

Im *Erbschleicher* sind die ersten dreizehn Szenen des ersten Akts (außer der Rolle Tosts) im Ton als ernst zu bezeichnen, dann wieder die beiden letzten des vierten Akts. (Umfangmäßig nach den Textseiten in SW ca. 23 Seiten von 99, also ein Viertel.) Dazu kommen noch die dazwischenliegenden eingestreuten ernsten Passagen.

Der *Erbschleicher* und ähnliche Nestroywerke sind also eher in der Tradition des internationalen Melodramas anzusiedeln.

Trotz diesem "Ernst"-Anteil gibt es mehrere recht typische Nestroysche Wortschöpfungen (um diesen leicht exzerpierbaren Aspekt herauszugreifen) — beim *Erbschleicher* alle im Scholz-Munde —, so daß die Kritik des Titus Feuerfuchs an den Lebensbildern (1840, also aus demselben Jahr) für Nestroys Melodramen nicht zutrifft:

TITUS: So schreiben Sie eine traurige Posse. Auf einem düsteren Stoff nimmt sich der matteste Witz noch recht gut aus, so wie auf einem schwarzen Samt die matteste Stickerei noch effektuiert.

HERR VON PLATT: Aber was Trauriges kann man doch keine Posse heißen?
TITUS: Nein! Wenn in einem Stück drei G'spaß und sonst nichts als Tote,
Sterbende, Verstorbene, Gräber und Totengräber vorkommen, das heißt man
jetzt ein Lebensbild! [. . .] gehört in das Fach der Haus- und Wirtschaftspoesie [. . .]

Und als Frau von Zypressenburg den Titus fragt, ob er Rührung nicht
möge, sagt er: "O ja, aber nur, wenn sie einen *würdigen* Grund hat, und
der find't sich nicht so häufig [. . .]" (*Der Talisman* II, 24) (GW III, 476).
Tost bemerkt z.b. über die als Pauline verkleidete Agnes: "an der ist
jeder Zoll eine Baroneß, jede Linie eine Herrvonin" (*Der Erbschleicher*
III, 11) (SW X, 346) oder später: "Eine Baronin um die Mitt' nehmen als
wie a Bauerndirn' au'm Kirchtag, das geht ja ins Attentatische hinüber"
(III, 15) (SW X, 353). Tost bietet schließlich seinen "Kopf zur gefälligen
Zerschmetterung an" (IV, 1) (SW X, 361), etc.

Man merke: bei Nestroy geht es nicht selten um Kriminalfälle (so beim
Erbschleicher, allerdings nicht so beim *Treulosen*) und nicht um Fried-
hofsatmosphäre. Offenbar muß Anlaß oder Gegenstand mit dem
Mitgefühl in gewisser Übereinstimmung sein. Ist dies bereits gegeben,
wenn der Gegenstand sozial erhaben genug ist?

Unter der Annahme, die hier aufgezeigten Beispiele sind für Nestroys
ernstes Schaffen typisch, stellt sich natürlich die Frage: Sind sie so
schlecht, wie ich vielleicht den Eindruck erweckt habe, daß sie es sind —
trotz der Vergleichbarkeit in vielen Fällen mit anerkannten Werken
Nestroys, wie die Beispiele hoffentlich zeigten —, oder sind hier
Tarnungen vorhanden, die wir noch nicht erkannt haben? Etwa die *relativ*
weniger verlogene Sprache des Treulosen gegenüber den Spießern und im
Zusammenhang damit die Tatsache, daß es der Standpunkt der Spießer
ist, der durch das Ende sanktioniert wird. Ist es ein Nachgeben einer
Mode? oder der Versuch, die Ernsthaftigkeit zuerst bei den erhabenen
Figuren im sozialen Gefälle auszutesten und durchaus absichtlich
klischeehaft zu bleiben, während in den Volksstücken, vor allem den
späteren, diese Erhabenheit der Gefühle und Motive Personen aus dem
Volk zugeschrieben wurde — wiederum in einer eigenständigen Sprach-
formulierung?

So viel wissen wir, daß sich die Zuschauer bei den ernsten Stücken in
der Regel sicher nicht langweilten (und sicher nicht beim *Treulosen*) und
daß ernste Ware nicht nur seit Friedrich Kaiser Teil des Vorstadt-
repertoires war, daß die internationale Melodramenliteratur nicht nur als
Vorlage für Nestroy und andere Lokalautoren wichtig war, sondern auch
als solche einem damaligen Theaterzuschauer präsent sein konnte — es
sich aber nicht um Formen handelte, die in der Literaturgeschichte
aufgegriffen wurden. Mit zunehmender Entfernung von Otto Rommel

und dem Blickwinkel des Folkloristischen und Bodenständigen am Wiener Volkstheater wächst unsere Chance auch die nicht possenhaften Züge und vorstadthaften sozialen Zusammensetzungen der dramatis personae im Volkstheater einzuordnen.

Es soll nicht der Eindruck entstehen, daß, weil wir über Nestroy reden, alles aus seiner Feder hinaufgelobt werden muß; man muß aber offen lassen, ob es notwendigerweise so bleiben muß, daß Aussagen, und vor allem die sprachliche Durchdringung der ernsten Stellen in ihrer Wertigkeit *vorerst* dem Satiriker und Wortkünstler, wie wir gewohnt sind ihn zu sehen, nicht einmal noch in die Nähe gerückt werden. Eines muß aber klar sein: Nestroy hat auch Auftragsarbeiten im heiteren Fach geschrieben, und man verzeiht sie ihm (*Der Affe und der Bräutigam*, *Moppels Abenteuer* u.a.), weil Bedürfnis herrschte oder weil es geweckt wurde. Seine ernsten Stücke wurden, wenn auch gewöhnlich nicht als Sensationserfolge so dennoch per Saldo ohne Gesichtsverlust gespielt, manchmal sogar nach Jahren wiederaufgenommen, wie *Der Treulose*, und stellen daher wohl keinen Fremdkörper in seinem Theaterselbst-verständnis dar.

Ich möchte mit der Behauptung schließen: Gerade am heiteren Nestroy haben wir gelernt zu sehen, daß Lachen, daß Possen nicht unbedingt mit bloßer Unterhaltung zu tun haben müssen. Aufgrund der Erfahrungen mit dem Geschäftstheater des 19. Jahrhunderts kann man auch umgekehrt sagen, ernste Theaterangebote (Melodramen) müssen nicht immer ernstgemeint sein, haben dann aber zumindest sehr viel mit Unterhaltung zu tun. Denken wir nur an die vielen populären Melodramen, die wir heute im TV sehen — in denen übrigens ebenfalls der Krimi mengen-mäßig sehr bedeutsam ist —, die Unterhaltung sind, ohne daß dabei gelacht wird. Es mag paradox klingen: Ich glaube, daß Nestroys ernste Stücke(Passagen) vielleicht mehr Unterhaltungswert für die Zeitgenossen hatten als viele seiner philosophischen, sozialkritischen und satirischen Possen für uns aufweisen.

Summary

While Nestroy's standing as a satirist is well-established, a considerable part of his work does not square with our conceptions (rooted principally in the research of Otto Rommel) of Viennese popular *comedy*. While fully recognizing that "comic" and "serious" are by no means mutually exclusive terms — in Nestroy's case the converse is clearly true — this paper uses the term "serious" in a special sense, to refer specifically to those plays, particularly *Der Treulose* and *Der Erbschleicher*, in which comic and satirical elements are least to the fore. These works tend to be either neglected or treated without understanding in modern Nestroy scholarship; but in Nestroy's day *Der Treulose* was repeatedly played, both in Vienna and elsewhere, and both with and without Nestroy himself in the cast. Moreover, while Nestroy's characteristic wordplay is rare in the "serious" (that is, non-comic) passages, parallels both in situations and in ideas between *Der Treulose* and some of his best-known *Possen* (*Der Talisman, Einen Jux will er sich machen, Der Zerrissene*) reveal that melodramatic effects and comic effects can be related, achieved essentially by the same formula.

In *Der Treulose*, though Nestroy's role is central, it contains no *couplets*, and the comic effect is concentrated in the role of Treuhold, played by Scholz (whose comic function generally increased in importance in the plays of more "serious" tone). If in the opening of *Höllenangst* a hackneyed theatrical idiom is used to serve an economical dramaturgical function, here too there are passages where linguistic clichés are used without an overt satirical function (though they may possibly suggest philistine qualities in their speakers). In other more "serious" plays like *Der Erbschleicher*, which conform to the international tradition of melodrama, Nestroy's own role remained comic, and the verbal jokes mean that the jibe directed in *Der Talisman* against the melancholy of the *Lebensbild* genre does not fit his own melodramas, for while he used plots involving crimes, he was not concerned with creating lachrymose atmosphere.

Investigation of this material prompts the question whether the intentions underlying it have yet been fully perceived. It is clear that contemporary audiences were not bored by a play such as *Der Treulose*. "Serious" material had indeed formed part of the repertoire of the Viennese *Vorstadttheater* since long before Friedrich Kaiser; and in the commercial theatre of the nineteenth century, melodrama was itself something entertaining.

7

M. A. Rogers

THE SERVANT PROBLEM IN VIENNESE POPULAR COMEDY

It seems to me that the strategies of comedy, and especially of stage comedy, remain remarkably constant from age to age and society to society, considering how radically all the other factors change that may have an influence on comedy and its methods. For the purposes of this paper, I should like to suggest that there is a basic vocabulary of comic structures to which each contemporary reality is adapted with more or less ingenuity by the writers concerned; that it is much more a case of material being cast into comic forms than the forms changing to accommodate the material. Unfamiliarity with the social background does not kill the joke, provided that the basic premise is made clear. We do not need to have a valet to appreciate the Jeeves-Wooster relationship, and the structure in which the servant is actually the master could no doubt be filled with a young man in marketing and his latest computer.

With this example, I have touched on one of the basic ways in which the servant-figure is used in comedy: for the reversal of roles and the reversal of expectations. Furthermore, like Jeeves, the servant may be the manipulator and initiator of intrigue; without necessarily assuming dominance over his master (or at least, without making it too evident), the servant suggests, as a conversation partner (another important role), the intricate plot required to get the girl from the aged guardian, who has this or that eccentric obsession. (Evidently enough, it is the nature of the obsession that offers room for topical comment and satire — though not necessarily put into the mouth of the servant.)

The position of the servant as manipulator and intriguer also puts him to some extent outside the action and gives him the opportunity for observations to the audience which undermine the statements of the other characters; furthermore, he can provide the necessary explanations or exposition.

These are only some of the possibilities, and it must be pointed out that these functions of the servant-role — functions to which it lends itself naturally — may be fulfilled by other characters in a play. Indeed, the position of the servant outside the action, as commentator, is one that Nestroy occupies in his own plays regardless of the part he is taking: where the servant is able to remain on stage after his master has left, or has been sent before him, and is able to speak to the audience alone, the Nestroy-figure's monologue or song brings him immediately into that relationship with the audience which he is able to exploit afterwards under all circumstances.

The servant, who is, by virtue of his position, privy to his master's secrets and to those of all the other masters and mistresses with whose servants he is acquainted, has a claim on our attention through his knowledge; the way in which he is used by his master — sent ahead, left behind, given errands — gives him the opportunity to be alone with the audience. Nestroy's appearance on the stage, to introduce his character and his opinions with a song and a monologue, is much more absolute and less motivated; if the servant has a freedom of action within the plot, the Nestroy-figure stands above the plot and is almost independent of it — for example, the way in which Titus Feuerfuchs refuses to carry through the final deception of Spund. A servant's observations remain within the framework of the play; the Nestroy-figure's transcend it, and become metaphysical.

In general, however, Viennese popular comedy envisages only two kinds of servant: the fool and the rogue. We are faced either with Kasperle, as in Hensler's *Die Teufelsmühle am Wienerberg*, or with a figure such as Wolf in *Der Verschwender*. Johann, in *Zu ebener Erde und erster Stock* I, 3, gives the simple recipe:

Was haben diese Leut', die Alchimisten, alles über Goldmacherkunst studiert! Ich weiß ein prächtiges Rezept. Man nehme Keckheit, Devotion, Impertinenz, Pfiffigkeit, Egoismus, fünf lange Finger, zwei große Säck' und ein kleines Gewissen, wickle das alles in eine Livree, so gibt das in zehn Jahren einen ganzen Haufen Dukaten. Probatum est! (GW II, 437–438)

Even the friendship between Faden and Strick in *Die beiden Nachtwandler* cannot change the nature of the servant-role; after the mysterious wealth has been snatched away, we hear:

FADEN: Ich hab' jetzt gar nix mehr, du wirst auch nit viel haben.
STRICK: Ich bin nur einen halben Tag Bedienter g'west, was kann ein Anfänger viel machen? Ich hab' Ihnen halt um dreißig Gulden betrogen, die will ich jetzt ehrlich mit Ihnen teilen.

(II, 23) (GW II, 619)

Evidently, livery has the same sort of effect as Bertram's coat in *Robert der Teuxel*.

To be sure, there is Valentin, for whom the master-servant relationship is something almost sacred. He begins as the fool and buffoon, subjected to crude practical jokes, for which he is rewarded, and even has his little drunk scene; but he also has the strong emotional relationship with his master.

This seems to be another of those instances in which Raimund succeeds

in taking a piece of theatrical convention and filling it with significance —
just as Die Zufriedenheit turns the painted backcloth into a moral lesson,
or like that most terrible of transformation scenes, when Wurzel is
stricken with old age: to be sure, Raimund had specialized in such things,
with *Zugkleider* and other effects, in the plays of Gleich — but it is in his
own plays that the allegorical figures actually acquire more than their
conventional force, and the visible shapes of age, decay, and beggary stalk
the stage and come between us and the beautifully painted sunsets.

If Valentin is the apotheosis of the loyal master-servant relationship, it
is Wolf who demonstrates in his brief, Edmund-like monologue (*Der
Verschwender* II, 29) and in the encounter with Flottwell (III, 4) the other
side of the coin and its reward — riches and misery.

However, it is characteristic of Raimund that he does not question the
relationship or its basis, but accepts it and explores the moral and
symbolic possibilities, both of the good servant and of the bad, without
falling into the resentful tone of Figaro's Act Five monologue in *Le
Mariage de Figaro:*

Parce que vous êtes un grand seigneur, vous vous croyez un grand génie! . . .
noblesse, fortune, un rang, des places, tout cela rend si fier! Qu'avez-vous fait
pour tant de biens? Vous vous êtes donné la peine de naître et rien de plus: du
reste, homme assez ordinaire! tandis que moi [. . .]

Wolf's concept of morality, though clearly hypocritical in its way, does
not challenge the social structure: he feels, as a good bourgeois, that
Flottwell is making a terrible waste of his resources; but then, it may be
argued that the Flottwells are not a family of hereditary nobles, but
precisely *nouveaux riches*.

From the examples I have adduced so far, it should be clear that the
servant-role can be used in many different ways: that it has a dramaturgical function which can be invested with further significance according to
the wishes and skill of the author and the actor. Contrasts and tensions are
inherent in the relationship between the master and the servant; and it is
not always clear from a written text whether the gross discrepancy in
behaviour between the two is to be taken as a criticism of the one, or the
other, or both. However much Wolf disapproves of Flottwell, the latter's
folly is Wolf's bread, butter, and jam. However much Leporello disapproves of Don Giovanni, he still takes a certain pride in the catalogue,
joins in the deceptions, and keeps watch at the seductions; the servant
lives his master's life vicariously.

This sort of interaction between two spheres is exploited in the
nineteenth-century and late eighteenth-century *Volkstheater* in terms of
the magic world and the real world: Papageno is Papageno, the bird-
catcher, and does not need to be introduced as Tamino's servant, though

that is the official relationship imposed on him in order to bring him into the action — certainly he does not function as his valet. The contrasts between the high and the low are, in general, presented crudely in the *Volkstheater:* in Bäuerle's *Der Fiaker als Marquis*, the cabby reveals his true identity and nature by his cries of uninhibited exuberance at the polite soirée (AWV VI, 52); the Gods in Meisl's parodies devote themselves to the lower-class kind of Viennese entertainment. Indeed, in the majority of cases it is clear that no social criticism can be intended, that the author is merely exploiting social incongruity for a purely comic effect, and it takes the consistency of Nestroy's approach and the ruthlessness of a character like Knieriem to expose the casuistic morality of Fairyland as self-deluding hypocrisy, rather than endearing indulgence.

If the gap between Fairyland and the mortals fulfils one function of the servant figure, in terms of contrast and parallelism, the "imposed test" and the "anecdotes on a theme" of the *Besserungsstück* fulfil another, in terms of plot organization and manipulation: the exposition is simple and clear-cut and brings with it a ready-made interpretative scheme, so that there is little left for the servant of either sex to do.

In case I may have been thought sexist for leaving out the female servant up to this juncture, I had better point out that the *Stubenmädl* is, as confidante, intriguer, and secondary love interest, played by a soubrette, a quite different matter, and one that lies beyond the scope of this present paper, though very important in the *dramatis personae* of the *Volkstheater.*

So, as I have said, the male servants are left as the fools or the rogues in the plays; and one may well wonder why. Should one attribute it to the "truth" of Viennese life — or is it really only "true" in the same way that all porters are surly, all chambermaids obliging, all stupid people lucky, and so forth: a proverbial piece of wisdom used as a premiss for allusive jokes? It is certainly surprising that the possibilities of the servant-master relationship are essentially left unexploited by Nestroy; but it may be that there was simply no actor in his company with whom he could have developed that kind of relationship successfully on the stage. With Scholz and Nestroy, the short fat one and the tall thin one, it is hard to think who could convincingly have played which; and it is really only in *Umsonst!* of 1857, with the High-German-speaking Treumann as Arthur, that Nestroy writes for himself, in the part of Pitzl, something like the servant of a young master, aping him and helping him, albeit inefficiently.

It may also be, of course, that the roles of fool or rogue were the only ones that the censorship would permit, and that this became tacit but common knowledge. Certainly one wonders how it was possible for Mozart and Da Ponte to get away with the strong material of *Le Nozze di Figaro*: even if the monologue in Act Five with its comments on the injustice of hereditary wealth and power is shortened to no more than the reflections on female infidelity, it must be assumed that audiences were aware of the controversial nature of the original, and the repeated "Se vuol ballare" still seems enough of a threat from a mere servant to his titled master, especially in post-revolutionary context.[1] A critical and intelligent servant, whose observations could not be dismissed as envy or stupidity, might be seen as a dangerous figure *per se*, almost regardless of actual utterances.

On the other hand, it also seems clear that the aristocracy as such disappear from the *Volkstheater* plays, unless they are travelling English lords fulfilling the function of *dei ex machina*, as in *Die beiden Nachtwandler*. The places of the aristocrats are taken by *Kapitalisten*, *Partikuliers*, *Rentherren* — and I should like to be permitted an aside here on the *Rentherr* in Stifter's *Turmalin*: how mysterious the man is, how disordered his existence, unlike all those other characters whose livelihood is *described* in loving detail! Indeed, it is presumably no coincidence that two of Raimund's major characters are essentially ordinary men who have become rich by magic means. Speculation in such matters is always problematic, and the theme of the artful bankruptcy runs through the whole of the *Volkstheater* up to *Frühere Verhältnisse*; but it is perhaps reasonable to assume that this change in the basic data of the plays, from the aristocrat to the wealthy man, could correspond to financial turmoil in the society watching them, especially in view of the jokes about devalued currency straight after the Napoleonic wars.

To some degree, Raimund is writing about the problem of wealth and its correct usage in *Der Bauer als Millionär* and *Der Verschwender*, though the origins of the problem in an unstable society are effectively disguised by the fairy-tale treatment and the moral standpoint taken: the characters' failings are personal and moral ones, related only symbolically to their acquisition of wealth — the acquisition itself being heavily symbolic in both cases. The loss of the money is not the tragedy in itself, but is the powerful expression of that tragedy: the tattered state of Wurzel and Flottwell is the visible presentation of that tragedy, and not a naturalistic depiction of tramps. Raimund is making symbolic use of the state of the society surrounding him — and indeed, the *Volkstheater* convention is essentially symbolic and not naturalistic.

However, if all that puts a master in the position of a master is his wealth, and if that wealth is continually being redistributed in one way or another, then there is essentially no place for the resentment against the *ancien régime* and the rights of birth which characterizes Figaro, since, as we see in the cases of Wolf, Johann, and Muffl, all that separates master and man is money: their positions are reversible.

Perhaps it is here that we can find a further explanation for the cupidity of the servants: they are aping their masters (another way of using the servant-role, for example Horváth's *Ein Sklavenball* that turned into *Pompeji*). Where wealth can be acquired and spent in such dubious ways, it is only natural for the servants to take their share, however they may justify it themselves: as *Das Mädl aus der Vorstadt* opens, it is clear that Dominik has been receiving commission from the makers of his mistress's wedding dress and trousseau, and that he will mention the tailor's name again — on receipt of similar consideration:

KRÄMER: Das versteht sich von selbst, wir wissen schon, was sich g'hört! Daß uns der Herr Dominik immer dran erinnert, is etwas schmutzig.

DOMINIK: Konträr, das is sehr reinlich, denn ich halt' drauf, daß eine Hand die andere wascht!

(I, 1)(GW III, 511)

However, one must be aware of taking all utterances that could be seen as "social criticism" at face value: this is to ignore the simple comic force of incongruity, and the comic force of exaggeration, for example, the extension of the servant's "knowing his place" beyond its sensible application, as in the case of Algy's butler in *The Importance of Being Earnest*, who "does not think it proper to listen" to his master playing Chopin.

On the other hand, it is one of Nestroy's talents to leave the exact interpretation open. When Salome Pockerl in *Der Talisman* II, 8 excuses her fainting at the sight of the black-haired Titus with the words "Und jetzt bitt' ich nochmal um Verzeihung, daß ich umg'fallen bin in Zimmern, die nicht meinesgleichen sind" (GW III, 456), it is not simply a slip of the tongue or a piece of naiveté. The question of the social divide has already been thematized in Titus's rise to fame and fortune, and even if the unavoidable stigma of red hair denies him the prospect of the *Gutsherrin* herself, after the first unwigging, the secondary talisman of money in the form of an inheritance is sufficient to keep him in the runner-up position with the maid; what magic did once is now accomplished by false blond or real gold. Nestroy fills the structure he has inherited with a new kind of meaning.

In *Zu ebener Erde und erster Stock* the social divide has also been thematized quite evidently: programmatically, with the divided stage, but not tendentiously, in view of the subtitle, "Die Launen des Glückes", the concluding chorus,

's Glück treibt's auf Erden gar bunt,
's Glück bleibt halt stets kugelrund,

and Goldfuchs's warning, "Mein Beispiel gebe warnend euch die Lehre: Fortunas Gunst ist wandelbar" (III, 32) (GW II, 549). But this juxtaposition of upstairs and downstairs is essentially crude in its outlines — and hence, presumably, to be regarded as harmless; it is, indeed, chance that alters the situation, aided and abetted by human folly; and whilst the contrasts are sharp — the miserable embers and the flare of goose-fat, the brilliant ball and supper and the bread and water — there is never any suggestion that the one is causally related to the other. Admittedly, there are remarks that could be taken in an egalitarian sort of way, such as Damian's in II, 5: "Wenn die reichen Leut' nit wieder reiche einladeten, sondern arme Leut', dann hätten alle genug zu essen" (GW II, 441); but then, Damian is a notable fool, played by Scholz into the bargain, and the statement is equally comprehensible as a foolish utterance, the "world turned upside down" kind of observation which misses the whole point of the social dinner. The same is true of the remark by François, the cook, in II, 1: "Wenn nur einmal die Mode aufkommet, daß die Köch' bei der Tafel sitzeten und die Herrschaft kochen müßt'; da wär' ich recht gern a Koch" (GW II, 467). The social positions are reversed, and the functions, too, but the joke lies in the reversal of the self-evident, not in the querying of the system. It is only with a certain degree of sensitization, and in a particular context, that the joke can transcend its position as a complaint in the form of nonsense, and be seen as a reflection on the fixed nature of an unjust society, in which some must always cook so that others can always eat. Certainly, the two utterances, suggestive though they are to the twentieth-century reader, can be accommodated within the system of "reine Herausarbeitung der Gegensätze", as Helmut Olles describes it.[2]

It is, however, naturally enough in Nestroy's own part, as the servant Johann, that the subtlest analysis of the relationship between the rich and the poor, the impotent and the powerful, the servant and the master, is to be found. Even before the reversal of fortune has given Johann the position of authority from which to castigate his former employer — authority deriving exclusively from wealth — we have seen the dropping of the mask in a drastic *coup de théâtre*: Emilie, who has entrusted the organization of her elopement to Johann, reproaches him with his jilting of her maid, Fanny; he replies:

(*sich verbeugend*) Oho, Sie scheinen mich beleidigen zu wollen. Sie vergessen, mein gnädiges Fraulein, daß Sie mir Ihr Geheimnis anvertraut haben. Auf so was muß man ja hübsch denken, wenn man sich einmal in die Hände der Dienstboten gibt — denn das ist a Volk — da muß man beim Böswerden hernach seinen Ton kurios moderieren. Schaun S', mich kost't es zum Beispiel nur ein Wörterl, so nimmt der Herr Papa ein Karbatscherl und treibt Ihnen die Lieb' aus'n Herzerl. Drum seit der Preisgebung Ihres Geheimnisses müssen Sie ja nicht mehr glauben, Sie sei'n meine gebietende Frau! (*Sich stolz emporrichtend und mit festem Tone.*) Jetzt bin ich der Herr! (*Gleich wieder ganz submiß.*) Übrigens das nur zur Privatnotiz. Sie zahlen mir jetzt das doppelte Honorar, und ich leite untertänigst bereitwilligst Dero Intrige. (II, 19) (GW II, 492)

The fearful proximity of servility and tyranny is here made quite evident in the abrupt transitions of tone and mood; but such abrupt transitions are commonplace theatrical devices — it takes Nestroy to fill them with such meaning; and it also takes Nestroy to let his servant use the words his masters have let fall and he has picked up: "das ist a Volk". Johann is conveying obliquely the simple truth: like master, like man. You get the servants you deserve; and it is clear from this passage alone that the only value of which he can conceive is a monetary one: satisfaction for the insult offered him is a double fee — and presumably the satisfaction of his position of power, which is so great that the overt role-reversal need only last for a single line, between the threatening diminutives and the eighteenth-century politeness.

In this context, the exchanges preceding the moment of mastery transcend the evident form of the "misapplied proverb":

EMILIE (*entrüstet*): Er ist ein Mensch ohne Grundsätze.
JOHANN: Ach ja, Grundsätze hab' ich.
EMILIE: Aber schlechte.
JOHANN: Mein Gott, ich denk' mir halt, für einen Bedienten ist bald was gut g'nug.

(II, 19)(GW II, 491)

If anything will do for a servant in one context, why not in another? It is the servant's revenge, to take his master's words literally.

And it is also Johann's revenge to drop his servile pose entirely towards the semi-ruined Goldfuchs in the first scene of Act Three (GW II, 514–517), and to respond to threats of violence entirely in terms of what it will cost the perpetrator per box on the ear: ". . .'s kost't 's Stück fünf Gulden, und Ihnen wird bald ein jeder Groschen weh tun." Johann's double comeuppance — the beating in Bonbon's place and the arrest for theft, after the loss of his "savings" invested with Goldfuchs — seems somehow a concession to comic tradition and poetic justice; it is improbable that Johann, however spiteful, would take a gratuitous risk, and almost unbelievable that he would commit outright theft: "an empty feat, When it's so lucrative to cheat."

At the beginning of his career, then, Nestroy uses the servant-role to explore the power of money and the relationship between servility and tyranny. In his penultimate work he presents the interchangeability of master and servant. By now, it is clear, the financial discrepancy need not be of the earlier fairy-tale proportions; but this makes the discrepancy in treatment all the more questionable. In fact, the scene between Muffl and Scheitermann in *Frühere Verhältnisse* (GW VI, 458–463) is all about the relationship between the individual and his social role — and how much of the social role remains attached to the individual when he transcends that role and assumes a new one.

The servant's role is clearly delineated: he is there to clean the boots and be beaten and sworn at by his master — even a master who has been a servant is unable to conceive of a different kind of treatment. Muffl makes his appeal to his former valet's "Dienertreue": "Na, du wirst deinen ehemaligen Prinzipal doch nicht vazierend lassen?". But Scheitermann is no Valentin; and his first objection to the arrangement, whereby his master would be his servant, shows how he feels servants should be treated: "Ich könnt' nie so gehörig grob werden mit Ihnen." Muffl's reply not only queries the automatic nature of this assumption; it also — subtly — implies that for all his present position he, Muffl, is still the one giving the orders: "Ich hab' dir die Höflichkeit nicht verboten." Searching for a further excuse, Scheitermann alleges a personal involvement which was manifestly not present in the purely social and financial relationship: "Der alte Respekt machet es unmöglich, daß ich mir von Ihnen die Stiefeln putzen ließ'." Scheitermann never felt that respect; what he felt then, as now, is fear; but Muffl takes him at his word and ironically presents himself as a servant who is above demarcation disputes: "Ich bin nicht eifersüchtig auf diese Dienstleistung, kannst dir s' putzen lassen, von wem du willst." With the next excuse there begins a fascinating alternation of viewpoints. Forgetting his own view of the need to be tough with servants, Scheitermann takes Muffl's previous treatment of him personally — the nearest he comes to admitting his fear in this "polite" and indirect conversation: "Dann kann ich auch keinen Menschen ins Haus nehmen, der sich bereits mehrmalen an mir vergriffen hat." The comic structure demands that Muffl should dismiss this excuse likewise — third time pays for all — but he does so by reasserting his role as the master, a gracious and forgiving one towards his former servant: "Ja, richtig! Ich hab' dich öfters durchkarbatscht — ich bin nicht unversöhnlich und hab' das längst vergessen." The master-servant relationship seems to be deforming all kinds of other logical relationships: the man who gives the beating forgives its recipient for being beaten; the master is always in the right. Small wonder that Scheitermann remains unconvinced and unreconciled:

> Ich aber nicht; es bleibt immer eine gewisse Erinnerung —
> MUFFL: Daß du alle Sonntag' b'soffen nach Haus kommen bist, liederlichs Tuch!

and the flat refusal of employment is followed by the proverbial accusations of thievery and the threat of blackmail, which produces the required effect, so that the negotiations can begin:

> MUFFL: Und was is denn wegen Lohn? Wieviel krieg' ich denn?
> SCHEITERMANN (*etwas zaghaft*): Ein Hausknecht hat bei mir acht Gulden monatlich und die Kost.
> MUFFL: Schmutzian! Du hast bei mir zehn Gulden g'habt; bin ich etwan weniger wert? Was du bist, das bin ich auch, du Lump, du!

Admittedly, unintentional self-revelation and self-denigration is a common comic device with Nestroy: for instance, Knieriem's self-analysis: "Wann ich mir meinen Verdruß nit versaufet, ich müßt' mich grad aus Verzweiflung dem Trunk ergeben" (*Der böse Geist Lumpazivagabundus* I, 6) (GW I, 593); but here it turns on the question of the equality between master and man, on the impossibility of switching between the differing roles and the differing perspectives. Scheitermann may object, but it is clear that Muffl still considers himself the master, even though he is now the servant:

SCHEITERMANN (*erbost*): Das verbitt' ich mir — ! Sie entwickeln eine Grobheit —
MUFFL: Erst entwickeln? Meine Grobheit datiert sich schon lang her, ich hab' ein historisches Recht, mit dir grob zu sein.

And in that little phrase is summed up, essentially, the whole of the aristocracy's claim to dominance: the perpetuation of the social relationships deriving from a specific economic order, even after that order has been replaced. This is indeed one of Nestroy's principal merits: that he makes clear the thought-processes behind behaviour as he explores and develops the implications of assumptions.

But it is also clear that it is the aggressive force of Muffl's character (*scilicet*: Nestroy's acting style) that triumphs over the submissive Scheitermann. If Nestroy's plays do not deal with the servant problem, this must be at least partly because the servant-role is not one that is suited to Nestroy as actor or author: the figures he plays are so multifarious within their own dramatic outlines that it would be highly inappropriate to subordinate them to clearly defined external functions. Nestroy as servant or Nestroy as master would make any relationship completely one-sided (the Muffl-Scheitermann duo succeeds because of the master-servant ambiguity, and because the play is a one-act piece with a mistaken-identity element in the plot — the master-servant relationship is in fact phased out after the initial encounter). The classic Nestroy-figures move questioningly through society and never become trapped in a single role, as even the most ingenious servant must be to some degree; and there is seemingly no room in Nestroy's *oeuvre* for the successful intrigue *à la* Figaro: the best-laid plots reach their happy end more by chance than by ingenuity; if the Nestroy-figure were in command, he could not stand so aloof from the action and make his comments on it.

What, then, is the servant problem in Viennese comedy? Perhaps that you simply can't get the right kind nowadays — if you ever could. The reasons which have been suggested are so manifold — censorship, changed social conditions, actors available to play the parts, the dramatic fashion — that this single aspect gives a good insight into the complexity of any theatrical analysis.

One point which does emerge clearly is that the functions of the servant-role in dramaturgical terms are fulfilled within the *Volkstheater* in different ways, and that with the removal of these functions from the servant-role, it simply becomes one of the stock characters that make up the *dramatis personae* of Vienna. But even though they are either fools or rogues, and no longer the ingenious fixers of past days, even though the presence of the middle and lower class on the stage in their own right removes the need for "the servant's point of view" for audience appeal and as a dramatic counterweight, the *Volkstheater* is still capable of using the servant-role and the master-servant relationship symbolically, as in the case of Valentin.

However, it must be remembered that Valentin is not simply a servant: he is a craftsman, who had his trade before he met Flottwell and returned to it afterwards; his greatest song is a fully-fledged *Metierlied* about being a carpenter; and in his way, he is showing an independence of the aristocracy and the claustrophobic master-servant relationship — if he did not have this independence, he could hardly help Flottwell. Generally, in fact, the lower orders, even the rag-and-bone-men and rope-makers, are independent craftsmen and tradesmen — one assumes, by both Viennese theatrical tradition and the economic development of society. The servants, it seems, can get along quite happily without their masters — but the reverse does not appear to be the case. Let us leave the last word on the servant-problem with Melchior:

MELCHIOR: Ich hab' g'hört, daß der Herr vermischte Warenhändler einen Haus-
    knecht g'habt hab'n, der ein reiner Lump war.
ZANGLER: Ich hab' ihn fortgejagt.
MELCHIOR: Und da, hab' ich g'hört, sind Sie in Desperation, daß Sie kein' Haus-
    knecht haben.
ZANGLER: In Desperation? Das is gar eine dumme Red', ich glaub', an solchen
    Schlingeln is keine Not.
MELCHIOR: Das is wahr, eher wird's an Prinzipal' eine Not sein. Ein Hausknecht
    halt't lang, aber Prinzipal geht alle Augenblick' einer z'grund'.
    (*Einen Jux will er sich machen* I, 6) (GW III, 608)

Zusammenfassung

In erster Linie will der Aufsatz auf verschiedene dramaturgische Funktionen der herkömmlichen Bedientenrolle hinweisen und ferner untersuchen, wie diese Funktionen von anderen Rollen und Strukturen innerhalb des Volkstheaters übernommen werden, z.B. wie der Hoch-Niedrig-Gegensatz durch die Polarität Erde-Feenreich dargestellt wird, und weit seltener durch das Herr-Knecht-Verhältnis.

Außerdem wird die Frage aufgeworfen, inwiefern sozialkritisch klingende Äußerungen oder Konstellationen in einem Stück mit Recht als solche zu bewerten sind, und nicht bloß als komische Effekte, Umkehrungen des Normalen, zu Erwartenden.

Im Zusammenhang damit wird auf die Wichtigkeit des selbständigen Handwerkers für die Wiener Volkstheatertradition hingewiesen — sei es als Theatertradition oder als Widerspiegelung tatsächlicher Verhältnisse.

Schließlich werden zwei Stellen aus den Bedientenrollen bei Nestroy eingehend analysiert: Johann (*Zu ebener Erde*) und Muffl (*Frühere Verhältnisse*).

Es wurde früher im Aufsatz festgestellt, daß schon Nestroys Spielweise viele Funktionen und Möglichkeiten der Bedientenrolle vorwegnimmt, ohne sich jedoch gesellschaftlich oder dramaturgisch im Rahmen des Stückes fixieren zu lassen. Bei der Analyse der ausgewählten Stellen geht es darum, zu zeigen, wie Nestroy das Konventionelle und Floskelhafte am Begriff der Herr-Knecht-Beziehungen mit äußerster Konsequenz gebraucht, um ein oft widerspruchsvolles, drastisch-schematisches Bild der nicht weniger grellen menschlichen Verhältnisse zu entwerfen.

8

W. E. Yates

NESTROY, GRILLPARZER, AND THE FEMINIST CAUSE

The aim of this paper is to argue that Nestroy's work, no less than Grillparzer's, shows considerable understanding of the social position of women in the Austria of the *Biedermeierzeit* — a time when the emancipation movement was still at a very early stage and when orthodox views of the role of women were still largely based on traditional prejudices.

The major Viennese dramatists of the period were, of course, notoriously unsuccessful in their personal dealings with women: Grillparzer impassioned but hesitant, never marrying; Raimund married unwillingly, and subsequently embattled in his tempestuously querulous relationship with Toni Wagner; Nestroy, too, unsuccessfully married, and then tied to the actress Marie Weiler in a common-law marriage which proved scarcely less tyrannous than the real thing, and from which he would escape in furtive dalliances. It is generally acknowledged that in Nestroy's case the experience has left its mark on his works in a succession of sour jibes against marriage as an institution. One typical example is the well-known passage in which Kilian Blau, punning on the word "Verein", defines marriage as a "wechselseitige Lebensverbitterungsanstalt" (*Der Färber und sein Zwillingsbruder* I, 10) (SW X, 202). In another piece of antithetical wordplay, Weinberl expounds the proverbial wisdom that marriages are made in heaven as meaning that they require of their participants supernatural patience (*Einen Jux will er sich machen* II, 7) (GW III, 643). Ledig's first monologue (*Unverhofft* I, 2) is one of many passages in which marriage is contrasted with love — in this case, in a characteristic theatrical allusion, as a commercially-inspired sequel of deadly tedium (GW IV, 447). Or again, Stegreif presents the act of marriage as a disaster to be avoided: "Ich bin immer gern bei Hochzeiten, schon das Bewußtsein, daß es nicht die meinige ist, macht, daß sich die Brust froh und frei erhebt" (*Nur keck!* I, 7) (SW XIV, 182). The list of examples could readily be extended, but these give us the picture: marriage is a series of quarrels; it is a trap, a torment, something essentially to be escaped; at best there is the consolation offered by Spitz in *Der alte Mann mit der jungen Frau* IV, 7: "[. . .] an Scheidungsgründen fehlt's nie, wenn nur der gute Wille da is" (GW V, 409).

Another received orthodoxy is that if long-term relations between the sexes are doomed to tension and disillusionment, it is the women who are the villains. The Nestroy of real life, as we know from the letter that has

93

survived to one Karoline Köfer (*Briefe*, 114–117), was in his mid-fifties still "auf Eroberungen ausgerüstet", and could commit himself to paper as finding the young woman "liebenswürdig und interessant in hohem Grade, der Gegenstand meiner glühendsten Wünsche". In the satirical world of the plays, on the other hand, he presents us with a gallery of portraits of female folly: man-hunters like Lucia Distl in *Liebesgeschichten und Heiratssachen* or the opportunist widows in *Der Talisman*; gold-diggers such as Aurora in *Glück, Mißbrauch und Rückkehr*; caricatures of affectation, from the simpering Marie and the gushingly sentimental Fräulein Blumenblatt in *Einen Jux will er sich machen* to the pretentious Frau von Cypressenburg (*Der Talisman*); and, no less gullible lower down the social order, young women falling for the clichés of romantic fiction, like Lisette in *Eine Wohnung ist zu vermieten*, or for a "Sehnsucht nach der Theaterwelt" like Peppi in *Frühere Verhältnisse* (GW VI, 452). Again there are many examples; and the proceedings of the 1982 Schwechat conference, which appeared in summarized form in the final number of *Nestroyana* for that year, include a useful typological summary of Nestroy's women characters by Barbara Rett.[1] There is no need to go over the same ground again; the general picture emerges from a passage such as Titus's résumé of the female constitution — fragile in nerves, soggy at heart, and impenetrable in mind: "Die Nerven von Spinnengeweb', d' Herzen von Wachs und d' Köpferl von Eisen, das is ja der Grundriß der weiblichen Struktur" (*Der Talisman* I, 16) (GW III, 437). We are given an impression of women as sex-objects, to be admired, as Sitzmeyer has it, for an ephemeral beauty: "Ja, Weiberschönheit is wohl recht eine schöne Schönheit, aber nix auf die Dauer" (*Alles will den Propheten sehen* II, 2) (SW XIII, 517). They are deceptive when young — "A Madl darf gar ka Luft haben," says Schippl, "in der Luft werden s' zu lüftig; eing'sperrt halten sie sich am besten, das hat mir a Türk g'sagt, der Deutsch können hat" (*Mein Freund* I, 1) (GW V, 457) — and unstoppably garrulous when older: "Es is a Kreuz mit euch Frauensleut', wenn's alt seids, red'ts zu viel, und wenn's jung seids, verschweigt's ei'm z'viel" (Schlicht in *Mein Freund* I, 20) (GW V, 481).

Any attempt to claim Nestroy for the feminist cause, then, is bound to be an uphill job. On the other hand it must be borne in mind that jokes against marriage (like music-hall jokes about mothers-in-law later) form part of a conventional routine of comedy; it is significant that Kilian Blau's description of marriage as a "wechselseitige Lebensverbitterungsanstalt" is one of the jokes that Nestroy's contemporary Friedrich Kaiser borrowed and reused verbatim a few years later in his play *Eine Posse als Medizin* (1849) (II, 4).[2] Similarly, type-roles of languishing wards and domineering wives belong to international comic convention, and are in no way peculiar to Nestroy.

In other respects too, the theatrical context for which his plays were written imposed significant limitations. He was by contract providing roles for a specific company including actresses with specific responsibilities.[3] The plot and characters in his plays were also to some extent dependent on the sources he adapted; when the process of adaptation involved making changes, these were determined either by the need to provide roles for particular members of the company (this has often been pointed out) or by the strategy of conforming to the conventions of theatrical comedy. In the novel (*La Maison blanche* by Paul de Kock) that served as the source of *Glück, Mißbrauch und Rückkehr*, the central figure is not forgiven at the end for his infidelity to his erstwhile sweetheart (see *Stücke 14*, 164); that Nestroy's Blasius and Babett *are* reconciled (and indeed set up in prosperity) is entirely in accordance with the orthodoxy of the happy ending, which requires both them and also Theodor and Friederike to be united at the final curtain.

Another comedy that ends with the lovers both united and rewarded is *Der Talisman*, where Titus dedicates himself to reproducing himself, in order to achieve the "Vervielfältigung" of red hair — a variation on a long-established pattern and particularly familiar from *Die Zauberflöte*, where Papageno and Papagena look forward in their final duet to their "liebe kleine Kinderlein" ("Erst einen kleinen Papageno!" / "Dann eine kleine Papagena!", and so on) (DL I, 317). The influence of *Die Zauberflöte* on Viennese popular comedy is, of course, pervasive. But in one respect at least *Der Talisman* stands very much in contrast to it. *Die Zauberflöte* — in this as in other respects a document of its age, and in particular of the ethos of Illuminist Freemasonry — is a markedly sexist work. Papageno instructs Pamina that the "first duty" of women is "die süßen Triebe mitzufühlen" (I, 14) (DL I, 280): no sooner is Tamino brought to the grove before the temples of wisdom, reason, and nature than he is disabused of all the Queen of the Night has told him: "Ein Weib thut wenig, plaudert viel" (I, 15) (DL I, 282); Sarastro instructs Pamina that she must be guided not by her mother but by a man, since women need male guidance:

> Ein Mann muß eure Herzen leiten,
> Denn ohne ihn pflegt jedes Weib
> Aus ihrem Wirkungskreis zu schreiten.
>
> (I, 18) (DL I, 286–287)

Finally, before Tamino embarks on his tests, the priests rehearse to him and Papageno their principle of distrustful misogyny: "Bewahret euch vor Weibertücken" (II, 3) (DL I, 292). — This element is strikingly lacking in *Der Talisman*.

Moreover, both Nestroy's gallery of foolish women and all the aphorisms about female deception need to be seen in the context of his gallery of equally foolish men. If we confine our attention merely to how his men behave in relation to women, we find infidelity on all sides, from the weakness of Blasius Rohr and the would-be-adulterous lechery of Gundlhuber to the calculating scheming of what Baumöhl calls "die Frauenentwendung" (*Das Gewürzkrämerkleeblatt* I, 10) (SW XII, 456) or the self-justifying resourcefulness of the (as he thinks) wounded Lorenz in *Die verhängnisvolle Faschingsnacht* (III, 1), who faces disappointment with an instant realignment of his affections (GW III, 403–404); and among male suitors too there are what Kampl calls the "Heiratskalifornianer" (*Kampl* III, 4) (GW V, 645). Nestroy's satire is not one-sided; his scepticism is universal.

The argument that because he satirizes women he is anti-feminist requires to be met with the same response as the argument that because he satirizes the Jews of Vienna in *Judith und Holofernes* his work is anti-Semitic. It has been argued that in *Judith und Holofernes* he was at least insensitive in subjecting a "buffeted and anxious minority" to satirical ridicule, "using themes that had been used in the political propaganda of the antisemites", and so "giving grist to the mill of the more zealous antisemites, those who saw Jewish vices as inherent and perennial".[4] In my view, this verdict is slanted by hindsight: it sees the satire not in its dramatic — more specifically, parodistic — context, where the anti-militarism of the Jewish traders is actually presented as a *positive* contrast to the militarism of Holofernes (which is what the play is centrally attacking), but primarily in terms of its reception, which acquires extrinsic significance because of later historical developments (see also pp. 130–132, below). After all, Nestroy *also* satirizes the Czechs and the English — just as he does lawyers, schoolmasters, and indeed the whole social scale from the vanity of noble birth (Vincelli in *Liebesgeschichten und Heiratssachen*) to the scheming of the meanest servant (Johann in *Zu ebener Erde und erster Stock*). His subject is mankind, where folly is universal — in Viennese and non-Viennese alike; in the female of the species, but no less in the male.

But it is a cardinal principle of satire that while the satirist may exercise a universal scepticism, his work may not be entirely destructive. The classic definition is Schiller's. Satire contrasts the defectiveness of reality with an ideal, which need not be made explicit, but which the satirist must evoke in the mind of his audience, so that the aversion from the shortcomings of reality which satire provokes is informed by the ideal with which that reality is — at least implicitly — contrasted:

In der Satyre wird die Wirklichkeit als Mangel dem Ideal als der höchsten Realität gegenüber gestellt. Es ist übrigens gar nicht nöthig, daß das letztere ausgesprochen werde, wenn der Dichter es nur im Gemüth zu erwecken weiß; dieß muß er aber schlechterdings, oder er wird gar nicht poetisch wirken. Die

Wirklichkeit ist also hier ein notwendiges Objekt der Abneigung, aber, worauf hier alles ankömmt, diese Abneigung selbst muß wieder notwendig aus dem entgegenstehenden Ideale entspringen.

(Über naive und sentimentalische Dichtung)[5]

It is precisely this function of providing a contrasting *standard* that the realistic good sense of the Jewish traders fulfils in *Judith und Holofernes*. Now it has often been pointed out that when we look for admirable characters in Nestroy, counterweights to the follies he satirizes, it is among his women that we find them. To the two most generally cited, the patient, loving and forgiving Kathi and Salome (in *Der Zerrissene* and *Der Talisman* respectively), we might add the equally forgiving Babett in *Glück, Mißbrauch und Rückkehr* and Sepherl in *Die verhängnisvolle Faschingsnacht*, or the faithful Peppi in *Moppels Abenteuer*. Most of these figures are, it is true, conventionally dependent on the central (male) character; and it could also be said that Peppi's faithfulness and the forgiveness shown by Kathi, Babett, and Sepherl are in part determined by a dramatic function, in that they serve to bring about the conventional happy ending. But in *Der Talisman* the issue is less simple. Not only does Salome have an eye to injustice herself; *Der Talisman* is also one of those plays where the ending carries its own significance, the convention being used to demonstrate a wider point — in this case the union of Titus and Salome represents the unspoken ideal informing the satire of the play, a union of intelligence and integrity.

Titus's position is that of a down-market Edmund — "Let me if not by birth, have lands by wit" *(King Lear* I, 2). (In Schreyvogel's adaptation, *King Lear* had in fact re-entered the repertory of the Burgtheater in May 1837.[6]) Like Edmund, Titus pursues his fortune by "wit" ("Witz" in Schreyvogel's version).[7] And as his opportunistic adventures prove, wit alone is not enough; in complete reversal of the wisdom of Sarastro, Titus needs the guidance of integrity as personified in Salome Pockerl — *das Ewig-Weibliche* pinned down in time and place, "die letzte hier im Ort" (I, 8) in 1840.

In the 1840s, half a century after Mary Wollstonecraft's *Vindication of the Rights of Women*, the emancipation of women was still only beginning to surface as a serious issue in Austria. In imaginative literature in German, such works as Gutzkow's novel *Wally, die Zweiflerin* (1835) had already begun to reflect the restrictions on women's lives.[8] It is true that even liberal thinkers were long very cautious in their support of the emancipation movement; nonetheless, in another of the 1982 Schwechat papers, Irmgard Neck was able to cite a work published in Vienna in 1846 and entitled *Gedanken über die angeborenen Rechte des Frauengeschlechtes*, in which the topic is described as being by then almost a *Zeitfrage*.[9]

Far from being a pamphlet in support of women's rights, this work is almost an anti-feminist tract. It is of interest, not for its intellectual cogency or originality of argument, but on the contrary because it demonstrates the survival of a conception of the role of woman more typical of the previous century — though in fact the author, Marie Baronin von Augustin (who came from a military background and wrote under the pseudonym Marie von Thurnberg) was some six years younger than Nestroy. Though she devotes a lot of space to the education of young women and argues for self-cultivation — the "Ausbildung unserer geistigen Kräfte" (p. 4) — this does not extend to the pursuit of scholarship or science, which are man's work (p. 79). In particular, woman has no intellectual function: "Sie ist nicht tiefsinnig, denn ihre Bestimmung ist nicht: zu ergründen, zu erwägen, zu prüfen [. . .]" (pp. 25–26); her chief responsibilities lie in the domestic sphere (p. 15), her fulfilment in love (p. 12).

It is against precisely these attitudes that we may set the case advanced by the early feminists of the *Vormärz* period. They made three principal demands:[10] first, for an improvement in education, which would lead to an end of tutelage and the limitations of domesticity, and would allow equal development of the female personality; secondly, for an end to the marriage of convenience; and thirdly, for wider occupational openings.

The openings were indeed very restricted. For young women of the poorer classes, there was service, or at best the kind of work represented by the seamstresses in *Das Mädl aus der Vorstadt* — and if the conventions of comedy allow Thekla to get her Gigl in the end, the role of the pre-datory Kauz is a reminder of the working girl's position in reality. Worse still, prostitution was rife, with the Theater in der Leopoldstadt one of the most notorious centres. (The figure later bandied about — that in the 1820s there were some 20,000 prostitutes in Vienna[11] — must surely be too high; the entire population, it must be remembered, was still under 300,000 in 1825.[12] But the problem was a real one, even if the censorship laws ensured that satire on the stage did not encroach on it.)

The woman who chose the orthodox domestic life was restricted to the portmanteau career of wife, mother, and nurse ascribed to his wife Eva by the cobbler Pfrim in *Höllenangst* III, 5: "Sehn Sie, ich hab ein vielseitig gebildetes Weib. Einmal is sie Gattin, nacher Mutter, gleich drauf wiederum Ammel und zur Abwechslung Krankenwärterin" (GW V, 318). This passage might almost be a satirical pastiche of Marie von Thurnberg. For, while her eye is of course on the middle and professional classes, it is precisely the domestic role of woman, the unchanging norm of wifehood and motherhood, that she extols: "Ihr Hauptgeschäft, — ihre Bestimmung, ihr Stolz, ist: eine gute Hausfrau und Mutter zu werden" (*Gedanken über die angeborenen Rechte des Frauengeschlechtes*, p. 15). And the one practical pursuit she commends is nursing the sick (*Kranken-pflege*), to which, indeed, a major section of her tract (pp. 123–147) is devoted. Employment might be had in teaching, too: in 1847 the journal *Der Humorist* thought it a proper subject for its women's section to report that in Paris there were currently 3,000 women working as teachers of music.[13] But almost the only openings for individual self-expression were those available to artistic talent. Ballets needed dancers, operas needed singers, stages needed actresses. And even there, the openings were hardly of a creative kind: there were next to no women dramatists, composers, even instrumentalists; and the stage was still a morally suspect environment, for while it may be true that by the end of the eighteenth century the serious actress was beginning to gain acceptance as a respectable artist,[14] the popular theatre did not confer similar respectability — "Der Wollüstling", wrote Bäuerle in 1811, "betrachtet das Mädchen auf der Bühne als eine Tochter der Freude."[15]

How little was achieved towards implementing the goals of the feminists of the mid-nineteenth century can be seen when we compare their demands with those being voiced half a century or more later.[16] After the rapid process of urban industrialization, the women's movement had by the turn of the century become linked with the socialist movement, and the need for better working conditions had been added to the earlier demands. But otherwise it is striking that the main demands of the turn-of-the-century feminists were exactly the same as those of the *Vormärz*: better education, an end to the marriage of convenience, and wider occupational openings.

One of the effects of the limitation in opportunities for women in the *Biedermeier* period was a restriction on the expression of the woman's point of view. Those who did publish were liable to be treated condescendingly.[17] As in other respects, Marie von Thurnberg sums up the conservative view: "Das Weib ist nach meiner Ansicht von der Natur weder zur Dichterin noch zu sonst einer Virtuosin berufen" (*Gedanken über die angeborenen Rechte des Frauengeschlechtes*, p. 15). She leaves open the possibility of exceptional genius (pp.149–150); but what she argues for is the cultivation of aesthetic appreciation (pp. 72–122), not for women to be creative artists (p. 91). Where she does imagine a young woman writing, it is to please her husband by keeping herself out of mischief:

Mancher Ehegatte würde sich glücklich fühlen, wenn seine Gemahlin, statt das Geld am Spieltische und im Putzladen zu versplittern, — statt in klatschsüchtigen Kaffee- oder Theegesellschaften ihr Herz zu verderben, an ihrem Schreibtische säße, um harmlose Gedichte zu schreiben. (p. 9)

For the young woman such writing would have a therapeutic function, casting off "die kleinen Reizbarkeiten der Seele" (p. 11).

Young women with literary aspirations were in fact liable not so much
to be helped and encouraged as rather to be positively discouraged from
pursuing them. There is an occasional poem, entitled "Einer jungen
Dichterin", by Johann Gabriel Seidl, that illustrates the point.[18] The
aspiring poetess is invited to cast aside her pen and paper to fulfil herself
instead in love and motherhood. Sitting at a desk is clearly an unfeminine
activity, damaging to one's looks:

> Willst du etwa kalt am Tische
> Schreiben, wie der Denker schreibt?
> Willst verkümmern deine Frische,
> Die so schöne Blüten treibt?

And the poem finishes with what purports to be an extolling of feminine
beauty but amounts in effect to a condemnation of emancipated self-
expression:

> Drum laß das Reimeschmieden,
> Denn der Jungfrau ziemt es nicht:
> Ist sie, was sie soll, hienieden,
> Ist sie selbst schon ein Gedicht!

What we have here is an equivalent in the literary life of the *Biedermeierzeit* to the phenomenon that Germaine Greer's study *The Obstacle
Race* traces in the field of the visual arts, the inhibiting assumption that
the pursuit of artistic activity was a denial of true femininity.[19] Even
Gutzkow, after all, was by 1838 rehearsing the old eighteenth-century
view "[daß] der Geist der Frauen nie schöpferisch wird".[20]

The outstanding example in post-Napoleonic Vienna of a work that goes
beyond this refusal of creative capacities to women is *Sappho*. *Sappho* has
recently been interpreted by Marianne Burkhard as exploring the conflict
between the heroine's creative independence and the role of women
conventional in Grillparzer's time, as represented in the play by Sappho's
love of Phaon and her longing for "häuslich stille Freuden" (v. 96) (WA
I/1, 268), so that her tragedy — her failure to achieve a workable
reconciliation of the two spheres of activity — illustrates the restrictions to
which women in the early nineteenth century were subjected.[21] Marianne
Burkhard quotes the monologue at the opening of Act Three, in which
Sappho rehearses an essentially stereotyped view of woman as dependent
for fulfilment on absorption in love; man by contrast cannot experience

> Wie all ihr Sein, ihr Denken und Begehren
> Um diesen einz'gen Punkt sich einzig dreht,
> Wie alle Wünsche, jungen Vögeln gleich,
> Die angstvoll ihrer Mutter Nest umflattern,
> Die Liebe, ihre Wiege und ihr Grab
> Mit furchtsamer Beklemmung schüchtern hüten;

Das ganze Leben als ein Edelstein
Am Halse hängt der neugebornen Liebe!

(vv. 827–834) (WA I/1, 305)

It is shortly after this, in her next monologue, that Sappho reaches her conclusion that her two spheres of activity are irreconcilable (vv. 952–953) (WA I/1, 310). The point is well taken that in elaborating his original conception of Sappho's tragedy Grillparzer expanded the resonance of the material; and indeed it is not really a new insight: it was Egon Friedell who summed up Grillparzer's treatment of the Sappho legend as "eine Wiener Vorstadttragödie", treating "die Neigung einer Operndiva zu einem jungen Menschen, der aber das 'süße Mädel' Melitta vorzieht".[22] Clearly Sappho does lose Phaon to a rival who is not only younger than herself but also wholly in the conventional mould —

nicht hohen Geists, von mäß'gen Gaben
Und unbehilflich für der Künste Übung

(vv. 756–757)

— and making her appeal "durch anspruchloses, fromm-bescheidnes Wesen" (v. 759) (WA I/1, 301).

Moreover, if Sappho's reflections on the conventional role of women imply a questioning of that role, that is entirely in keeping with other works of Grillparzer's. The sympathetic realism and candour of his portraiture of women has long been recognized, and is indeed increasingly appreciated.[23] But it is not just that his characterization, especially of the psychology of affection, seems full of insight — as, for instance, when he shows truthfulness and modesty battling with sensual attraction in Erny in *Ein treuer Diener seines Herrn*, or the sensations of love gradually burgeoning in Hero. If we go back to the first act of *Des Meeres und der Liebe Wellen* and ask *why* Hero has ever embarked on becoming a priestess, for which she is patently not cut out, we find that among the motivating factors are a resentment at the second-class position of women in the outside world from which she is escaping, in which they are expected to be the unquestioning playthings of male whims (vv. 207–208) (WA I/4, 90), and a rebellion against the kind of subservience in marriage which she has seen exemplified in the married life of her own mother (v. 204) and which makes her dismiss with scorn the cliché she is offered, "Das Weib ist glücklich nur an Gattenhand" (v. 320):

Das darfst du sagen, ohne zu erröten?
Wie? und mußt hüten jenes Mannes Blick,
Des Herren, deines Gatten? Darfst nicht reden,
Mußt schweigen, flüstern, ob du gleich im Recht?
Ob du die Weisre gleich, stillwaltend Beßre?
Und wagst zu sprechen mir ein solches Wort?

(vv. 321–326) (WA I/4, 98)

Still more modern is the fiery Kunigunde in *König Ottokars Glück und Ende*, who complains explicitly about having been excluded from an equal say in political power (vv. 2138–2140) (WA I/3, 127), and whose rejection of Ottokar in Act Four — a rejection twice expressed in terms of refusing him the marriage bed (vv. 2183–2184, 2405) (WA I/3, 129, 141) — seems to have its roots in specifically sexual disappointment: her bitterness at Ottokar, expressed in Act Two after she has been serenaded by the dashing Zawisch, not only brings out her resentment at the subservience required of her; it emerges too that she clearly expected to find him an impassioned and vigorous lover, and has not done so (vv. 973–983) (WA I/3, 60–61).

Though nowadays, with our sensibilities blunted by *Cosmopolitan* and the like, this may not make us turn a hair, it is a long way from the orthodoxies of the *Biedermeierzeit* — a long way, even, from the demands of the early feminists, which did not stretch to sexual emancipation. Free love might be advocated by the *avant garde* of the Young German movement; but that was male wishful thinking — and actually seemed preposterous to a right-thinking satirist like Nestroy. Ultra in *Freiheit in Krähwinkel* (I, 12) takes up an extremist position against marriage: "Ehstand is Sklaverei, und ich bin Freiheit durch und durch" (GW V, 79). It looks like another of Nestroy's aphoristic jibes against marriage; but in context, like all Ultra's declarations of policy, it is a piece of absurd unrealism, all of a piece with his equally untenable attitude towards political freedom. Ultra gets his just deserts in the end, as his hand and heart are captured by Frau von Frankenfrey (GW V, 133). Barbara Rett's reading of this is that Frau von Frankenfrey is sacrificing her freedom.[24] But that is surely not the principal force of the scene, for the focus is mainly on Ultra. And it is he, the apostle of liberty, who is succumbing (as Heugeig'n in Nestroy's next play also does); and if his attitude to marriage is indeed intended to function as a correlative to his political attitudes, the obligatory union of lovers at the final curtain implicitly bodes ill for the revolution.

It has constantly to be recalled how hollow the routine happy ending is. In fact the notion of marriage as a happy ending stands in glaring contrast to the plays themselves, and the artificiality of the convention is repeatedly brought out — for example, in the laughable improbability of the domestication of Zwirn at the end of *Der böse Geist Lumpazivagabundus*, or in the sudden blessing of the union of Eduard and Amalie at the end of *Eine Wohnung ist zu vermieten*. "Aber heirate so schnell als möglich", says Eduard's father, "und werde solid" (*Stücke 12*, 80) — the patent hollowness of the advice making this one of those places where Nestroy draws ironic attention to the implausibility of theatrical convention, which brings happy endings where real life would not.

It is true that because his central characters are mostly unmarried, the whole dimension of family life is necessarily given short shrift in his plays.[25] This is indeed determined precisely by his adherence to the convention that comedies end with the union of the principals as lovers. But such glimpses of marriage as we get in the plays cannot but cast doubt on the health of the institution. The reality of poverty and what it meant in bringing up a family, for example, is stated realistically enough by the unfortunate Sepherl downstairs in the second scene of *Zu ebener Erde und erster Stock* — "Ich bin doch ein recht unglückliches Weib. Mein' Mann sein Verdienst so schlecht und die Schar Kinder zum Abfüttern!" (GW IV, 432) — and is shown equally well in the plight of Eva in *Höllenangst* I, 8, running a home with the support of no more than her faith in better things to come in the after-life (GW V, 266). Among the well-to-do we meet a figure such as Kunigunde in *Eine Wohnumg ist zu vermieten*, who has no wish to leave her present home but has to submit to the whim of her husband, and is constantly subjected to his high-handed instructions, his insults, and even deceptions. (That he does not in fact manage to be unfaithful to her is a result solely of his own incompetence.)

Furthermore, the device of the solo scene, though basically providing a theatrical set-piece for himself (or for Scholz, or later for Karl Treumann), does also provide Nestroy with the opportunity to give direct — albeit of course comic — expression to a woman's view. On marriage he does this notably in *Der Kobold*, in the opening scene of the second act. Thekla (who was played by Marie Weiler) is wondering why Staberl has been spying on her: has her beloved Folletterl put him up to it? Is it a symptom of jealousy? She feels unsure about marriage — and the uncertainty leads her into reflecting on what it will hold:

> Der Ehstand is an und für sich schon betrübt,
> Und nur zu ertragen, wenn man wahnsinnig liebt,
> Als Frau soll man gsetzt sein, sonst richten s' eim aus,
> Nur ewig mi'n Schlüsselbund umgehn im Haus,
> Nicht tanzen, nicht lachen, welch trauriges Lebn,　　　　5
> Nur immer fürn Mann auf die Wirthschaft Acht gebn,
> Und "er soll dein Herr sein", heißt's noch oben drein,
> Nein, nein, nein, nein, das geht mir halt durchaus nicht ein.
>
> Jetzt kann sich's dann treffen das is 's Ärgste gwiß
> Daß man d' wahre Lieb kennen lernt wann's zu spät is,　　　　10
> Und so a Malheur kann gar [g]schwind gschehen sein,
> Die Eh macht ja 's weibliche Herz nicht zu Stein,
> Man wirft einen Blick auf den, den 's Herz sich erkohrn,
> Da brummt eim der Ehmann dann hinein in die Ohrn:
> "Was schaust auf ein Andern? au'm Mann schaust allein!" —　　　　15
> Nein, nein, nein, nein, das geht mir halt durchaus nicht ein.
>
> 　　　　　　　　　　　　　　　　(*Stücke 14*, 118–119)

Far from being the starry-eyed bride of convention, Thekla spells out in this song — an attractive allegretto tune in three-four time (see *Stücke 14*, 332) — that marriage presents a dismal prospect (v. 1) which requires total love if it is to be tolerable (v. 2): the role of a wife is to be stuck at home (vv. 4–5) — "welch trauriges Leben" — keeping house and having to recognize her husband as lord and master (vv. 6–7); and all of that, she concludes in the refrain, makes no sense to her. Here, in 1838, Nestroy is already in effect summarizing two of the main plaints of the *Vormärz* feminists, the rejection of tutelage and the restrictiveness of domesticity. And what the second stanza goes on to consider is another of the central topics of feminist writing, the loveless marriage. One could, she reflects, meet true love when it is too late (vv. 9–10) — the female heart is susceptible (vv. 11–12) — but she would be tied to a husband demanding total fidelity (v. 15). And that too, she concludes, makes little sense.

Still more significant is Salome's song in *Der Talisman* I, 15 (GW III, 435–436). The play is about prejudice against inequalities in material and social good fortune, arbitrarily dispensed by Providence and symbolized in the red hair of the two principals, which in Titus's case is replaced by chance for the duration of the comic fiction — the injustice of Providence suspended for him, though not for Salome. It is important for the dramatist to establish that the prejudice against which the satire is directed is not limited to the specific trivial example of red hair — that the red hair has merely an illustrative function. He does this in the first place in Titus's two short monologues in scenes 5 and 7, which serve to suggest wider perspectives by generalizing about prejudice (I, 5) and suggesting the animosity of society as a whole (I, 7). But the breadth of reference still requires to be brought out in further exemplification. The function of Salome's song is precisely to establish this wider reference; and the particular example of prejudice chosen is the lot of women. The nub of the argument, led into by the monologue — "Die Mannsbilder haben's halt doch in allen Stücken gut gegen uns" — and summarized in the refrain ("Ja, die Männer hab'n's gut, hab'n's gut, hab'n's gut"), is that it's a man's world. A man can chase a girl who catches his fancy; women are denied that liberty (stanza 1). This is a comic rephrasing of the very point Sappho makes about the unseriousness of male affection in her monologue in Act Three:

> Und findet er die Lieb', bückt er sich wohl,
> Das holde Blümchen von dem Grund zu lesen,
> Besieht es, freut sich sein und steckt's dann kalt
> Zu andern Siegeszeichen auf den Helm. [. . .]
> Ein Kuß, wo er ihm immer auch begegnet,
> Stets glaubt er sich berechtigt ihn zu nehmen;
> Wohl schlimm, daß es so ist, doch ist es so!
>   (vv. 821–824, 839–841)(WA I/1, 305)

Salome continues: if a man is thwarted, he can take refuge in the ale-house, and can launch another affair when he pleases:

> [. . .] Kränken wir einen Mann, thut's ihn nit stark ergreifen,
> Er setzt sich ins Wirtshaus und stopft si sei Pfeifen;
> Wir glaub'n, er verzweifelt, derweil ißt er ein' Kas,
> Trinkt ein' Heurigen und macht mit der Kellnerin G'spaß,
> Schaut im Hamgehn einer andern glei hübsch unter'n Hut [. . .]
>
> (stanza 2)

Women, by contrast, are tied to a rigid convention of propriety, so that their whole repute depends on standards of far greater strictness (stanza 3):

> Hat a Madel die zweite oder dritte Amour,
> Is ihr Ruf schon verschandelt, und nachher is zur [. . .]

A feminist tract would put it more theoretically; but though the terms would be different, the point — that hypocritical double standards applied in a patriarchal society — would be the same.

These two solo scenes are not isolated examples of insight. In *Das Gewürzkrämerkleeblatt* II, 8 Madame Zichori gives us a woman's eye view of male superiority (SW XII, 488–489), and similar solo scenes in other plays also treat relations between the sexes, spelling out the inequalities of social expectations and emphasizing the deceptiveness, unreliability, and self-indulgence of the male.[26] Romantic love is a fine dream; but reality, Nestroy's constant touchstone, brings brutal disillusionment. A proposal of marriage may be the supreme romantic moment — in romance; but for Lisette romance is swiftly dispelled:

> CAJETAN (*vor ihr auf die Kniee stürzend*): Engel! Göttin! Du mußt die Meinige werden.
> LISETTE: Wie gschieht denn dem Herrn?
> CAJETAN: Sei meine Geliebte, sag ich, oder ich thu dir alle möglichen Grobheiten an.
> (*Eine Wohnung ist zu vermieten* I, 15) (*Stücke 12*, 23)

And as for marriage itself, all the points of the nineteenth-century feminists about the unjust imbalance in social conventions are comically summarized in *Die verhängnisvolle Faschingsnacht* II, 2 as Lorenz spells out his expectations:

> NANI: [. . .] Ist die Sepherl so streng?
> LORENZ: Unendlich! Das ist auch ein Hauptfehler von ihr. Sie glaubt, was dem Weibe verboten ist, das darf der Mann auch nicht tun. Wie arrogant! Und es ist doch das konträre Verhältnis. Erlaubt sich das Weib das geringste, so leidet die Ehre des Mannes dabei; je mehr sich aber der Mann erlaubt, je niederträchtiger als er sie behandelt, und sie ertragt das Ding alles als stille Dulderin, desto mehr Ehre macht es ihr. Es gibt gar nichts Ausgezeichneteres für ein Weib, als wenn sie im Renommee als stille Dulderin ist.
> (GW III, 382)

This scene is part of a secondary action, in which Lorenz makes advances to Nani, that is not based on the Holtei drama (*Ein Trauerspiel in Berlin*) being parodied in the play. Lorenz's sense of "honour" *is*, of course, parodistically based on the original; but in elaborating it, Nestroy chooses to build in a satirical reflection on the most self-evidently absurd principle of injustice, in the relations between the sexes.

To sum up: Nestroy viewed women satirically, as his many aphoristic formulations mocking them and the world of marital domesticity make clear. But that is how he viewed all mankind. Women are no more picked out for *prejudiced* satire than the Jews of "Bethulien". On the contrary, in his treatment of social contrasts, what his plays provide cumulative testimony to is his general sympathy for the under-dog; and in the uneven battle of the sexes he sees very clearly — just as his contemporary Grillparzer does — the extent to which in early and mid nineteenth-century Austria the underprivileged were women.

Zusammenfassung

Nestroys Stücke enthalten bekanntlich viele bissige Aphorismen sowohl über die Ehe (was die Forschung gewöhnlich mit seinem eigenen desillusionierenden Eheerlebnis in Zusammenhang bringt) als auch über die Frauen, deren vergängliche Schönheit sich mit Dummheit und Betrug paare. Diese Witze sind aber z.T. konventionell. Das Motiv des Vorurteils gegen "Weibertücken", das für *Die Zauberflöte* bezeichnend ist, fehlt etwa dem *Talisman* gänzlich, und die törichten Frauengestalten in Nestroys Werken sind von ebenso törichten Männern umgeben. Seine Satire ist unparteiisch. Daß die Frauen in seinen Possen oft in einem satirischen Licht erscheinen, zeugt so wenig von Vorurteil wie seine satirische Darstellung der Leopoldstädter Juden in *Judith und Holofernes*. Im Gegenteil: Der Satiriker muß ein Ideal andeuten, das als Kriterium der Satire dient, und gerade diese Funktion haben sowohl die jüdischen Kaufleute in der Hebbel-Parodie als auch etliche Frauengestalten in anderen Possen. So erweist sich etwa der Verstand Titus Feuerfuchs' als etwas Einseitiges und Irreführendes, das der Ergänzung durch jene Integrität bedarf, die Salome Pockerl verkörpert.

In den vierziger Jahren wurde die Frauenemanzipation erst allmählich zur Zeitfrage in Österreich. Marie von Thurnberg vertritt den konservativen Standpunkt, indem sie die häuslichen Pflichten der Frau betont und ihr solche männlichen Eigenschaften wie den "Tiefsinn" abspricht. Die Gelegenheiten zur Berufstätigkeit, die der Frau in der Biedermeierzeit offenstanden, waren sehr begrenzt. Als Norm galt noch jene Rolle als Gattin, Mutter und Krankenwärterin, die Nestroys Pfrim an seiner Frau Eva preist, und wie wenig es den Frauenrechtlerinnen des Vormärz gelang, die Umstände zu ändern, ist daraus zu ersehen, daß die Frauenbewegung der Jahrhundertwende im Grunde noch die gleichen Reformen verlangte. Auch in den Künsten fehlte der Frau weitgehend die Möglichkeit, sich schöpferisch auszudrücken: Seidls Gedicht "Einer jungen Dichterin" zeigt, wie der literarisch veranlagten Frau von solcher Tätigkeit abgeraten wurde.

Wenn Grillparzers *Sappho*, wie Marianne Burkhard argumentiert hat, sich gerade mit den Beschränkungen auseinandersetzt, die der Frau der Biedermeierzeit auferlegt waren, so entspricht die in diesem Stück bewiesene Einsicht in die Stellung der Frau und in die weibliche Persönlichkeit einem Grundelement in Grillparzers Werk, das sich ebenfalls in Heros Ablehnung des demütigenden Klischees vom häuslichen Glück und in Kunigundes Enttäuschung über ihre Ehe mit Ottokar manifestiert. Es reichten allerdings nicht einmal die Plädoyers der vormärzlichen Frauenrechtlerinnen bis zur Sexualfreiheit, und die Ablehnung des Ehestands durch den freiheitsbesessenen Ultra erfährt am Schluß von *Freiheit in Krähwinkel* eine bezeichnende Niederlage. Daß die Liebenden in einem künstlich herbeigeführten Happy-End vereint werden, gehört zur Routine der Komödie, und bei Nestroy wird häufig auf das Unglaubwürdige an der Konvention aufmerksam gemacht. Das Bild von der Ehe, das seine Stücke vermitteln, steht in starkem Kontrast zur konventionellen Vorstellung eines fröhlichen Ausgangs. Darüber hinaus geben dem Satiriker solche Soloszenen wie die Theklas in *Der Kobold* ii, 1 and Salomes Couplet in *Der Talisman* i, 15 die Gelegenheit, die Einstellung der Frau zur Ehe und zu anderen Grundproblemen der Frauenemanzipation unmittelbar — wenngleich komisch — von einer Frauengestalt ausdrücken zu lassen, und bestätigen, daß Nestroy mit der gleichen Klarheit wie sein Zeitgenosse Grillparzer erkennt, wie sehr die Frauen noch zu den Unterprivilegierten in der Gesellschaftsordnung der Zeit gehörten.

9

Günter Berghaus

REBELLION, RESERVATION, RESIGNATION: NESTROY UND DIE WIENER GESELLSCHAFT 1830–1860

Nestroys Entwicklung im Vormärz

Als Nestroy seine theatralischen Wanderjahre absolviert hatte und 1831 seinen ersten Vertrag bei Carl unterschrieb, traf er im Theater an der Wien keineswegs auf ein Publikum, das sich in einem politischen Dornröschenschlaf befand. Die Wiener Vorstädte waren durch die dortige Konzentration der Industrie zum Ausgangspunkt einer politisch-oppositionellen Bewegung geworden:

Das Theater war in der Zeit vor 1848 und eine Zeitlang nach diesem denkwürdigen Jahre das Forum der Donaustadt. Einzig und allein hier durfte die Gesellschaft Wiens, als Körper vereinigt, offen und frei ihre Meinung äußern, ihren Willen kundgeben, Lob und Tadel ungestraft austeilen. Im Theater allein konnte das Volk Souveränität der Gedanken-Freiheit üben; da hatte es gelernt, sich zu fühlen, da machte es von dem Rechte der Selbstbestimmung Gebrauch. Im Theater wurde Wien mit dem Vereins- und Versammlungsrecht bekannt.[1]

Als Nestroy seine Wiener Karriere begann, besaß er zwar kein revolutionär gesinntes, jedoch ein mit den politischen und sozialen Verhältnissen unzufriedenes Publikum, auf das er mit seinen Stücken großen Einfluß nehmen konnte.

Die künstlerische Situation der Wiener Vorstadttheater war jedoch im Vergleich mit dem politischen Bewußtsein seines Publikums desolat. Entgegen Rommels apologetischen Beschreibungen charakterisiert Wangermann die Lage der Vorstadttheater zutreffender als "a mixture of elaborate mechanical gimmicks and vulgar buffoonery".[2] Der Typus des gemütlichen, fröhlichen Wieners, dessen Spießbürgerlichkeit jede Kritik am Staat und der herrschenden Ordnung ausschloß, beherrschte die Bühne. Daher war es für die staatlichen Obrigkeiten möglich, die Vorstadttheater als eine gute Einrichtung zu loben, "womit die Leute von denen privat und öffters zu gefährlichen Absichten veranlassenden conventiculis oder Zusammenkünften abgehalten werden".[3]

Nestroy empfand dieses vordergründig naiv-heitere Theater als Verdrängung der realen gesellschaftlichen Widersprüche, und in seiner ersten Phase, die bis etwa 1834 dauerte, sah er seine Aufgabe darin, dieser Welt des "Guten, Schönen, Wahren" den Schleier vom Gesicht zu ziehen und die häßliche Kehrseite der heiteren Biedermeierfassade aufzuzeigen.

Mit der Juli-Revolution 1830 war die Zeit gesellschaftlicher Um-
wälzungen, die Zeit des Kampfes gegen das Ancien Régime der Heiligen
Allianz angebrochen. Er wurde in Österreich jedoch nicht vom mittleren
und höheren Bürgertum geführt (sie waren wirtschaftlich zu schwach und
zahlenmäßig noch zu unterentwickelt), sondern von den kleinbürgerlichen und plebejischen Unterschichten. Das Bessere Bürgertum war der
einzige Nutznießer der Metternichschen Restaurationspolitik. Es war das
Rückgrat der Wiener Biedermeierdramatik, deren verlogener Senti-
mentalität und Idyllik Nestroy den Kampf angesagt hatte. Diese Gesellschaftsschicht repräsentierte einen wichtigen Zuschaueranteil in den
Wiener Vorstadttheatern. Doch bis etwa 1835 besaß es einen Gegenpol in
den kleinbürgerlichen und Dienstbotenschichten, die die billigeren Plätze
in den Theatern einnahmen und Nestroys eigentliches Zielpublikum
darstellten.

Nestroys frühe Possen hatten nichts mit der harmlosen und idyllischen
Biedermeierdramatik eines Raimund, Meisl oder Gleich zu tun. Er fühlte
sich der sozialen Wirklichkeit der Wiener Nachkongreßgesellschaft
verpflichtet und griff in seinen Stücken realhistorische Probleme auf, die
das kleinbürgerliche — und nicht etwa das großbürgerliche — Publikum
im Theater behandelt sehen wollte.

Ähnliches läßt sich über den Schauspielstil Nestroys sagen, der in
genauem Gegensatz zu Raimunds psychologischer Darstellungsweise
stand. Nestroy griff auf die alten Hanswurstgestalten, die komischen
Outsiderfiguren der Gesellschaft zurück und entblößte mit seinem
aggressiven Witz die Dummheit und Brutalität der gesellschaftlichen
Stützen des Metternich-Regimes. Nestroys häßlicher Naturalismus und
seine wahrheitsgetreuen Milieuschilderungen waren für das Wiener
Theaterpublikum ein Novum, mit dem es sich nur schwer anfreunden
konnte:

Um der Wahrheit die Ehre zu geben, muß constatirt werden, daß Wien, das sich
so lange an Raimund's und Korntheuer's "solider" Komik ergötzte, von der
grotesken Darstellungsweise und der "Scharfzüngigkeit" Nestroy's anfänglich
nicht gleich vollkommen gepackt fühlte, vielmehr gegen den verwegenen
"Umstürzler" sich etwas reserviert hielt.[4]

Zahlreichen Theaterrezensionen ist zu entnehmen, daß sich das
gutbürgerliche Publikum entsetzt von den frühen Stücken Nestroys
abwandte. Doch die kleinbürgerlichen und plebejischen Zuschauer, die
sich nur einen billigen Platz auf der Galerie leisten konnten, verhalfen der
realistischen Drastik und dem outrierten Stil Nestroys zum Durchbruch.
So heißt es z.B. in einer Rezension zu *Die beiden Herren Söhne* in den
Sonntagsblättern: "Das Stück erhielt in den obersten Regionen des
klatschbefehligten Olymps einigen Beifall, von dem gebildeten

Publikum wurde es mit ausgesprochenem, wenn auch weniger lärmendem Mißfallen zurückgewiesen."[5]

Der Einfluß Nestroys auf sein Publikum wuchs von Jahr zu Jahr. Besorgt urteilte Sedlnitzky: "Sehen Sie! dieser Nestroy hat anfänglich nicht recht gefallen, *jetzt* ist er der Abgott der Wiener. Hat Nestroy sich geändert? Nein! *Er* ist derselbe geblieben, aber die *Wiener* sind Andere geworden!"[6] Natürlich hatten sich die Wiener nicht durch Nestroy geändert, sondern Nestroy griff in einen historischen Prozeß ein, dessen auslösendes Moment die Juli-Revolution gewesen war. Nach einem Besuch der Wiener Vorstadttheater 1833 befand Willibald Alexis, daß sich auch Österreich nicht länger völlig von der geistigen Bewegung in Europa habe abschließen können. Die harmlose Luft der Biedermeierzeit sei verflogen, die Wiener fingen an zu reflektieren und sich zu erbittern.[7]

Doch das Publikum, bei dem Alexis diese Veränderungen festgestellt hatte und auf das Nestroy einen so großen Einfluß ausübte, verschwand in der zweiten Hälfte der dreißiger Jahre immer mehr aus den Theatern. Die konstante Erhöhung der Theaterpreise, die Verschlechterung der wirtschaftlichen Lage der Unterschichten und schließlich die zyklische Wirtschaftskrise der vierziger Jahre vertrieben Nestroys Zielgruppe selbst aus den Galerien. Zurück blieb das mittlere und höhere Bürgertum, das von nun an den Ton in den Vorstadttheatern angab. Da Carl den Stil seines Theaters am Geschmack des jeweils trendsetzenden Publikums ausrichtete, hielt er seinen Starkomiker und Hausdramatiker Nestroy dazu an, sich den Wünschen des nun vorherrschenden Publikums anzupassen.

Dieses konservative, wirtschaftlich wohlgestellte Bürgertum verlangte nach humorigen Lokalfiguren, die in einer heiteren und verständlichen Sprache ein harmonisches Volksleben vorführten, aus dem die Schattenseiten der Biedermeiergesellschaft ausgeklammert waren. Nachdem Nestroy glücklich die Überreste des Altwiener Zauberspiels beseitigt hatte, standen ihm nun die Vertreter des Neuen Volksstücks gegenüber. Der Hauptrepräsentant dieser retrospektiven Volkstheatertheorie war Moritz Gottlieb Saphir. Er war das Sprachrohr des gemäßigten Großbürgertums, dessen Forderung nach kerngesunden Gestalten mit Geist und Gemüt, sprudelnder Lebendigkeit und rosaroter Herzenswärme Nestroy ästhetisch wie auch politisch ablehnte. Für ihn war das "neue" Volksstück nur eine zeitgemäßere Fortsetzung der alten Zauberspiele mit der Aufgabe, die politischen und gesellschaftlichen Widersprüche, die nach 1830 immer offener zutage traten, zu übertünchen.

Nestroy aber war nicht bereit, die gesellschaftlichen Zustände der Restaurationsepoche, die mit der Juli-Revolution ins Schwanken geraten waren, idealisierend abzubilden und die häßliche Realität unter den Tisch fallen zu lassen. Nach außen hin war er gezwungen, Anleihen bei der von

ihm so verachteten "Haus- und Wirtschaftspoesie" (*Der Talisman* II, 24)
(SW X, 456) zu machen. Er kolportierte die Kriminal- und Sittenstücke,
das Lustspiel oder das Genre der Rühr- und Besserungsstücke, doch das
verlogene Pathos und die realitätsferne Idyllik seiner Dramatikerkollegen
Kaiser, Berla oder Elmar suchte er wenn irgend möglich zu umgehen.
Manche der Stücke, die er in dieser Zeit aufs Papier brachte, gehören zu
den Schlechtesten, die er je produzierte (z.b. *Der Treulose oder Saat
und Ernte* (1836), *Glück, Mißbrauch und Rückkehr oder Das Geheimnis des
grauen Hauses* (1838), *Gegen Torheit gibt es kein Mittel* (1838), *Der
Erbschleicher* (1840), *Die Papiere des Teufels* (1842)). Diese Werke, die
prinzipiell dem Geschmack des großbürgerlichen Publikums entgegen-
kamen, fielen so offensichtlich hinter die Qualität eines Rührstückes von
Iffland und Kotzebue, hinter die Familien- oder Dorfgeschichten der
Birch-Pfeiffer zurück, daß sich diese Versuche Nestroys im "ernsten
Genre" nicht auf dem Spielplan durchsetzen konnten. Einzig *Glück,
Mißbrauch und Rückkehr* konnte sich wegen Nestroys Glanzrolle als
Blasius Rohr im Repertoire halten.

Bloß in den Possen dieser Zeit gelang es ihm, die ihm eigentümliche
Schreibart beizubehalten. Zwar mußte er auch hier sein Dynamit in Watte
wickeln, doch auf die Dauer wirkte es nicht minder effektvoll. Nestroy
mußte sich jedoch immer mehr mit dem Gedanken abfinden, nicht für,
sondern gegen sein Publikum spielen zu müssen. Er wollte die Kanaille im
Zuschauerraum zusammenkartätschen und doch war er gezwungen, sein
Publikum mit lustigen Sprüngen zum Lachen zu bringen (s. SW XV, 195).

Die Folge war eine pessimistische und manchmal sogar resignative
Tendenz in seinem Werk, die sich nach 1848 zum vorherrschenden
Charakteristikum seiner Stücke entwickelte. Der Grund dafür waren
keine individuellen Charakterschwächen, sondern objektive Gegebenheiten, die Nestroys politische und künstlerische Entwicklung von allen
Seiten einschränkten. Zuerst ist sein Publikum zu nennen, das von 1835
bis 1845 in der Überzahl dem biedermeierlich reaktionären Untertanen-
geist verpflichtet war. Die *Theaterzeitung* warnte Nestroy: "Möge er stets
die Anforderungen des Publikums beachten, das [. . .] seinem Streben
eine feinere Richtung anbefiehlt und jetzt Ausdrücke, die z.b. in
'Lumpazivagabundus' belacht wurden, entschieden zurückweist."[8] Da
Carl sein Theater ganz wie ein Wirtschaftsunternehmen führte und seine
Warenproduktion einzig von den Bedürfnissen des Marktes bestimmen
ließ, wurden Nestroy nicht weniger Restriktionen von seinem Direktor als
von seinem Zensor auferlegt. Haffner gibt eine gute Beschreibung dieser
Umstände, als er über einen Besuch Nestroys bei Carl berichtet:

"Vielleicht kann mir der Herr Direktor Auskunft geben, ob mein neues Couplet
zensuriert worden ist?"

"Oh, schon gestern. Sie haben nur eine einzige Strophe zu ändern. Alle anderen sind gestrichen worden."

"Schön! Ich werde mir einen anderen Sedlnitzky verschreiben."

"Die Strophen waren auch viel zu freisinnig! Berühren Sie doch um Himmels willen nicht die Politik. Sie haben ja noch andere Quellen, die unerschöpflich sind für eine reiche Phantasie."[9]

Unter diesen Produktionszwängen war es kein Wunder, daß Nestroys Darstellungsart und Schreibweise immer mehr an satirischer Schärfe einbüßte. Seine Possen verloren viel von ihrer ursprünglichen bissigen Aggressivität, und die grotesken Satiren wandelten sich zu humorvollen Moralitäten. Über den Wandel in Nestroys Schauspielstil äußerte sich Gutt 1844 so:

Die Charaktere sind nicht (wie es Nestroy früher so häufig geschah) bis in's Ungeheuerliche chargirt, sondern mit der Wahrheit und Zierlichkeit des Lustspiels, nur mit etwas satteren Farben ausgeführt. In seinen neueren Arbeiten hat Nestroy, ohne irgend an Kraft einzubüßen, eine Mäßigung, einen Formsinn, den man früher nur zu häufig vermißte.[10]

Mit dem Einbruch des Vaudevilles 1842 sah es sogar so aus, als würde Nestroy völlig von der Vorstadtbühne verdrängt. Er konnte erst dann wieder seine Schaffenspause beenden, als auch das Großbürgertum von der Wirtschaftskrise der vierziger Jahre erfaßt wurde und den realitätsflüchtigen Vaudevillisten das Lachen im Hals verstummte. Der oppositionelle Geist sprang nun auch auf die großbürgerlichen und adligen Stände über, und dies bot Nestroy die Chance, seine fortschrittlichen Gedanken erneut auf dem Theater verbreiten zu können.

In dieser letzten Phase vor der Revolution tritt uns Nestroy als überzeugter Demokrat entgegen. Seine politischen Aussagen sind reifer, seine Charaktere lebenswahrer geworden. Nun, wo er die Opposition gegenüber dem Publikum abbauen konnte, entwarf er seine bürgerlichen Figuren nicht länger als reine Karikaturen, sondern gestaltete sie als psychologisch einfühlsame und komplexe Charaktere. Nestroy hatte die politische Bündnisfähigkeit des höheren Bürgertums erkannt. Daher kritisierte er sie nun sehr viel milder als in den vorangegangenen Stücken. Er gab seine Leidenschaft als Fassadenzertrümmerer und Entlarver von falschen Illusionen auf und stand von nun an den menschlichen Schwächen sehr viel konzilianter gegenüber.

Gleichzeitig erhöhte sich die Klarheit seiner Gesellschaftsanalyse und seiner politischen Anschauungen. Im *Schützling* verwendete er zum ersten Mal den Begriff der Arbeiterklasse (I, 4) (SW VII, 123), im *Unbedeutenden* sprach er sogar von einer "angeborenen Feindschaft zwischen arm und reich" (III, 23) (SW VII, 90). Nestroy, der die Armut bisher immer nur als individuelles Schicksal und Resultat einer lieder-

lichen Lebensführung gesehen hatte, begann nun nach dem wahren
Grund für die erbarmungswürdige Lage der Unterschichten zu fragen.
Die extreme Verschärfung der Klassenwidersprüche nach 1844 führte
auch Nestroy zu der Erkenntnis, daß Armut nicht einfach vom Schicksal
bestimmt war, sondern das Resultat eines Ausbeutungsverhältnisses
zwischen den antagonistischen Hauptklassen der österreichischen Gesellschaft darstellte. Hatte er früher noch angenommen, daß Fleiß und
Redseligkeit jedem Menschen eine akzeptable gesellschaftliche Stellung
verschaffen würden, so mußte er nun erkennen, daß selbst so begabte und
tüchtige Kräfte wie Gottlieb Herb auf der Straße landeten.

Nestroys Gesellschaftsbild

Die Präzision der Klassenanalyse in den Stücken vor der Achtundvierziger-Revolution deutet an, welchen Wandel Nestroys politisches
Bewußtsein in den nahezu zwanzig Jahren seiner dramatischen Tätigkeit
durchgemacht hat. Zwar hatte er auch in der Frühzeit die menschlichen
Schwächen, die er geißeln wollte, in einen gesellschaftlichen Rahmen
gestellt; doch während seiner frühen Theatertätigkeit kann man nicht
davon ausgehen, daß er einen ausgeprägten Klassenbegriff besessen habe.
Zwar lassen sich die meisten seiner Theaterfiguren in ein soziologisches
Klassenschema einordnen, doch dramaturgisch arbeitete Nestroy nur mit
dem Gegensatz von arm und reich. Seine armen Leute waren überwiegend
positive Charaktere, während die Reichen meist grell und überzogen
karikiert wurden.
  Der Grad von Nestroys politischem Wandel wird deutlich, wenn man
seine beiden Stücke *Zu ebener Erde und erster Stock* (1835) und *Der
Schützling* (1847) miteinander vergleicht. Während in dem früheren Stück
Schlucker und Goldfuchs noch friedlich unter einem Dach leben konnten,
speist sich die Dramatik im letzteren aus den antagonistischen Klassen-
widersprüchen zwischen Arbeitern und Kapitalisten. In den Stücken der
mittleren Phase fällt die unrealistische Darstellung des Elends der
Unterschichten auf. Der märchenhafte Gleichmut, mit dem die am
Hungertuch Nagenden ihr Schicksal erdulden, läßt sich nicht allein damit
erklären, daß Nestroy Rücksicht auf die Zuschauer nahm, die die
"Wahrheit zum Seekrankwerden"[11] nicht länger ertragen wollten,
sondern legt nahe, daß Nestroy die realen Erfahrungen fehlten, um die
soziale Lage der Unterschichten realistisch beschreiben zu können. Daher
erschöpft sich sein politisches Programm in diesen Stücken in einem
liberalen Reformbestreben. Wie anders dagegen sehen die Unterschichten
in seinen Stücken Ende der vierziger Jahre aus! Willibald spricht in *Die
schlimmen Buben in der Schule* von der Erde als einem "Himmelskörper,

auf dem die Unglücklichen ein höllisches Leben haben" (10. Szene)
(SW XIII, 224). In *Höllenangst* wird der Arme zum geborenen Revolutionär: "Kein Wunder, wenn der Arme ein Mißvergnügter is.
Mißvergnügter, Verschworner und Revolutionär, das sind Geschwister-
kinder" (SW V, 702).

Dem Industrieproletariat hat Nestroy erst relativ spät seine Auf-
merksamkeit zugewandt. Die Arbeiter in seinen früheren Stücken waren
alle pauperisierte Kleinbürger, Dienstboten, arbeitslose Gesellen etc. Erst
das Gußwerk im *Schützling* III, 1–6 und Gottliebs Frage, ob die technische
Entwicklung auch zum Wohl der Arbeiterklasse beitragen könne (SW VII,
216), zeigen, daß Nestroy ein Problembewußtsein in Bezug auf das
Industrieproletariat entwickelt hat. Der erste selbstbewußte moderne
Proletarier aber betritt erst 1852 mit Bernhard Brunner im *Kampl* die
Nestroysche Bühne.

In keinem der Nestroyschen Stücke kann jedoch ein Zweifel darüber
bestehen, auf welcher Seite des sozialen Spektrums seine Sympathien
lagen. Die armen Leute sind in allen Stücken grundsätzlich positiv
gezeichnet. Ausnahmen bilden nur die unzufriedenen Gestalten, die aus
ihrer gesellschaftlichen Stellung auszubrechen suchen und vom Weg der
"Mittelstraße" abweichen. Doch auch hier läßt es Nestroy nie zu einer
rein negativen Darstellung kommen. Er zeigt die armselige soziale
Realität, in der Blasius, Titus, Nebel, Faden, Damian etc. leben und wie
die Armut deren phantastische Aufstiegswünsche gebiert. Dadurch
erhalten die Ausbruchsversuche der kleinbürgerlichen Gestalten eine
tragische Seite, die Nestroy oft in seinem Darstellungsstil unterstrich.

Die armen Gestalten haben zeit ihres Lebens nur die Schattenseiten des
Lebens kennengelernt. Dies bewirkt bei ihnen, daß sie den Glanz und
Prunk der oberen Schichten für bare Münze nehmen. Nur der Gegensatz
zwischen Arm und Reich ist letztendlich dafür verantwortlich zu machen,
daß sie aus dem Gleichgewicht gebracht werden und der Aura des Geldes
verfallen. Nestroy stellt sich nie hochmütig über seine irrenden Kleinbürger, sondern hat Mitleid mit ihrer Beschränktheit. In der Art, wie er
den Grund für ihre Flucht in die Chimäre erkenntlich macht, zeigt sich
seine pädagogische Absicht. Er versucht die Kleinbürger von ihren
falschen Illusionen zu befreien und sie zu einer positiven Haltung
gegenüber ihrer sozialen Stellung zu erziehen.

Daher ist es falsch, Nestroy Menschenhaß und Menschenverachtung
vorzuwerfen. Er kritisiert die gesellschaftlichen Schichten, in denen er
Heuchelei, Lüge, Hochmut, Kaltherzigkeit, Egoismus etc. antrifft. Doch
sein Haß ist zielgerichtet und nicht universell. Den armen, einfachen und
bedrückten Leuten begegnet er mit liebevollem Verständnis. Er zeichnet
ihre Lebensumstände mit einer solchen Einfühlsamkeit nach, daß der
Zuschauer die Qualen und Demütigungen der Protagonisten mit

empfinden muß und angeregt wird, sich gegen die aufgezeigten Mißstände zu empören.

Weniger verständnisvoll verfuhr er jedoch mit den bourgeoisen Gestalten. Es waren vor allem zwei gesellschaftliche Typen, die es ihm angetan hatten: die geldgierigen Spekulanten, Rentiers oder Unternehmer und die pharisäerhaften Spießer.

Die Kapitalisten in Nestroys Stücken sind fast alle Geldprotze mit ausgeprägtem Eigendünkel und Kastendenken. Sie kümmern sich nicht um ihre Mitmenschen, sondern verprassen ihren Reichtum, während ihr Nachbar hungert. Oder sie erweisen sich als geldgierige Ausbeuter, die ihre Abhängigen bis aufs Blut aussaugen.

Einer besonders harten Kritik wird der Parvenü unterzogen, der in einen Geldrausch verfällt und zum Sklaven seines Reichtums wird. Die Herren Geldsack, Massengold, Goldfuchs, Fett etc. besitzen eine Ethik, die sich nur nach dem "kategorischen Imperativ des Geldes" (*Nur keck!* II, 5) (SW XIV, 227) ausrichtet. Der Reichtum zerstört ihre persönlichen Bindungen, und ihre Herzen schrumpfen in dem Grade ein, wie sich ihr Geldbeutel erweitert.[12] Das Geld wirkt als Katalysator, der die bisher verborgene Gemeinheit ihres Charakters voll zur Entfaltung bringt.

Als Prototyp des Wiener Spießers hat er den Rentier von Gundlhuber in *Eine Wohnung ist zu vermieten* gekennzeichnet. Er ist ein Reaktionär, dessen Krähwinkelgeist nicht weiter als von Wien bis Hietzing reicht. Er ist nicht nur dumm, sondern auch selbstgefällig. Er ist ein scheinheiliger Pharisäer und unterwürfiger Konformist, ein Antityp zu dem revolutionären Kleinbürger und damit eine Stütze des Metternich-Staates. Er ist anpassungsfähig und gehorsam nach oben und brutal und verschlagen nach unten. Seine ökonomische Lage versetzt ihn schon im besten Mannesalter in den Frührentner-Stand. Er lebt von seiner Grundrente und kann sich ganz dem Müßiggang widmen. Was bei dem Großbürgertum nicht selten in "Zerrissenheit" ausartet, gestaltet sich bei Herrn Gundlhuber in rastloses Nichtstun. Um seine Zeit totzuschlagen, stürzt er sich in eine sinnlose Geschäftigkeit und terrorisiert damit seine Umgebung.

Das Gegenbild zum geschäftigen Gundlhuber ist der ruheliebende Biedermann Schafgeist in *Nur Ruhe!*. Er gehört zu jenen Spekulanten und Glücksrittern, die im Fahrwasser des allgemeinen wirtschaftlichen Aufschwungs mit viel Glück und ohne Anstrengung ein Vermögen erworben haben, das selbst nur zu verwalten sie zu faul sind. Er will nur Ruhe, d.h. persönliche Ungestörtheit, Ordnung im Staat und wirtschaftlichen Gleichlauf. Er ist Metternichs idealer Bürger, ein Nutznießer der politischen Verhältnisse und daher eine verläßliche Stütze des Staates.

Eine Gesellschaftsschicht, die wir bisher nicht erwähnt haben, ist der Adel. Doch die Aristokratie nimmt im Werk Nestroys nur eine untergeordnete Funktion ein. Einzig in *Liebesgeschichten und Heiratssachen* und im *Unbedeutenden* macht er die Adelskritik zum Hauptthema eines seiner Stücke. Da Nestroy kein Freund ererbter feudaler Privilegien war,[13] erscheint ihm die Feudalstruktur der österreichischen Gesellschaft als ein Relikt vergangener Zeiten. Der Adel ist ein Fossil, aus dem jegliches Leben gewichen ist. Das übertriebene Ehrbewußtsein und der Standesdünkel macht die Aristokraten lächerlich. Wegen ihrer gesellschaftlichen Schmarotzerstellung werden sie überwiegend unsympathisch gezeichnet.[14]

Nestroy und die Achtundvierziger-Revolution

Bei Nestroys so gearteter Gesellschaftsanalyse und Weltanschauung ist es kein Wunder, daß er der Achtundvierziger-Revolution überaus skeptisch gegenüber stand. Als aufrechter Demokrat befürwortete er den Märzaufstand, da nur so das verhaßte Metternich-Regime gestürzt werden konnte; doch in typisch josephinistischer Distanz zum politischen Handeln blieb er den Kämpfen selbst fern. Er, der in seinen Vormärzstücken immer wieder das Bürgertum Wiens kritisiert hatte, fand nun genügend Bestätigung dafür, daß der Bourgeoisie Reife und politisches Bewußtsein fehlte, um in der Revolution eine politische Führerrolle einnehmen zu können. In seinen Revolutionspossen machte er keinen Hehl daraus, daß er das Ereignis der Märzrevolution unterstützte. Doch gleichzeitig kritisierte er die Revolutionsführung, die den Märzaufstand in einen Ulk ausarten ließ.

Als distanziertem Beobachter blieb ihm der Dilettantismus in der Verwaltung der revolutionären Errungenschaften nicht verborgen. Die Verbrüderungsfeste, die Umtrünke und die militärischen Sandkastenspiele der Nationalgarden konnten kein klares Programm und einheitliches Vorgehen ersetzen. Daher mußte die Freiheitseuphorie bald in Lächerlichkeit umschlagen. Nestroy sah den Widerspruch zwischen der revolutionären Idee, deren Verfechter er selber war, und der Mediokrität ihrer Durchführung in Wien.

Auch hier erwies er sich wieder als der nüchterne Realist, der seinen Mitmenschen ihre falschen Illusionen auszutreiben suchte. Er kritisierte die deklamatorischen Tendenzen, die pathetischen Phrasen und das abstruse Krakeelertum, mit dem die Wiener Bürger die anstehenden politischen und sozialen Probleme vom Tisch zu wischen suchten. Während die geschäftigen Revolutionsakteure sich noch an der Märzdekoration erfreuten und der Freiheitskampf nur noch in den Beiseln weitertobte, sah Nestroy, wie die Reaktion hinter den Kulissen stand und nur auf den günstigen Moment wartete, um die Regie wieder an sich reißen zu können.

Nestroys Haltung im Nachmärz

Doch Nestroys Warnung vor der Konterrevolution verhallte ungehört. Als 1849 das alte Regime wieder installiert war, gab er seine Hoffnungen auf eine baldige politische Veränderung auf. Nicht nur seine Stücke wurden einer rigideren Zensur unterworfen als unter Sedlnitzky,[15] sondern auch seine alte Technik des politischen Extempores war unmöglich geworden. Denunzianten und sogenannte "Vertrauensmänner" kontrollierten systematisch die Theater und meldeten ihren Vorgesetzten sogleich die leiseste Regung einer vermuteten Oppositionshaltung bei den Künstlern.

In der Vormärzzeit hatte Nestroy immer einen Weg gefunden, um die Theaterkommissäre zu überlisten und seine politischen Kommentare beim Zuschauer anzubringen. Doch was sollte er nach 1849 machen, als er sich einem Publikum gegenüber befand, das gar keine Extempores mehr hören wollte? Die fortschrittlichen Besucherschichten waren endgültig aus den Vorstadttheatern vertrieben worden. Was übrig blieb, war eine Mischung aus Konservativen, "Gutgesinnten" und Reaktionären, die ein Verlangen nach den neuesten Pariser Vaudevilles hegten, vielleicht ein wenig lokalisiert und mit Wiener Talmi-Glanz angereichert. Doch Politik war das letzte, über das man in den Wiener Vorstadttheatern der Nachmärzzeit sprechen wollte.

Ein Konfidentenbericht für die Wiener Polizeidirektion aus dem Jahr 1857 zeigt, daß das Carltheater fast ausschließlich von reichen Müßiggängern besucht wurde, die hier einem unkomplizierten *dolce far niente* nachgehen wollten (s. SW xv, 392–393). Mit der politischen und sozialen Realität wollte man im Theater nichts zu schaffen haben. Die Stickigkeit der Altwiener Gemütlichkeit zog wieder auf, nur wenig aufgelockert mit ein paar Spritzern Erotik und Pariser Eleganz. So entstand die Wiener Operette, die sich nach dem Tode Nestroys über die Vorstadtbühnen verbreitete und nach und nach selbst die Erinnerung an die drastische und gesellschaftskritische Komik Nestroys verblassen ließ. Ilsa Barea faßt die kulturelle Atmosphäre im nachmärzlichen Wien treffend zusammen, wenn sie sagt:

It was ironical that the picture of Merrie Old Vienna, a Biedermeier Paradise Lost, was painted in retrospect [. . .]. It was even more ironical that the legend gained strength while, and because, any discussion of the un-cosy reality was banned from the printed page.[16]

Kein Wunder also, daß Nestroys Stücke nach 1848 mehr und mehr die politische Realität verlassen und sich z.B. der Theaterwelt zuwenden. Als er noch einmal die politische Wirklichkeit zum Thema eines Stückes wählte wie im *Alten Mann mit der jungen Frau*, sah er sich gezwungen, das Werk, das zu seinen besten zählt, im Schreibtisch liegen zu lassen.

Nachdem in Wien wieder "normale" Zustände eingekehrt waren, d.h. nachdem die Oppositionellen im Gefängnis saßen oder ins Ausland geflüchtet waren und der unterschwellige Widerstand der Bevölkerung zusammengebrochen war, in dieser Friedhofsruhe blieb Nestroy nur noch eine vage Hoffnung:

> Weil uns traumt hat von Freyheit, muß's a wirkliche geb'n,
> Wenn s' auch in Jahrhunderten erst tritt ins Leben.

(SW v, 692)

Diese Mischung aus Resignation und vager Hoffnung für eine bessere Zukunft, die man selbst nicht mehr miterleben wird, tritt uns im *Alten Mann mit der jungen Frau* immer wieder entgegen. Die autobiographische Komponente im Charakter Kerns ist unverkennbar.

Trotz seiner Sympathien für die Revolution hat Kern nicht an ihr teilgenommen. Rückblickend glaubt er den gesetzmäßigen Verlauf solcher Aufstände zu erkennen. Er bewertet Rebellionen als prometheushafte Anstrengungen, die den Zweck verfolgen, das unbezwingbare Schicksal dem menschlichen Willen zu unterwerfen. Er hat die Aussichtslosigkeit solcher Unternehmen erkannt und daraus die Schlußfolgerung gezogen, sich in die Welt des Privaten zurückzuziehen und sozialrevolutionäres Engagement mit christlicher Nächstenliebe zu vertauschen.

Auch Nestroy ergab sich nach der Niederschlagung der Revolution in den Glauben an die Schicksalhaftigkeit der menschlichen Zustände. Er war nicht länger davon überzeugt, daß der Mensch den Verlauf der Weltgeschichte beeinflussen könne. Solange Nestroy wie in den dreißiger und vierziger Jahren Kontakt mit einer oppositionellen Bewegung hatte und eine Rückkoppelung mit einem historisch progressiven Prozeß besaß, vermochten sich die pessimistischen Züge seiner Weltanschauung nicht voll auszuwirken. Die Ansätze dazu sind in seinen Vormärzstücken feststellbar; doch erst nach der Niederlage der Revolution von 1848 kommen sie voll zum Tragen.

Pessimismus und Resignation im Spätwerk

Nestroys politische Ermüdungserscheinungen nahmen in den Stücken nach *Höllenangst* einen offensichtlichen Charakter an und breiteten sich in den Werken nach 1849 immer stärker aus. Doch trotz aller Resignation und allem Pessimismus entwickelte sich Nestroy nie zu einem Menschenhasser. Als Gegentendenz zu seiner negativen Beurteilung der menschlichen Entwicklungsmöglichkeiten tauchte der "Ausweg des Herzens" auf, der bewirkte, daß Nestroy nie seine humanistische Grundposition verließ. Er entwickelte eine Haltung christlicher Demut und suchte sich in Akten der Mitmenschlichkeit zu bewähren. Diese "Strohalman-

klammerungsversuche" (*Mein Freund* II, 12) (SW VII, 315) bewahrten ihn
vor Ausbrüchen in eine "Kotzebuesche Verzweiflung" (*Umsonst!* I, 5)
(SW XIV, 321). In Aphorismus 18 bekannte er: "Ich habe auch meine
Stunden der Empörung, aber ich verstecke sie, weil ohnmächtige
Empörung lächerlich ist. Da ich nicht stolz sein kann, bin ich demütig
geworden, um mir die Scham zu ersparen, niederträchtig zu werden"
(SW XV, 683).

In einer Zeit, in der sich seine Hoffnungen auf eine gesellschaftliche
Erneuerung zerschlagen hatten, blieb ihm nur noch ein demütiges Sich-
Fügen in die realen Gegebenheiten und das Refugium der individuellen
Mitmenschlichkeit. Von dieser Resignation sind fast alle Hauptfiguren des
Netroyschen Spätwerkes befallen. Sie hatten sich wie ihr Autor "nach und
nach an der schroffen Wand der Hoffnungslosigkeit den Schädel"
(SW XV, 705) eingestoßen und ließen sich nun "in resignierter Delinquen-
tenmanier noch nach Möglichkeit gut g'schehn mit einer Gustospeis"
(*Mein Freund*, Vorspiel, 3. Szene) (SW VII, 246).

Doch die resignativen, pessimistischen und skeptizistischen Züge
waren nicht die einzigen Charaktermerkmale, mit denen Nestroy seine
nachrevolutionären Hauptfiguren ausstattete. Sie waren begleitet von
einem engagierten Philanthropismus, der für die Beurteilung von
Nestroys Weltanschauung nach 1848 wichtiger ist als eine Blütenlese von
Aphorismen à la "Ich glaube von jedem Menschen das Schlechteste" (*Die
beiden Nachtwandler* I, 16) (SW VI, 311) oder "Die Menschen muß man
hassen, ehe man sie kennt, verachten, wenn man sie kennt" (SW XV, 701:
Aphorismus 238). Die hier ausgedrückte Meinung muß zwar ernst
genommen werden, doch man sollte sie nicht als Nestroys endgültige
Weltanschauung mißinterpretieren. Diese Gedanken stellten eher gele-
gentliche Anwandlungen dar, die wieder überwunden wurden und über
die Nestroy dann später urteilte: "Ich lass' nix kommen über die Welt,
wenn auch dann und wann was über mich kommt" (*Mein Freund*,
Vorspiel, 3. Szene) (SW VII, 248).

In den nachrevolutionären Stücken stellt Nestroy keine in selbst-
gewählter Einsamkeit an der Menschheit verzweifelnden Misanthropen
als Vorbilder hin, sondern enttäuschte Skeptiker, die weiterhin unter
Menschen leben, sich an den kleinen Dingen des Lebens erfreuen und ihr
begrenztes Dasein mit Taten aktiver Mitmenschlichkeit ausfüllen. Dieses
Leben entbehrt nicht der hedonistischen Komponenten, wie die Gestalt
Schlichts in *Mein Freund* am deutlichsten zeigt. Trotz der schlechten
Behandlung, die ihm zuteil wird, verliert er nicht die Freude am Leben.
Er wendet sich gegen die Weltverleugner und entgegnet ihnen: "Legen
wir keinen Spott auf das Irdische. Die Welt ist schön" (*Mein Freund*,
Vorspiel, 3. Szene) (SW VII, 248).

Dieses christliche "Dennoch" war wesentlicher Bestandteil von

Nestroys Weltanschauung und ist letztendlich dafür verantwortlich zu machen, daß sich Nestroy auch später nicht in einen Nihilisten verwandelte. Trotz seiner Verzweiflung über die Weltenordnung und seiner Kritik an den sozialen Zuständen hat er nie die positiven Seiten des Lebens außer acht gelassen. Gottlieb brachte es im *Schützling* auf die Formel, "daß das miserabelste Leben mehr wert ist als der brillanteste Tod" (I, 12) (SW VII, 140), und Finkl in *Karikaturen-Charivari mit Heiratszweck* sagt zu diesem Thema:

> Zwar in d'r Erd'n is Ruh', doch niemst sehnt sich danach,
> 's schönste Grabmal gibt a Toter für a Kammerl au'm Dach.

(I, 8) (SW XIII, 395)

Selbst die Ärmsten der Armen besitzen trotz ihrer erbärmlichen Lebensumstände eine ursprüngliche Kraft, die ihnen hilft, ihre innere Würde und die Freude am kleinen Glück im Leben aufrechtzuerhalten. Wie sagt Schlicht? "Die Welt ist schön. Es gibt zwar lauter Unzufriedene drauf, das soll von der menschlichen Ungenügsamkeit kommen" (*Mein Freund*, Vorspiel, 3. Szene) (SW VII, 248).

In seinem nachrevolutionären Werk nahm Nestroy wieder die Linie auf, die er mit Figuren wie Federl und Schnoferl begonnen hatte. Einer Zeit des Zerfalls ethischer Werte und politisch-sozialer Hoffnungen trat Nestroy mit seinen Gestalten wie Kern, Schlicht oder Kampl und einer Strategie der Befreiung durch die aktive Tat des Dienens entgegen. Das "Alle Menschen werden Brüder", das er in *Die beiden Herren Söhne* 1845 noch politisch verstanden hatte (IV, 7) (SW XII, 417), wandelte sich nun zum philanthropischen Wunsch, "daß ein Herz für's andre schlägt brüderlich warm" (1850).[17] Erst als Nestroy ganz die Hoffnung auf eine soziale Erneuerung zu seinen Lebzeiten aufgegeben hatte, erhob er den Dienst am Nächsten zum eigentlichen Sinn des menschlichen Daseins. Die Nestroysche Weltanschauung nach der Achtundvierziger-Revolution ließe sich daher mit dem Aphorismus überschreiben: "Es gibt Augenblicke im Leben, in welchen man nicht würdig ist, Mensch zu heißen, wenn man nicht alles andre vergißt, als nur Mensch zu sein" (SW XV, 688: Aphorismus 81).

Summary

Nestroy's theatrical career may be divided into two principal phases: the first, rebellious phase (1830–48) in which he observed the Viennese bourgeoisie and criticized their social and political attitudes; and a second, more resigned phase (1849–60) in which sharp criticism gave way to more general observations of an increasingly pessimistic nature.

The tendency towards pessimistic resignation in Nestroy's work was the result of incessant confrontations with the established political, social, and theatrical order. From 1830 to 1848 he was associated with a historically progressive movement, and his belief in human progress prevailed. After 1835 the lower strata of Viennese society — petty bourgeoisie, craftsmen, domestic servants etc., who had become politically aware after the July Revolution of 1830 — were gradually forced out of the theatre as a result of the economic crisis and the rising price of theatre tickets. Nestroy was consequently faced with the fact that the critical section of his audience was diminishing in number, while complacent, conservative "Biedermeier" now filled the auditorium, demanding superficial, escapist entertainment which bore no relation to the deteriorating political, social, and economic reality of *Vormärz* Vienna.

His situation was further aggravated by his constant battles with the censor and the police invigilators, and by the restrictions and interference of the theatre director Karl Carl. From this background arose the pessimism that was to predominate in his *oeuvre* after the failure of the 1848 Revolution. What prevented him from becoming wholly nihilistic, however, was his adherence to the values of basic humanity and affection, and his appreciation of the small pleasures of life.

10

John R. P. McKenzie

NESTROY'S POLITICAL PLAYS

Nestroy, as much as any literary or dramatic writer, and perhaps even more than most, offers himself as easy prey to commentators with a preconceived world-view. We learn from one that "Nestroy characteristically became an enthusiastic revolutionary",[1] from another that he was "a whole-hearted partisan of the democratic movement",[2] and from a third that *Der alte Mann mit der jungen Frau* is "ein kühnes Bekenntnis zur Revolution".[3] On the other hand we are also told that "Nestroys Skepsis gegenüber allem entschärft die Satire ins Possenhafte",[4] that "Nestroys Gedanken in politische Terminologie zu übersetzen, zerstört sein Wesen",[5] and we are assured that "den politischen Verfassungskämpfen, die die Restaurationszeit erfüllen und zur Revolution von 1848 führten, steht Nestroy gleichgültig, ja man könnte fast sagen mit einer dämonischen Künstlermentalität gegenüber".[6] Contemporary reaction to Nestroy's political works demonstrates the same lack of unanimity; *Der Humorist* complained that Nestroy had trodden "die edle Sache der Revolution in den Kot",[7] while an anonymous flysheet extolled his revolutionary fervour: "Ich hätte nie geglaubt, daß Nestroy so ultraliberal sein kann."[8]

Given this degree of critical disarray — often passionate disagreement — are there any criteria we can propose for approaching the political material in Nestroy's works; indeed, to what extent are his political plays truly political? In attempting to answer these questions I shall concentrate on those works that deal to a greater or lesser degree with the events of 1848. First, I shall consider the kinds of problem we face in approaching political comedy, then I wish to examine the two overtly political plays, *Freiheit in Krähwinkel* and *Judith und Holofernes*, and finally I shall look briefly at the political attitudes revealed in the plays written in 1849.

The first question to resolve is what we mean by the terms "political" and "political play". While in common usage the word political is becoming more and more a synonym for "party political", and even "tendentious", I prefer to use the term in its broader sense to include the affairs and organization of society in general. This is an important distinction to bear in mind when dealing with Nestroy, for whatever conclusions one may reach about his own political persuasions, his plays do not present a *systematic* analysis of politics, rather a collection of comments that have political implications.

In an essay on social drama Ronald Peacock has a number of useful observations to make on this, the relation between the raw political or social material and its presentation in drama. While some plays, he argues, deal primarily with social problems, in many more the social comment is implicit in the overall picture they present, and the moral stance they adopt. Peacock states: "The crux of the matter nearly always is not so much a specific 'social problem' as the situation of the individual in relation to the society he lives in."[9] Accordingly, what we are faced with is not simply establishing the nature of the political and social criticism in a given work but attempting to discover the author's moral standpoint, his attitude to the problems his plays depict; this is no easy task.

Bearing in mind that Nestroy as a practising man of the theatre wanted to, indeed was required to, produce comedies that were comic, we have also to take into account the nature of comedy, its aims and conventions. For, inevitably, the nature of comedy conditions the way in which the social and political material is moulded into a comic form.

I would argue, therefore, that in dealing with social and political comedy it is important to recognize that there is a two-way relationship between the dramatic mode and its material. The text of a drama is not a historical or sociological document, and even if, as is the case with a politically committed work, its primary aim is to make a political statement, it does so through the dramatic medium. Comedy is essentially an artefact, as is any work of imaginative literature. It creates an apparently self-contained world, a fictive world that is distinct from the real world. The relation between this fictive world and social and political reality operates on two levels: the play deals with a known social and political context, which it exploits to create comic effect; it also makes statements about the particular social or political conditions it depicts. In short, a study of Nestroy's political comedies must take into account not only *what* he says about society and politics at the time of the 1848 Revolution, but *how* he presents his comments, *how* he handles the conventions of comedy.

More than any dramatic or literary form, perhaps, comedy lends itself to widely differing interpretation — if only for the simple reason that what appears comic to one man does not necessarily appear comic to another. For comic effect is not simply determined by the author's intention — it is the product of comic intention and audience receptivity.[10] This introduces a further complication in interpreting Nestroy's political plays: whether to judge them from the point of view of what audiences at his time found comic, or what a present-day audience would laugh at. The implications of this for a theatre producer are clearly not the same as those that confront the academic critic. It is our job to understand as best we can the reception of the works by contemporary audiences as well as assessing their relevance to the present day. This seems to me to be especially important when dealing with Nestroy's political works because if we fail to give full weight to their impact at the time they were written we can all too easily concentrate our attention on those aspects that appear to us to be eternally valid, at the expense of those whose relevance is limited to the immediate context of the mid-nineteenth century. In my view we should attempt to do both. Equally, we can fall into the trap of reading into a writer's work ideas that are not his own but, rather, reflections of our curious wish to find that our current preoccupations have been anticipated by writers in the past.[11]

In attempting to determine Nestroy's attitude to the events of 1848 we must tread carefully. Nestroy, the unswerving sceptic, did not wear his political heart on his sleeve, nor did he betray sympathy for any particular political philosophy. Constructing a picture of his political outlook is essentially an exercise in counter-suggestibility: we have to build it up bit by bit *ex negativo*, and from the welter of satirical comments we have to try to deduce his own standpoint.[12] We should also not lose sight of the fact that Nestroy was a dramatist first and a satirist second.

In acknowledging that the playwright is concerned with selecting, moulding, and adapting the raw material of politics into a dramatically effective form, we can see that his task is quite distinct from that of the academic historian. Political historians readily accept that historical truth is not absolute because it is not knowable in full, and in their more cynical moments will admit that much historiography consists in evolving a theory and finding the facts to support it. There is a constant risk of this happening to the student of Nestroy's politics. As we have seen, he is variously claimed to be a champion of democracy, to be a political *ingénu*, and to be wholly apolitical. I would argue that no-one can write about a time of political upheaval without being political — however inconsistent that political view may be. That brings us to an important difference in the aims and methods of the political historian and the dramatic critic of a political play. The political historian is confronted by an infinite body of information from which he cannot but select in his attempt to create a consistent historical picture, and this process of selection is inevitably one of evaluation. It can, of course, be argued that it is likewise the duty of the critic of social and political drama to deal as best he can with a wealth of historical data — the dramatic tradition and cultural context of the plays he is discussing — but while this is true, at least the *immediate* bounds of his task are set by those particular texts.

I would like also briefly to rehearse some points that are common currency to anyone involved in the study of Nestroy, for I believe them to be *peculiarly* relevant to the problem of interpreting political comedy. (Having said they are common currency, though, I must also acknowledge that they are often sadly disregarded.) Nestroy wrote for a particular audience, and had to create roles that matched the abilities of a particular troupe of actors. He had to come up with a certain number of plays in each season and therefore normally borrowed his plots and characters from existing works, material he then adapted to conform to the Viennese tradition of farce (see pp. 56–57, above). Farce is patently not a realistic form: its essence is exaggeration and distortion; it favours unlikely intrigue, contrived situations, and caricature, all of which have as their primary aim the creation of comic effect; and, in common with all comedy, farce traditionally has a happy ending.

Nestroy's particular brand of farce, the *Posse mit Gesang*, has its own traditions and conventions; in particular, we must take into account his process of adaptation, *Verwienerung*. It has to be recognized that the dialogue makes no attempt to be realistic, and this is especially true of the verbal acrobatics performed by the *Zentralfiguren*; its aim rather is to be comic and to expose the workings of the language. We must also be aware of the multiple function of the *Zentralfigur* as a character in the plot and a *raisonneur* outside the action who delivers his independent commentary in *couplets* and monologues. Nestroy treats his plots and his characters as *vehicles* for an expression of his sceptical, often fatalistic view of life, for satirical comment, for verbal flights of fancy and for unsophisticated fun; it is, therefore, inappropriate to demand plausibility of a Nestroy play. This quality of deliberate contrivance, combined with his predilection for aphorism and extended metaphor, aggravates the reader's difficulty in establishing the writer's purpose.[13] Above all else, we should never assume that the opinions voiced by the characters are automatically shared by the dramatist, any more than we should confuse character, narrator, and author when dealing with a work of prose fiction.[14]. This is an obvious point, but all too often professional commentators unthinkingly treat the characters' views as if they were automatically underwritten by Nestroy himself.[15]

In May 1848 Nestroy produced *Die Anverwandten*, the first of his plays to be staged without the constraint of censorship; it thrust him into the middle of a political controversy. By no means a political work, it nevertheless contains several topical references, in particular in the two *couplets* and monologues. These appear to have been inserted into an already complete text, as work on the play must have been far advanced by the time the Revolution broke out.[16] The second *couplet* contains a sceptical appraisal of the events of the previous two months, alluding to the perversion of the revolutionaries' aims, to the disastrous lack of unity among delegates to the newly established Austrian parliament, and to the personal ambitions of would-be politicians. Significantly, these are the satirical butts that Nestroy was to return to time and again during the following eighteen months. Edelschein's disparaging comment on the political ignorance of the population caused an uproar:

Bei die Wahlen durch Stimmen is der Fehler auch das,
Es gibt mancher sein' Stimm' und er weiß nicht, für was;
Gar mancher is als Wähler für Frankfurt 'nein g'rennt,
Der auß'r d' Frankfurterwürsteln von Frankfurt nix kennt.
                              (*Die Anverwandten* IV, 4) (SW V, 94)

The audience was divided between those who applauded what they saw as an acute perception, and those who considered the observation to be too near the knuckle for their liking. Thus, from the outset Nestroy fell victim to the political satirist's fate: it was assumed that Edelschein's sentiments were his own — which, admittedly, is a not wholly unreasonable assumption in this case — and for daring to put unflattering comments into the mouth of his *Zentralfigur* Nestroy was condemned for lacking sufficient revolutionary fervour.[17] The short-circuitry of this argument is familiar. The curtain-line to the third act neatly captures what was to be Nestroy's sceptical attitude of wait-and-see throughout 1848: "O Freiheit und Gleichheit! Wie du dich noch auswachsen wirst, das is schon a Passion!" (*Die Anverwandten* III, 15) (SW V, 85). This mixture here of a mute approval for the suspension of absolutism, and of world-weary, fatalistic anticipation of the outcome is, of course, typical of Nestroy's life-long sceptical stance, and if he habitually and temperamentally viewed human motives and actions with extreme scepticism, politics and politicians, not surprisingly, provided him with ideal subject matter. *Freiheit in Krähwinkel* and *Judith und Holofernes* supply an extensive answer to this rhetorical question about the course and outcome of the Revolution, the one seen from the standpoint of a commentator of current events, the other offering a retrospective view.

As I indicated earlier, it is unreasonable to demand of a Nestroy farce that it should present us with an artistically perfect blend of comic plot and satirical material — and there is no reason to suppose that Nestroy paid particular attention to such an aim. The integration of form and content is, of course, something to which academics are constitutionally addicted, even if, doubtless, the average theatre-goer does not accord it such high priority. When, however, a play elegantly integrates the satirical material in the plot, we are entitled to see this as a welcome bonus, and I would argue that part of the attraction of *Freiheit in Krähwinkel* and *Judith und Holofernes* is their remarkable coherence of comic plot and satirical matter. How is this coherence achieved; and how does Nestroy exploit the possibilities of his farcical plots — and in the case of *Judith und Holofernes* the possibilities of parody — to make political comedy?

Freiheit in Krähwinkel is one of the last in the tradition of *Krähwinkeliaden* begun some half a century earlier, and this pedigree must be taken into account.[18] The play's genesis is well known: the plot is lifted freely from an earlier example of the type, Bäuerle's *Die falsche*

Primadonna, and subjected to Nestroy's usual method of adaptation —
while its location in a petty German state is superficially maintained it is,
in effect, wholly translated to a Viennese setting and into the Viennese
idiom of 1848.[19] This translation can be interpreted in two ways. Some
commentators have dismissed it as simply the application of political
material to the surface of a well-tried and also well-worn plot; but I would
argue that Nestroy's achievement is greater than this, that *Freiheit in
Krähwinkel* is an accomplished amalgam of traditional farce and contemporary politics. To take an example: the hackneyed plot of the "Heirat mit
Hindernissen" is not only comic in its three-fold realization, it also has an
important structural function in that it provides a vehicle for the series of
revolutionary scenes which make up the larger part of the action. The love
intrigue becomes a satirical weapon in its own right: the courtship of a rich
widow by the leading figures of the revolutionary and the reactionary
forces makes good farce, and it is also a comment on the role of venality
and personal ambition in the world of politics. Similarly, *Judith und
Holofernes* is peculiarly successful in its blending of parody and political
satire, a blend in which each element reinforces the other. If we take the
example of the character of Holofernes we can see that in ridiculing
Hebbel's hero Nestroy not only parodies the original; he also establishes a
satirical parallel between the bombastic, bloodthirsty commander of the
Assyrian army and Windischgrätz, the commander of the Imperial forces
who supervised the bloody siege of Vienna in October 1848.

  Nestroy's stategy of locating the action of his two plays nominally in
South Germany and Babylonia results, I believe, from his recognition that
to achieve maximum comic effect his criticism had to be oblique. The
fiction that the butt of his satire is someone else — that while Krähwinkel
may be seen as Vienna in miniature it is not formally Vienna — this fiction
is sufficient to remove the natural inhibition one has of laughing *openly* at
oneself, even though the ploy is transparent and there can be no doubt
about who is the real victim. In other words, this process of oblique
Verwienerung is dictated by Nestroy's awareness of the psychological
workings of comedy.[20]

  The blend of the farcical and parodistic elements on the one hand and
the political satire on the other is further reinforced by the role of the
Zentralfigur. In addition to the traditional double function of Nestroy's
Zentralfiguren as character and *raisonneur*, a personal union which provides
its own cohesion, their function in these two plays is more complex. Ultra
is involved in the love intrigue, he steps out of his role to deliver two
couplets and monologues in which he makes political comments on
contemporary events, and, in a political development of the *Kräh-
winkeliade* tradition, he dons a variety of disguises to impersonate an
emissary of the *Europäische Freiheits- und Gleichheitskommission*, a member

of the proletariat, and two representatives of absolutism, Metternich and a Russian prince. The role of the *Zentralfigur* in *Judith und Holofernes* is likewise unusually complex: in parodying Hebbel Nestroy has Joab, a soldier in the Hebrew army, impersonate his sister, Judith, in order to outwit Holofernes; stepping out of his role, Joab also functions as a political *raisonneur* and establishes anachronistic links between the Babylonian captivity and the siege of Vienna. In this way the two strands of the play, the dramatic parody and the political satire, are united.

What are the main objects of Nestroy's satire in the two plays and what can we deduce about his own political stance towards the events of 1848? The structure of *Freiheit in Krähwinkel* offers a useful starting point for an understanding of his attitude. The play is divided into two sections: the first two acts are grouped together under the heading *Die Revolution* while Act Three is entitled *Die Reaktion*. In terms of the events portrayed, this division is wholly arbitrary — indeed, given the happy ending, the heading *Die Reaktion* would appear to be a misnomer. The answer to this apparent discrepancy is to be found in the series of dreams experienced by the mayor. Enacted as tableaux at the end of the first act, the first two dreams depict two major events in the course of the Revolution;[21] the first shows the outbreak of the Revolution on 13 March, the second depicts the popular revolt of 15 May. But the third is a vision of the future: it presents the mayor arm-in-arm with a Russian general surrounded by cossacks and knout-swinging grenadiers. One could legitimately expect the three dreams to be realized later in the action, and, indeed, the first two are. The question is why the third dream remains the odd one out. It is not to be explained away simply as a piece of wishful reverie on the part of the mayor; rather, the third dream would seem to represent Nestroy's conviction in the summer of 1848 that the Revolution was bound to fail. The dream tableau was as far as he was prepared to go in voicing his fears: good comedy cannot be made out of predicting bloody counter-revolution, and for that reason, if for no other, the tradition of the happy ending had to be upheld. When the mayor awakens from his nightmarish reenactment of 15 May, Klaus offers him the following words of comfort, which, like so much of the text, appear to be contained within unseen quotation marks: "Ich kenn' die Krähwinkler — man muß sie austoben lassen; is der Raptus vorbei, dann werd'n s' dasig, und wir fangen s' mit der Hand" (*Freiheit in Krähwinkel* I, 24) (GW v, 94). Here, I believe, speaks the pessimistic student of human nature.

A reading of *Freiheit in Krähwinkel* confirms that Nestroy had recognized by early July 1848 that the revolutionaries' resources, both political and military, were hopelessly inadequate, and that the population of Vienna had little genuine revolutionary zeal. In the contrived happy ending the forces of reaction are routed neither by military superiority nor by a united popular front, but by the young women of Krähwinkel who, sporting Calabrese hats, the uniform of the *Akademische Legion*, impersonate revolutionary students, mount the barricades, and force the mayor to flee to London. It is worth noting that though this ending is contrived in dramatic terms, Nestroy's theatrical portrayal is barely an exaggeration of reality, and in this sense the contrived quality of the fiction reveals the fragile nature of the revolutionaries' achievement in May 1848. The fragility of their success is articulated by Ultra's final rallying call: "Die Reaktion ist ein Gespenst, aber G'spenster gibt es bekanntlich nur für den Furchtsamen; drum sich nicht fürchten davor, dann gibt's gar keine Reaktion!" (*Freiheit in Krähwinkel* III, 25) (GW V, 134). To my mind this splendid piece of false logic and political eye-wash is clearly a thinly veiled expression of Nestroy's foreboding, and one cannot overlook — at least from our viewpoint with the benefit of hindsight one cannot overlook — his prediction that a counter-coup was inevitable.

If *Freiheit in Krähwinkel* omits the realization of the mayor's final dream, *Judith und Holofernes* makes up for the omission. The siege of Vienna provides the anachronistic background to Nestroy's devastating parody of Hebbel's tedious and ill-conceived tragedy. In his parodistic portrait of Holofernes he is able to satirize the military mind in general and to censure the ruthlessness of the Imperial military command in particular. The object of Nestroy's satire is all too obvious when, for example, proclaiming his belief in might over right and slapping his sword, Holofernes anachronistically refers to the power of modern weapons: "Hier ist die Götterfabrik! Was in der neuen Zeit durch Bajonette geht, das richten wir, die grauen Vorzeitler, mit dem Schwert" (*Judith und Holofernes*, sc. 7) (GW V, 224). Windischgrätz's decision to bombard Vienna is alluded to in Holofernes's grotesque order: "Der Koch soll sich Bethulien anschaun, morgen zünd' ich's an und ich weiß nicht, ob's ihm Glut genug geben wird, ein' Kartoffelschmarn für mich zu schmoren" (*Judith und Holofernes*, sc. 21) (GW V, 240–241). And in seeking to reassure Judith/Joab, Holofernes betrays the unthinking destructive urge of the fanatical militarist: "Es ist nicht so arg; ich hab' nur die Gewohnheit, alles zu vernichten" (*Judith und Holofernes*, sc. 24) (GW V, 245). In the wake of the siege of Vienna, summary martial law was imposed in November 1848; popular response to this is pithily satirized in the opening chorus of the play where Holofernes's followers display their political realism:

> Weil er uns sonst niederhaut,
> Preisen wir ihn alle laut!
>
> (GW V, 221)

But this equation of Holofernes with the Imperial military commanders and of Bethulien with Vienna is more complex. The play operates on three

parallel planes: Hebbel's biblical setting, the parodistic milieu of the
Leopoldstadt with its Jewish immigrant population, and the wider
context of Vienna as a whole. Perhaps it is not surprising that Nestroy
should have been accused of conscious anti-Semitism — though there is no
evidence elsewhere in his works of hostility towards the Jews — but I
believe the charge to be mistaken.[22] Just as Krähwinkel functioned as a
psychological alibi for contemporary audiences, by ascribing to Hebbel's
Hebrews the supposed characteristics of Viennese immigrant Jews
Nestroy was able to create the necessary distance for his audience: in
laughing at the antics of the Leopoldstädter Jews, the Viennese were really
laughing at themselves.[23] And one may surmise that the comic potential
offered by parody, topical allusion, and the available equation of the
Leopoldstadt with Bethulien proved irresistible to the practised parodist
and satirist. The controversy brings us back to the question of point of
view: present-day observers who view the play against the backcloth of
mounting hostility towards the Jews legitimately argue that the play is
susceptible to anti-Semitic interpretation; and, indeed, it is clear that,
however unexceptionable Nestroy's intention may have been, anti-Jewish
elements in Vienna at the time of the Revolution welcomed *Judith und
Holofernes* as an affirmation of their prejudice.[24]

Central to Nestroy's satirical purpose in both plays is his depiction of
popular reaction to the events of 1848. In his opening monologue Ultra
steps out of his role to predict that the Revolution will fail because the
Krähwinkler are indolent and faint-hearted:

> Wahrscheinlich werden dann von die Krähwinkler viele so engherzig sein und
> nach Zersprengung ihrer Ketten, ohne gerade Reaktionär' zu sein, dennoch
> kleinmütig zu raunzen anfangen: "O mein Gott, früher is es halt doch besser
> gewesen — und schon das ganze Leben jetzt — und diese Sachen alle —", aber das
> macht nichts, man hat ja selbst in Wien ähnliche Räsonnements gehört.
>
> *(Freiheit in Krähwinkel* I, 7) (GW v, 73)

The pervading indolence and faintheartedness determine the response of
many of the inhabitants, and here Nestroy exposes the fatal discrepancy he
saw between the revolutionary ideals and the inadequacy of popular
response to them. The people are more interested in the prospect of
personal financial gain and in protecting their own skins than they are in
pursuing political objectives. Revolution for the man in the street is
reduced to the level of a free spectacle — as one character puts it: "A
bisserl Revolution anschaun [. . .] Wer weiß, wann wieder a Revolution
is!" (*Freiheit in Krähwinkel* II, 11) (GW v, 105). Another, a widow, makes
the following illogical, telling comment: "Ich bin froh, daß der Meinige
schon tot is — wie leicht könnt' ihm da was g'schehn bei der G'schicht!"
(*Freiheit in Krähwinkel* I, 12) (GW v, 105). These observations are echoed

and reinforced in *Judith und Holofernes*: the antics of the National Guard are satirized in the behaviour of the Hebrew forces — they are shown to be poorly disciplined, more interested in acting the part of soldiers than in preparing for battle, and even more concerned with deriving financial profit from the food shortages that arise during the siege.[25] The parallel with October 1848 could hardly be more striking, and must have been all the more so to an audience in the Leopoldstadt. It was also an audience that had recently seen Nestroy and his fellow actors man the barricades in the Jägerzeile under the unlikely command of theatre director Carl, who as an astute entrepreneur had an eye for cheap publicity. Thus before the Revolution had been suppressed by the intervention of Imperial troops, professional actors had already turned it into a farce on the streets of Vienna.

Apart from his scepticism about the revolutionaries' ideals, about popular commitment to political change, and his sense that the Revolution was bound to fail, what can we deduce of Nestroy's personal political stance, as revealed by the two plays? It would seem clear that he shared the general contempt for the excesses of the Metternich régime, in particular corruption in high places, censorship, bureaucratic chicanery, the role of the clergy, and financial speculation. Other social and political ills are either not mentioned or are sidestepped in superficial references that have no satirical force. There is, for example, no acknowledgement of the widespread destitution that unemployment, crop failures, and inflation had produced in the years before 1848. Whatever the reason for these omissions may be, whether Nestroy was consciously making concessions to his audience, instinctively avoiding issues that might undermine the comic effect, is a question we cannot, of course, resolve; it would in any case be unreasonable to accuse Nestroy of wilfully concealing the economic causes of the Revolution, for at the time a knowledge of economic science was not available to the average citizen. Other than a couple of inconsequential witticisms in *Judith und Holofernes* about "Wachteln" and "Preßburger Zwieback" which are described as falling like manna from heaven, there are no references in either play to revolutionary events in the Bohemian and Hungarian provinces.[26] Nor is the role of the Imperial family in the events of 1848 alluded to. But this is an area where we do not have to deduce Nestroy's attitude *ex negativo*. For him as, surely, for his audience the continued existence of the Habsburg Empire was an unchallengeable article of faith. He would have no truck with the nationalistic aspirations of the constituent nations, a phenomenon he disparagingly dismisses as "Nationalitätschwindel".[27] Ultra's second *couplet* contains sentiments that in their almost religious fervour stand out from the rest; despite the upheaval of recent weeks he proclaims his belief in the glory, unity, and stability of Austria:

Eine Freiheit vereint uns,
So wie a Sonn' nur bescheint uns;
G'schehn auch Umtrieb' von Ischl
Oder von Leitomischl,
Wir kommen zur Klarheit,
G'sunder Sinn find't schon d' Wahrheit;
Und trotz die Diff'renzen
Wird Östreich hoch glänzen
Fortan durch Jahrhundert'
Gespriesen, bewundert [. . .]
(*Freiheit in Krähwinkel* III, 22)(GW V, 131)

However readily the audience would have lapped up this patriotic appeal — and the hostile attitude of German-speaking Austrians to the separatist movements of 1848 is well documented — this goes far beyond a conventional patriotic appeal: it is the affirmation of an unchallengeable creed.

What of Nestroy's political attitudes in the period after 1848? Political references are to be found not only in *Judith und Holofernes* but also in *Lady und Schneider, Höllenangst*, and *Der alte Mann mit der jungen Frau*, all written in 1849. I shall not deal with these plays in any detail, but select a handful of references that help to answer two questions which I believe to be basic to Nestroy's political stance. Did Nestroy, as is often maintained, renege on the spirit of 1848 and throw in his lot with the forces of reaction? Or do these three plays rather show his growing indifference to political matters, an indifference motivated by his increasingly fatalistic view of the world?[28]

One can discern two distinct phases in his response to the reimposition of absolutism: *Lady und Schneider* and *Judith und Holofernes*, first performed in February and March 1849 respectively, look closely at the reasons for the failure of the Revolution, while *Höllenangst*, first performed in September, and *Der alte Mann mit der jungen Frau*, written at approximately the same time, are characterized by a much more sober, even pessimistic attitude. The shift may be explained, I believe, by the natural course of events: early in 1849 a sense of outrage at the brute force of the military intervention still dominated, by the autumn he realized that the restoration of absolutism was a *fait accompli* and that the political outlook was bleak.

In attempting to answer the question whether Nestroy changed his political spots between 1848 and 1849 and to deal with the assertion that he reneged on his former views, we should recognize that it is all too easy for commentators to fall foul of the danger I mentioned earlier, the danger of assuming that Nestroy and his *Zentralfiguren* are somehow identical, if not in their roles then in their function as *raisonneurs*. But Nestroy was not an Ultra or a Wendelin and he certainly was no Heugeig'n.[29]

There is also the vexed question of censorship. We can only surmise the extent to which Nestroy indulged in self-censorship, but there can be no doubt about the stifling effect of the official censor.[30] Contrary to the opinion held by some, theatre censorship was as severe after 1848 as it had been before.[31] It was, moreover, backed up by *Gutgesinnte*, a highly effective nineteenth-century listeners' and viewers' association who eagerly pounced on any scrap of suspect material they could find. For this reason Nestroy appears to have bought the censor and his accomplices off, as it were, by including a certain amount of apparently reactionary material in his later plays. This allowed him to get away with his critical observations on the restoration.

The political interest in the three plays centres on a handful of characters — for the main part *Zentralfiguren* — who typify certain political positions. Heugeig'n is characterized as a ruthless political opportunist, an ale-house politician, devoid of principle, and hell-bent on achieving his political ambition. He is convinced, wholly without justification, of his mission to abandon his job of tailor and to occupy a position of political power and authority: "Sie müssen mich noch wo an die Spitze stellen, sei's Bewegung oder Klub, liberal, legitim, konservativ, radikal, oligarchisch, anarchisch oder garkanarchisch, das is mir alles eins, nur Spitze!" (*Lady und Schneider* I, 10) (GW v, 154). Stepping out of his role of unprincipled would-be demagogue, he comments as a *raisonneur* on the phenomenon of the political turn-coat. And developing an extended commercial image he remarks upon the existence of hundreds of thousands of opportunistic "Umsattler":

> Nur ein G'schäft tut z' kurz kommen,
> Was, metaphorisch genommen,
> Grad z' tun hat am meisten,
> Das sind d' Sattler, die leisten
> Enorms in der Zeit,
> Wo von gestern auf heut'
> Hunderttausend' von Leut'
> Hab'n umg'sattelt so g'scheit —
> Und kein einz'ger von all'n
> Tut dem Sattler was zahl'n.
> Ja, beim Umschwung der Zeit
> Lernt man s' kennen, die Leut'.
>
> (*Lady und Schneider* I, 8) (GW v, 147)

In the monologue that follows his *couplet* Heugeig'n utters the cynical observation about the political immaturity of the common man, often taken to be sure evidence of Nestroy's change of heart: "Das Volk is ein Ries' in der Wiegen, der erwacht, aufsteht, herumtargelt, alles zusamm'-tritt und am End' wo hineinfallt, wo er noch viel schlechter liegt als in der

Wiegen" (GW v, 148). But do these opinions necessarily indicate a shift in Nestroy's attitude towards 1848? They are in no way inconsistent with those voiced in *Freiheit in Krähwinkel* about the inadequacy of the popular response to political challenge. And though Nestroy makes Heugeig'n the mouthpiece for criticism of the shortcomings, excesses, and impracticalities of the revolutionary period, this does not necessarily imply that Nestroy has thrown his lot in with the other side. Equally, when egalitarianism, political disunity, and the promoters of communism come under attack it has to be recognized that these comments are double-edged: Heugeig'n is an unreliable commentator and his testimony is unsure. But what Nestroy had to say was inevitably welcomed by the conservatives and equally unthinkingly condemned by the progressives; such is the fate of the non-partisan in troubled times.

By contrast *Der alte Mann mit der jungen Frau* has none of the sharpness of the earlier plays, though it does contain a number of telling political comments. Although the fact that Nestroy worked out a cast list shows that he clearly intended to stage the play, it is the only one of these works not to be performed in his life-time. The likeliest explanation for this is that Nestroy realized it would never pass the censor's scrutiny and, as Kern's political attitudes and actions are an indispensable part of his character, we must assume that Nestroy rejected the possibility of excising the offensive material: the play could not have survived such major surgery.[32] Total suppression of the work, the ultimate in self-censorship, appears to have been his only option.

Kern's views on the events of the previous year are contained in two poignant passages. He voices his respect for those who have had the courage of their convictions and who now suffer imprisonment for their views, and he recognizes that in different circumstances — were he a younger man — he could well have been a political victim in the same way as Anton, the political refugee to whom he offers asylum:

Was Sie getan haben, das haben Hunderttausende, das hat — sie's durch Tat oder Wort oder Gesinnung — fast jeder getan. Wer kann bei der jetzigen Krisis in Europa sagen: "Ich war nicht dabei" —? Die Revolution war in der Luft, jeder hat sie eingeatmet und folglich, was er ausg'haucht hat, war wieder Revolution. Da muß sich keiner schön machen woll'n.

(*Der alte Mann mit der jungen Frau* i, 15) (GWv,365)

This allusion to the summary justice to which political suspects were subjected under martial law also makes an important philosophical point: that an individual's involvement in the Revolution was not necessarily the result of a conscious decision but was often due to the heady atmosphere of 1848 which, after years of repression, was peculiarly intoxicating. Maintaining this sovereign point of view Kern continues his political reflections with an acute observation about the necessarily arbitrary way in which punishment was meted out:

> Nach Revolutionen kann's kein ganz richtiges Strafausmaß geben. Dem Gesetz zufolge verdienen so viele Hunderttausende den Tod — natürlich, das geht nicht; also wird halt einer auf lebenslänglich erschossen, der andere auf fünfzehn Jahr' eing'sperrt, der auf sechs Wochen, noch ein anderer kriegt a Medaille — und im Grund haben s' alle das nämliche getan.   (GW v, 366)

The recognition that there cannot be adequate justice in such circumstances, that some will be executed while others are rewarded (as indeed was the case), together with the earlier observations that no-one could be blamed for participating in the Revolution, and the degree of self-awareness that "there but for the grace of God go I" — all these suggest an attitude of resignation to the workings of the world, of fatalistic acceptance of man's helplessness in dealing with the blows of an irrational fate.

This fatalistic view of life is expressed at some length in the "Schicksalsmonolog", intended for inclusion in *Höllenangst*, but suppressed by Nestroy — an act of self-censorship doubtless motivated by the knowledge that the professionals would not let it pass.[33] This is not the place to look at the "Schicksalsmonolog" in detail, nor can I enter the thorny debate about whether, despite its sustained political imagery, it marks, as many have argued, Nestroy's total rejection of politics and his recognition of the fact that man's condition cannot be materially altered by human intervention since he is at the mercy of an irrational, malevolent higher force.[34] But I would counter this argument with the basic observation that the effectiveness of imagery depends on the extent to which there is a demonstrable connexion between the image and the object it describes; this interaction is well demonstrated in the following extract:

> Revolutionairs stürmen in der Regel gegen die irdischen Regierungen an. Das is mir zu geringfügig, ich suche das Übel tiefer oder eigentlich höher, ich revoltiere gegen die Weltregierung, das heißt gegen das, was man eigentlich Schicksal nennt, ich trage einen unsichtbaren Calabreser mit einer imaginären rothen Feder, die mich zum Giganten macht; Giganten waren antediluvianische Studenten, sie haben den Chimborasso und Lepoldiberg aufeinandergestellt . . . und sie haben Barrikaden gebaut, um den Himmel zu stürmen. Das war so eine Idee, dabei schaut doch was heraus, den gräulichen Absolutismus des Schicksals vernichten, das Verhängnis constitutionell machen, daß es Rechenschaft ablegen müßt, sowohl über Verschleuderung als über die universelle Staatsschuld an Glücksgütern.   (GW v, 705)

The spirit of the political imagery is clearly fatalistic, but I would nevertheless argue that the effectiveness of the metaphor is not simply rhetorical: in establishing such a sustained parallel between political absolutism and fate, and by referring in such detail to the events of 1848,

Nestroy is making both a political and a more general philosophical statement. The relationship between the metaphor and the image is, as we have seen before, two-way: the one informs the other. This interpretation means that even if Nestroy's main point here is to rail against the tyranny of fate, by describing it in terms of political repression and arbitrariness, he is at the same time rehearsing his condemnation of the political reality of 1849. And although the conclusion he reaches is that there is nothing the individual can do to counter the blows of fate, that conclusion also has a political dimension, the recognition that pessimistic, fatalistic resignation is the only appropriate response to what, at the end of 1849, must have seemed to be a politically hopeless situation.

What conclusions may be drawn from this discussion of 1848? I would suggest that the most important consideration in reading Nestroy's plays is the question of point of view, aesthetic, political, and personal. When dealing with political comedy the following determinants of point of view must be taken into account. First, we must recognize that the point of view of the political historian is different from that of the dramatist: the playwright is not primarily concerned with presenting a historical pageant or a socio-political analysis but with creating a dramatically effective play. Secondly, the moral concerns of the dramatist normally override the claims of historical accuracy, just as the comic playwright's obligation to create comic situations and dialogue must, to a greater or lesser degree, determine his view and presentation of contemporary events. Thirdly, the perspective of the theatre producer is inevitably different from that of an academic critic; this is an important consideration when we are dealing, as here, with *Theaterstücke* rather than *Buchdrama*. Fourthly, the perspective of the dramatist and audience of 1848 must necessarily differ from those of later generations who have the benefit — or handicap — of hindsight. Fifthly, we must recognize that the selection of political material is further conditioned by the intellectual and cultural horizons of the audience for whom the play was intended; we must also acknowledge that the creation of comic effect is a cooperative venture between the author's comic intent and the receptivity of the audience or reader. Their receptivity is in turn conditioned by their point of view, the time when they see the play, the nature of their political persuasions, and their familiarity with the comic tradition. And, finally, we must not lose sight of the particular comic tradition in which Nestroy wrote and performed. From the corpus of conventions that fashion the presentation of his satirical material we should remember in particular the multi-perspective of the *Zentralfigur*, and we should constantly be wary of assuming that the characters' point of view is one shared by the dramatist. While it is tempting to assume that whatever we consider to be reasonable opinions in the plays must be Nestroy's opinions, that in turn implies that we would agree about what is reasonable, an assumption that is itself unreasonable; and, equally, we have no right to impose our own particular views either on Nestroy or on his works.

Zusammenfassung

Nestroys politische Stücke haben gegensätzliche Reaktionen hervorgerufen. Einige Literaturwissenschaftler betrachten ihn als Verfechter der 48er Revolution, anderen erscheint er ganz und gar apolitisch. Angesichts dieser Uneinigkeit in der Literaturwissenschaft legt dieses Referat die wichtigsten Kriterien dar, nach denen wir seine politischen Stücke beurteilen sollten. Dabei muß man die allgemeinen Ziele und Konventionen der Komik und des Lustspiels beachten, und insbesondere die eigentümlichen Konventionen des Nestroyschen Volksstücks, sowie Nestroys Arbeitsbedingungen und -verfahren, und die politischen und sozialen Umstände der Jahre 1848–1849.

Da Nestroy in erster Linie als Dramatiker-Schauspieler auf die Revolution reagiert, darf man von seinen Stücken keine systematische Analyse der politischen Ereignisse und sozialen Umstände erwarten. Will man Nestroys persönlichen Standpunkt verstehen, kann man ihn nur *ex negativo* aus seiner skeptischen Haltung und der Vielfalt seiner satirischen Bemerkungen ableiten.

Der Schwerpunkt der Analyse liegt auf *Freiheit in Krähwinkel* und *Judith und Holofernes*, deren eigentliche Bedeutung darin besteht, daß sie die komische Handlung und den satirischen Stoff geschickt vereinen und die Möglichkeiten der Krähwinkeliadentradition und der Parodie auswerten.

Im letzten Teil des Referats wird die Frage gestellt, ob Nestroys politische Ansichten eine grundsätzliche Wandlung erleben, wie es oft behauptet wird: Will sich Nestroy mit *Lady und Schneider* und *Der alte Mann mit der jungen Frau* von der Revolution distanzieren; entwickelt er politischen Angelegenheiten gegenüber eine fatalistische Gleichgültigkeit, oder ist sein Standpunkt nach 1848 die logische Entwicklung seiner früheren skeptischen Haltung?

Das Referat kommt zu dem Schluß, daß es bei der Analyse eines Nestroystücks und vor allem seiner politischen Komödien von entscheidender Bedeutung ist, verschiedene Perspektiven zu beachten, ästhetische, politische, wie auch persönliche, die unsere Bewertung weitgehend mitbestimmen.

11

Patricia Howe

END OF A LINE: ANZENGRUBER AND THE VIENNESE STAGE

In *The Death of Tragedy* George Steiner speculates, "Do art forms have their prescribed life cycle? Perhaps there is in poetic energy no principle of conservation".[1] If we consider Viennese theatre in the light of this, we find something of a mystery. From Stranitzky to Nestroy it conserves and renews itself, only to decline precipitously after Nestroy's death. To understand this decline, I think we have to look at the sources and kinds of poetic energy that sustain it for so long and then, suddenly, no longer. I suggest that this energy, which Steiner does not define, is found in three areas: first, in the individual work, as that inherent energy of plot, character, dialogue etc., the "Motor des Dramas" that propels the work along and is concerned with mimesis;[2] secondly, as that energy which strives to make every work an extension of its predecessors, created by the interaction of tradition and individuality, and is concerned with novelty, or, at a higher level, with originality; thirdly, as the energy of collaboration between the work and its audience. Ultimately all three are necessary for survival.

Historians of Viennese theatre tend to attribute its decline to the dwindling energy of collaboration.[3] This energy is generated jointly between performers, author, and audience. It originates in the interaction of the artistic form and the reality it reflects. The author creates and the actors present an image of Vienna and its people that is derived from but not identical to the reality of Vienna. This is received, modified, and reflected back in the audience's reactions, in a theoretically endless process of modulation.[4] Dialect, local setting, and the "restlose Verwienerung" of foreign elements conserve the form's energy. Actor, author, and producer may be one and the same person, hence uniquely close to the audience's tastes. It is thus a collaboration of a particularly intimate kind.

Intimacy, however, is both strength and limitation. The frontiers of the genre are, more or less by definition, the outskirts of Vienna. Even its most protean talents can be fulfilled only by a specific audience. Its emergence from and dependence on a particular cultural context and its use of dialect make it inaccessible to outsiders and unsuitable for performance elsewhere. It is therefore unusually vulnerable to fluctuations of taste and fashion.

This vulnerability prompts historians to explain its decline in social terms, to say, in effect, that the history of the genre is the history of a

139

changing society.[5] Thus the hectic period between the French Revolution and the Congress of Vienna, whose frenzy Steiner sees as a rival to the excitements of high tragedy, seems to favour Viennese comedy.[6] A city united and made doubly patriotic by a common foe warms to the portrait of its own integrity and humane good sense in a play like Bäuerle's *Die Bürger in Wien*. The Congress of Vienna confirms the message of the *Lokalstück* that precisely this city and its citizens stand at the heart of the universe. The ensuing peace and relative prosperity favour the *Zauberposse*, where much that seems to be accomplished by magic is really achieved by money, and the *Besserungsstück*, where the exercise of benign authority combines with a romantic belief in the perfectibility of man.

This congruence of political climate and personal taste ends, however, about 1830, as Vienna experiences shocks and defeats that threaten its unity and thus the intimate form of its popular theatre. The 1848 Revolution, the defeats of the 1850s and 1860s, the problematic alliance of church and state, the expansion of Vienna, industrialization, and social change from a cohesive society with common beliefs to a disparate and competitive one deprive the popular theatre of its initiated and indulgent audience. To a diffuse and divergent public its intimacy appears self-satisfied and introspective. As wealth declines, so the theatre becomes, as elsewhere, the playground of the rich, who prefer, or so it seems to Anzengruber, to be lulled and distracted by a froth of French domestic dramas and operettas.

These changes may explain the decline of the energy of collaboration, but I am reluctant to believe that they alone explain the decline of the form. For this implies that Anzengruber and others fail only by an accident of birth and that popular theatre knows no permanent values or aesthetic criteria, nothing that is not subject to the vagaries of time and taste. If, as Steiner says, poetic temperament and inadequacy collude with a disappearing public in the death of tragedy, then this must be true in some measure of other, even popular, forms.[7] It seems to me rather that a changing society brings with it aesthetic problems for the author who is so dependent upon it. In responding to them he may undermine the genre, but not to do so would jeopardize his artistic integrity.

Increasingly the Viennese dramatist finds it hard to present a portrait of his city that is truthful, not trivial, and yet flattering. He may struggle with this awkward trio, as Nestroy seems to struggle to reconcile his outraged sense of society's vices with the immediate need to please in order to survive. He may abdicate in favour of triviality, and it seems to Anzengruber at times as if his entire profession has faded away before "die ununterbrochene Aufeinanderfolge von Ehebruchsdramen und Demimondekomödien und Demimondedramen und Ehebruchskomödien" (GA xv/iii, 24), or, speaking more forcefully of operetta, "das sittenloseste Machwerk, das je zynischer Blödsinn mit der blasierten Raffiniertheit zusammen gezüchtet" (GA xv/iii, 5); or he may attempt to reform, using the traditions of popular drama in a new way. This means using the technical assurance that a long tradition bestows, while creating an individual style. The encounter with tradition creates that poetic energy which makes the new work an advance on those that went before. This is the task Anzengruber sets himself.

Anzengruber begins from the belief that his age needs a theatre that confronts its own problems and anxieties:

Unsere Zeit steht an gewaltigen, weltgeschichtlichen Ereignissen gewiß keiner anderen nach; vor unseren Augen zersplittern alte Reiche und neue Staaten erstehen, der Kampf für Gewissensfreiheit gegen jeden Glaubenszwang wird mit den schneidigsten Waffen geführt und die Humanität, die den Schwerpunkt durchaus nicht auf fromme Untätigkeit, sondern geradezu auf die Werktätigkeit legt, wird als das Evangelium der Zukunft gepredigt; doch all die treibenden, leitenden, bewegenden Ideen kommen auf unseren Bühnen zu keinem Ausdrucke, kein "gespielter" Zeitgenosse läßt viel von der Zeit merken, in der wir leben.

(GA xv/iii, 23)

His aim is to bring social awareness into the theatre, to enlighten and free humanity from literal-minded and hence narrow-minded beliefs, its pious inertia and unthinking acceptance of traditional authority. In place of these he suggests a joyous awareness of man's central importance and his rootedness in nature. The specific issues of his time, such as industrialization, religious tolerance, poverty, and loss of community, serve as the impetus for such enlightenment. By comparison with his predecessors' aims, Anzengruber's is more overtly serious, even didactic. But he preaches it, as the quotation suggests, with religious zeal and in the belief that it represents not merely a private insight but the public temper of his age.

The question is, how far is it compatible with entertaining a public accustomed to popular theatre? He must have thought that the Viennese would accept his more serious aims if these were clad in a familiar garment. For he retains the most obvious traditional mimetic elements. He uses conventional plots: that of thwarted lovers trying to outwit their feuding fathers, for example, a staple plot of the *commedia dell'arte*, found later in Bäuerle's *Die Bürger in Wien* or Nestroy's *Freiheit in Krähwinkel*, appears in comic guise in Anzengruber's *Doppelselbstmord* and more seriously in *Das vierte Gebot*; *Der Fleck auf der Ehr* and *Aus'm gewohnten Gleis* contrast the ways of town and country, as do such plays as Nestroy's *Der Zerrissene*, Friedrich Kaiser's *Stadt und Land*, and many earlier plays; the theme of misused or misappropriated fortunes, a minor aspect of *Die Bürger in Wien* or of Gleich's *Der Eheteufel auf Reisen*, the central problem of Raimund's *Der Verschwender*, emerges in Anzengruber's *'s Jungferngift, Der ledige Hof,* and, most clearly, *Der Meineidbauer.* Like his forerunners, he writes in dialect, though not in Viennese, and incorporates into his dialogue songs, long monologues, and jokes on familiar topics, such as marriage, mothers-in-law, occupations etc., and local allusions, including the puns on Viennese street names that go back at least as far as Abraham a Santa Clara's polemic *Merk's Wien* and survive in Hofmannsthal's *Der Schwierige,* when the courtship of Hans Karl and Helene is concluded "auf der Freyung". There are specific debts, as W. E. Yates has shown: a stylistic debt to Nestroy, whose influence on plot and characterization are evident in Anzengruber's plays set in Vienna, especially *Aus'm gewohnten Gleis.*[8] Anzengruber draws generally on Nestroy's verbal techniques, on antithesis, hyperbole, repetition and accretion, if more diffusely and to different ends. There is also a debt to Friedrich Kaiser, who likewise tried to confront the problems of the age, but who was obliged by a tyrannical director and the speed of production to undermine their seriousness with comic trappings and happy endings. Kaiser's legacy to Anzengruber is perhaps the possibility of the unhappy ending.[9]

Yet, despite his debt to tradition, Anzengruber's dramatic aims and procedures also subvert it. While there is some reason to think that the individual drama was originally sustained by the energy of its plot — by the urge of the characters to displace each other, by chance and coincidence — Anzengruber's dramas derive their energy from the tension between an intellectual idea and a character. If anything, the idea dominates. He says of his method: "Ich nehme erst den Menschen, hänge ihm das Standeskleid um und dann gebe ich ihm soviel von der lokalen Umgebung, als sich mit den künstlerischen Intentionen verträgt" (GA II, 392). He is not interested in naturalistic portrayal, but in the limits of the idea: "Ich bin nicht dafür vorhanden, daß ich naturwahre Bauerngestalten mache, sondern ich schaffe Gestalten, wie ich sie brauche, um das darzustellen, was ich darzustellen habe" (GA II, 393). The choice of "Bauerngestalten", as of *Bauernstücke,* is itself an aspect of the poetic idea. Such figures had been part of the comic tradition since Stranitzky's Hanswurst appeared as a Salzburg peasant, but Anzengruber, who neither knew nor cared about the countryside for its own sake, chooses its settings and inhabitants for the apparent simplicity of their lives:

An den Bauern ist nicht viel zu lernen; der Typus ist bald gegeben. Mir handelt es sich um den Menschen! Das Kostüm ist mir das bequemste, weil darin der ursprüngliche Mensch noch am deutlichsten zum Ausdruck kommt, ohne daß ich notwendig habe, die Kulturschminke und Konvenienz des modernen Menschen erst abzukratzen. (GA II, 391–392)

In contrast to the city, the simple village community is still coherent enough to make the isolation of an individual obvious. The proximity to nature shows the correspondence between human behaviour and natural phenomena, and measures human values against a world that changes so slowly as to seem timeless. The authority of church and state seems irrelevant because its sources are physically remote.

Anzengruber also believes that stripping away the trappings of a sophisticated society makes human reactions to fate and circumstance clear: "Der Aufweis: wie Charaktere unter dem Einflusse der Geschicke werden oder verderben [. . . ist] klarer zu erbringen [. . .] an einem Mechanismus, der gleichsam am Tage liegt, als an einem, den ein doppeltes Gehäuse umschließt und Verschnörkelungen und ein krauses Zifferblatt umgeben" (GA X, 370). Although he seems here to perceive what later dramatists practise, namely that paring away inessentials of character and circumstance throws a set of values more obviously into relief, his own practice is more uncertain. For his central characters emerge distinctly, not because inessentials are pared away, but because their essential qualities, ideas, or ambitions are exaggerated, even monumental.[10] However, their dramatic magnitude makes them singular and separates them from the corporate experience in which popular theatre is rooted.

Their singularity emerges when we compare Anzengruber's idea of *Bildung* with the traditional *Besserung*. *Besserungsstücke* suggest, sometimes by their titles, the improvement or return to conformity of an amiable fellow with a single moral blemish — the insouciance of *Der lustige Fritz*, the misogyny of *Der Eheteufel auf Reisen*, the prodigality of *Der Verschwender*. The single sinner is converted to the majority's virtue; the means are vicarious — dreams, illusions, kindly benefactors. Magically, the mere sight of his vice reforms the sinner, for belief in man's perfectibility underpins the process. Nestroy, of course, takes a more sceptical view of humanity, and Anzengruber follows him in perceiving not a single fault, but the basic faultiness of society. But he attributes this to the fact that man's innate goodness has been distorted and misused, and retains what he calls "einen treuen Glauben an die Menschheit im allgemeinen und an das Volk im besonderen" (GA XV/iii, 350). Like Nestroy he isolates virtue in a few individual characters, but through them preaches reform and enlightenment. Moreover, the chief means of enlightenment is suffering, not vicarious, but profoundly individual. This alters the balance of the drama. Where previously the audience watched the return of the errant individual to the virtue of the many — by implication, its own virtue — Anzengruber asks his audience to watch the efforts of isolated individuals to redeem corporate folly.

An example is Steinklopferhanns in *Die Kreuzelschreiber*, in which a group of Bavarian peasants, having made their marks on a petition against clerical reforms, are punished when their priest orders their wives to banish them from bed and board until they have repented by going on a pilgrimage. Two couples exemplify the prohibition: an elderly pair whose lives are so entwined through shared hardship and happiness that the husband drowns himself when banished from the home, and a young couple, tormented by the frustrations of physical separation. The religious issue is confusing and marginal, merely a point of departure, for Anzengruber wants to show clerical squabbles as irrelevant to the peasants' real hopes and fears, and yet as a damaging intrusion. It is an outsider, Steinklopferhanns, whose experience is as remote from theirs as that of the priest, who rescues them by forming a band of young girls to accompany the husbands on their pilgrimage, so that the wives are forced to relent. The problem, created by remote clerical sophistry and demands for obedience, is solved by humane good sense.

But this good sense owes more perhaps to Anzengruber's reforming intentions than to psychological plausibility. For Steinklopferhanns is an outcast, deprived and rejected by the community as an illegitimate child, sent to war, and on his return given the meanest task in a quarry; he survives an almost fatal illness because he resolves to die not in his cave but under the open sky, and is instead revived by sunshine and fresh air. The nearness of death and his miraculous survival reveal to him that he, apparently the lowest of men, is in nature imperishable:

Es kann dir nix gschehn! Selbst die größt Marter zählt nimmer, wann vorbei is! Ob d' jetzt gleich sechs Schuh tief da unterm Rasen liegest oder ob d' das vor dir noch viel tausendmal siehst — es kann dir nix gschehn! — Du ghörst zu dem alln, und dös alls ghört zu dir! Es kann dir nix gschehn!

(*Die Kreuzelschreiber* III, 1) (GA IV, 73)

The man who has always been rejected and isolated has an almost mystical vision of belonging. However, he interprets it not just as private revelation but as a message: "Und dös war so lustig, daß ich's all andern rundherum zugjauchzt hab: Es kann dir nix gschehn! — Jujuju! — Da war ich 's erstmal lustig und bin's a seither bliebn und möcht, 's sollt a kein andrer traurig sein und mir mein lustig Welt verderbn!" (*Die Kreuzelschreiber* III, 1) (GA IV, 73). Improbably, this gives him an urge to redeem and rescue those who rejected him. Another such character is Horlacherlies in *Der Gwissenswurm*. Brought up in ignorance of her true parentage, she returns unknown and unknowing to her father's house as a servant, and cures his hypochondria through her good-hearted cheerfulness. Like Steinklopferhanns, she is sustained through degradation and suffering by her affinity with nature. When Grillhofer, her neurotic father, thinks of dying as he sees the stars shining over the cemetery, she replies:

Geh zu, was kümmert dich der Freithof? Dö er angeht, dö wissen nix davon, und dö davon wissen, dö geht er nix an! Schau lieber, wie heunt dö Stern funkeln und 's Mondschein leucht. Bin hizt durch'n Wald hergfahrn, im Gezweig habn dö Johanniskäferln ihr Gspiel triebn und über der stillen Nacht is der ganze Himmel voll Lichter glegn. Und wann ma so hinaufschaut, wie's leucht und funkelt über der weiten Welt, da is ein, als ziehet's ein d' Seel aus der Brust und reichet dö weit über d' Erd in sternlichten Himmel h'nein.

(Der Gwissenswurm III, 6) (GA IV, 165)

Further examples of characters who combine suffering, insight, and affinity with nature are found in *Doppelselbstmord* and in the heroines of *Der Meineidbauer* and of *Der Fleck auf der Ehr*; but in all of these, in contrast to the *Besserungsstück*, virtue is individual and vice collective; virtue is won from suffering and isolation so profound that the sufferer turns away from society to a primitive oneness with nature. In short, while *Besserung* confirms the wisdom of corporate experience and taste, Anzengruber's idea of *Bildung* challenges and undermines it.

There is another, more technical sense in which the isolation of his characters undermines the drama. Although outsiders who comment on and tacitly judge their society in monologues are familiar figures in Viennese theatre, Anzengruber's outsiders and their monologues are different. The passages I have quoted are abridged from much longer ones, whose function is not comment, witty exposé, or the endearing self-justification of a figure like Bäuerle's Staberl, but epic representation. Both Steinklopferhanns and Horlacherlies play important dramatic roles because of experiences that are not dramatic but solitary and prolonged and can be reproduced only as narrative. This narrative cannot be omitted because without the accounts of their formative experiences they would lose credibility. This is a shift towards narrative — and indeed Steinklopferhanns lives beyond *Die Kreuzelschreiber* in *Die Märchen des Steinklopferhanns* — but it also slows down the pace of the drama and suggests a decline in its inherent energy.

Similarly Anzengruber both refers to and revises the traditional relationship between the physical and metaphysical worlds. This relationship, brought into Viennese theatre from Baroque drama, originally set out to show the poverty of human life and the riches of eternity. But, in time, the metaphysical world recedes, becoming worldly and mechanical, so that gods and other spirits come to exist to improve human lives — to smoothe the paths of thwarted lovers, to guide the errant, to favour the deserving. Metaphysics also becomes mechanical as an excuse for spectacular feats of stagecraft — transformations, revelations, assumptions to realms of bliss. Anzengruber takes this to a logical conclusion, showing the misery of men who come to believe that God exists to provide for their wishes, when religion is only a rationalization of egotism. In doing so he turns what has become form back into theme.

Religion as egocentricity finds its clearest expression in *Der Meineid-*

bauer, where Franz Ferner, having knowingly cheated his brother's intended heirs of their inheritance, rationalizes his false oath and act of misappropriation by so-called signs from God. A series of random happenings appear to him as divine intervention justifying his lies, and over the years he comes to believe that God will always step in to safeguard his interests. To salvage his vestigial conscience he has sent his son to train for the priesthood, so that, when the time comes, he may give him absolution. All this predates the play, and, again, is recreated in narrative. The play shows instead his son's rebellion and the defiance of the rightful heirs to his property, the exposure of his crime and the shattering discovery that his "hot-line" to God is a delusion of his monumental egocentricity. That Ferner is a pillar of the community proves only the alliance of this egocentricity with the institutions of church and state.

This alliance is also shown in *Der Pfarrer von Kirchfeld*, directly inspired by the Concordat that gave the church a monopoly over education and marriage, where Anzengruber juxtaposes compassion and bigotry, enlightenment and indoctrination through the trio of Pfarrer Hell, a liberal priest, Finsterberg, a reactionary aristocrat, and Wurzelsepp, an embittered peasant. Hell preaches "Teilnahme, Mitleid, Erbarmen, [. . .] Menschenliebe" (*Der Pfarrer von Kirchfeld* III, 7) (GA II, 82), telling a man who can find God in nature but not in a church, "Sei du brav und geh ehrlich deiner Wege, so sind's Gotteswege" (*Der Pfarrer von Kirchfeld* I, 1) (GA II, 8). To Finsterberg this is revolutionary talk, "[. . .] tu Er mir das neumodische Reden ab! Merk Er's, das leid ich nicht! Weg und Weg, das ist ein Unterschied" (*Der Pfarrer von Kirchfeld* I, 1) (GA II, 8). Hell is destroyed as a priest by the unholy alliance of Finsterberg, who identifies his worldly interests with the church's, and Wurzelsepp, who believes it has denied his. He predicts that Hell will be destroyed by the church he serves, which has taught people to think negatively, so that they will believe rumours about the priest's love for a servant girl, "[. . .] *ihr habt s' ja mehr 'n Satan als unsern Herrgott fürchten gelernt* und so glaubn s' auch eher 's Böse als 's Gute von ihrn Nebenmenschen!" (*Der Pfarrer von Kirchfeld* II, 4) (GA II, 59).

In *Das vierte Gebot* religion bolsters domestic tyranny, the treatment of children as possessions allied to a demand for filial piety. One father insists on his daughter's loveless but prosperous marriage; another father and mother abdicate their moral duties and produce a daughter edging helplessly towards the gutter and a son who murders; a priest preaches the unquestioning obedience of children, failing to see that all parents are not as good as his own. As the murderer goes to his death, he tells the priest, his childhood friend, "Du hast's leicht, du weißt nit, daß's für manche 's größte Unglück is, von ihre Eltern erzogen zu werden. Wenn du in der Schul den Kindern lernst: 'Ehret Vater und Mutter!', so sag's auch von der Kanzel den Eltern, daß s' darnach sein sollen" (*Das vierte Gebot* IV, 5) (GA V, 235).

Religion is contrasted with nature. Those who reject the church still find "sermons in stones". And nature, as we see in *Doppelselbstmord*, a sort of comic *Romeo und Julia auf dem Dorfe*, sustains them. Here the thwarted lovers run away, leaving a note saying that they are to be eternally united. In spite of a spate of such suicides, the father of Agerl, the heroine, believes she has too much common sense to kill herself, and, indeed, his instinct proves right, when the runaways are found celebrating their eternal union up a mountain in a disused shed. To Anzengruber suicide is not a sin, as it is to the church, but a denial of the will to survive, a sentimental perversion.

Anzengruber rejects religion as aberrant self-centredness because basically, like his characters, he too feels that the ways of God, an absent but looming force in his dramas, should be explicable in humanistic terms. What he perhaps does not see is that they might more effectively be made explicable in dramatic terms. Otherwise motivation and causality collapse and this undermines his reforming purpose. The unseen divine adversary of his resentful peasants is ultimately less dramatically effective than the more worldly spirits of his predecessors, with whom human characters can at least debate their material and spiritual needs and failings.

The loss of tension that results from a loss of direct access to the spiritual protagonist in the drama becomes part of the wider problems of plot. Anzengruber's concentration on poetic idea and its human embodiment in character saps the plot's energy. True, his plots are in some ways like traditional ones. The desire to displace, to usurp the position of another while guarding one's own, which sustains the genre from the *commedia dell'arte* onwards, still provides the basic impulse for his dramas. In response to social change it becomes more urgent, no longer a simple wish for improvement or wealth that can be accommodated because, in theory at least, there is enough improvement and wealth for everyone, but, in a more fragmented and competitive society, an impulse to exclude and deprive. In spite of what this might suggest, Anzengruber's plots are not more dramatic as a result. For the struggle to displace predates the play's action, which deals with the uncovering and results of earlier actions. It is thus all dénouement, as in Ibsen or the works of some German Naturalists. The revelation of the past gives much space to narrative; the endings are arbitrary, depending on accident, and this is also connected with his belief that man is inherently good and with the avoidance of tragedy. Their credibility rests on epic representation of the truly dramatic and decisive events that form character.

These few aspects of Anzengruber's dramatic practice point to a move away from the immediacy, the convergence, the rootedness in place of

Viennese theatrical tradition. His language underlines this. For he proposes his alternative values in a dialect that borrows from existing Austrian and Bavarian dialects but finally conforms to none. In a sense it is a radical expression of new ideas, but it also suggests a gap between language and experience that real dialect seems to bridge. Further, his other stylistic mannerisms underline this. As W. E. Yates has pointed out, Anzengruber's use of puns, hyperbole, aphorisms etc. differs from Nestroy's because he does not have Nestroy's antithetical cast of mind.[11] Nor does he have the conciliatory cast of mind of earlier dramatists. He does not make links, even the negative connexions of antithesis, but exposes gaps.

Let us consider a few examples: first, some comments on marriage. Bäuerle's Redlich offers a charming, antithetical, and not very meaningful comment: "Die lachende Liebe besingen die Herren in Versen und dann beweinen die Mädchen den Ehestand in Prosa" (*Die Bürger in Wien* I, 3) (AWV v, 6). W. E. Yates gives two examples from Nestroy, the rather brusque "Die Liebe ist ein Traum, die Ehe ein Geschäft" (GW VI, 575) and the more picturesque comment, "Der Ehestand verwandelt die feenhafte Villa des Ideals in einen ergiebigen Meierhof" (GW VI, 571).[12] All these depend for effect on antithesis and the connotations of the metaphor, which becomes more aggressive and pointed. Anzengruber's comments attenuate the antithesis and abandon the metaphor; in *'s Jungferngift*, for example, a widower asked why he does not remarry replies: "Der heilig Ehstand ist a schöne Sach und jung entschließt mer sich leicht, aber einmal alt, ist mer nimmer so dumm" (*'s Jungferngift*, I, 7) (GA IV, 284). This more diffuse wisdom is scarcely aphoristic, although a few aphorisms exist, based on a sardonic reversal of logic, as in: "Ja, freilich, wer d' Schläg kriegt, hat allmal unrecht" (*Der Pfarrer von Kirchfeld* I, 3) (GA II, 29). The cynicism of these remarks links them with the bitter experience of Anzengruber's characters and the seriousness of his poetic idea. This emerges also in his puns, for example, "reaktionnarrisch" (*Der Pfarrer von Kirchfeld* I, 3) (GA II, 23) imitates Nestroy's "millionärrisch", but expresses the confusion of a peasant about the new laws, and "Zuvielehe" (*'s Jungferngift* V, 12) (GA IV, 366) links the mismatching of two couples with the introduction of civil marriage.

But perhaps the most obvious development away from conciliation towards divergence and exposure is to be found in the humorous comments on occupations. Many of these involve the writer's own profession or a similarly artistic one. Bäuerle's Redlich spars thus with the poet found embracing his daughter: "So? [. . .] Sie dichten kurios — und du, meine liebe Tochter! Ich glaube, ihr macht Hexameter oder wie man die Verse heißt. Verhext bist du wenigstens" (*Die Bürger in Wien* I, 3) (AWV v, 5). And later, "Das könnt' ich brauchen, verliebte Zusammen-

künfte hier im Haus; da könnte zuletzt der Herr Dichter und meine
Tochter Werke miteinander herausgeben, die kein Mensch kaufen möchte
(*Die Bürger in Wien* I, 4) (AWV v, 7). In *Das vierte Gebot* Anzengruber's
heavy father dismisses his daughter's music teacher, ironically called Frey,
for the same reasons, that he is poor and thus an unsuitable match. They
have the following exchange:

> FREY: [. . .] obwohl Ihr Fräulein Tochter ein sehr hübsches Talent besitzt und
> ich mein möglichstes getan habe, so war doch die Dauer des Unterrichtes zu
> kurz.
> HUTTERER: Eben, Sie hätten mit der Zeit auch Unmögliches leisten können.
> FREY: Mit einem Wort, es fehlt dem Fräulein noch an Geläufigkeit.
> HUTTERER: Ja, ja, sehn S', Sie könnten meiner Tochter vielleicht mehr Geläufigkeit
> beibringen, als der ihrem Zukünftigen lieb wär.
>
> (*Das vierte Gebot* I, 5) (GA v, 157)

In the more comfortable climate of Bäuerle's play, the poet's talent for
writing is assimilated, when, having purged himself of his more dramatic
impulses by diving into the Danube to rescue his beloved, he becomes a
clerk. By contrast, Frey abandons music to become a soldier, and
Hutterer drops from this exchange into Odoardo-Galotti-like threats to
kill his daughter if she disobeys him. Here the gap between art and the rest
of life is not bridged. Even more obvious comedy is represented by
unbridgeable misunderstandings, suggesting the ability of language not
only to unite, but also to divide. A final example: in *'s Jungferngift* Regerl,
a country girl, asks Foliantenwälzer, a scholar bent on stealing a priceless
copy of *The Golden Ass*, which no one in the village wants anyway, about
his occupation:

> REGERL: Du, fürs erste, sag mir amal, was bist du eigentlich?
> FOLIANTENWÄLZER: Linguist.

She is suspicious:

> REGERL: Dös is gewiß nix Rechtschaffens, weil d' dir's net deutsch z' sagen traust.

Foliantenwälzer retreats into pomposity as he defines linguist and she
redefines it so that it means something to her:

> FOLIANTENWÄLZER: Sohin bezeichnet Linguist einen Gelehrten, der sich mit
> Sprachwissenschaft befaßt.
> REGERL: Also ein Sprachmeister?
>
> (*'s Jungferngift* v, 10)(GA IV, 359)

Language fails to bridge the gap between them and they must make do
with a tacit agreement to misunderstand. Precisely the same gap exists
later between Hofmannsthal's Ariadne and Zerbinetta in *Ariadne auf*

Naxos, and this scant camouflage for profound divisions seems to me to be something of a reversal of intimate, univocal Viennese popular drama. Recently I heard a commentator on Austrian music say that the Viennese scale of values goes: good — better — Viennese — traditional. If this is true of drama, Anzengruber sets himself an almost impossible task. His Viennese plays are generally too derivative to be successful, and *Bauernstücke* have no natural audience. Tradition gives him themes, plots, and comic trappings, but also imprisons him, so that he cannot confront the problems of his age with the same freedom as Ibsen or the German Naturalists. If Nestroy's Titus is right in seeing the *Lebensbild* as a dreary genre — "drei G'spaß und sonst nichts als Tote, Sterbende, Verstorbene, Gräber und Totengräber" (*Der Talisman* II, 24) (GW III, 476), it is the "drei G'spaß" that separate it from Zola's "tranche de vie" and cause Anzengruber trouble. He is not a natural comic, yet even *Das vierte Gebot* has moments of sardonic humour, and the first audience of *Die Kreuzelschreiber* did not know whether it was watching a tragedy or a comedy until after the final act. He has to harness his jokes, often through cynicism, to an overtly serious aim. His directness, the robust language, the monumental characters, the moral earnestness of his ideas, were perhaps discomfiting to a city where drama had used humour to achieve indirectness. But Anzengruber's tendency to epic representation is only part of a trend whereby drama shifts towards narrative forms.[13] Perhaps the long theatrical tradition of Vienna makes this more difficult to accept than it is elsewhere.

Yet, for other reasons and in other ways, this theatrical tradition had been slowly changing for a long time, and while we have celebrated Raimund and Nestroy as its twin pinnacles, one or two of Raimund's contemporaries and most of Nestroy's saw each of them as its gravedigger. When Otto Rommel records this and Reinhard Urbach states, "Nach Raimund und Nestroy beginnt der Historismus der Wiener Komödie. Bisher hatte es kein Nachspielen gegeben",[14] they are, I think, registering a very specific form of change. It is a loosening of the drama's rootedness in its own time, as Anzengruber's *Bauernstücke* are a loosening of the rootedness in place. It is also a change towards the emergence of individual poetic talents and thus a loosening of folk theatre's rootedness in corporate experience, in which the individual writer was less highly prized than the form itself. This means, too, that popular drama begins to obey more obviously the laws of a literary genre, to prefer individuality to familiarity, eclecticism to the well-tried pattern, to distinguish between novelty and originality. The literary dramatist also tends to suppose that what is great and true in art lies in the universal rather than the local and particular, which becomes the prerogative of the novel.[15] This belief, perhaps, leads Anzengruber to push specific, contemporary problems to the margins of his works and abstract their wider implications. Those later writers, like Hofmannsthal and Horváth, who draw on traditional theatre as one among many sources of inspiration, are aware of this need for selectivity. They realize that it is not dialect, either real or synthetic, but a contrived simplicity of speech which suggests dialect, that best conveys fundamental experiences and gives them an air of universality; not monumental characters based on traditional types, but individuals pared down to their essential motivation give the illusion of life. Anzengruber is thus the last dramatist to take over the tradition as it stands, and it is in this limited sense that he can be described as the end of a line. He offers this explanation, and, if necessary, excuse:

Ich hatte ererbtes dramatisches Talent, genaue Kenntnis der Bühne, erworben durch mehrjährige Verwendung als Schauspieler, ein zurückhaltendes, stets auf Hören, Sehen und Beobachten angewiesenes Wesen und einen treuen Glauben an die Menschheit im allgemeinen und an das Volk im besonderen [. . .] Ein anderer wollte sich nicht finden, welcher der Zeit von der Bühne herab das Wort redete, und einer mußte es tun, also mußte ich es sein!   (GA xv/iii, 350)

Zusammenfassung

Der Verfall des Wiener Volkstheaters nach dem Tode Nestroys ist bisher als Begleiterscheinung der gesellschaftlichen Entwicklung Wiens im späteren neunzehnten Jahrhundert erklärt worden. Mit dem gesellschaftlichen Umbruch der einheimischen Bevölkerung durch Industrialismus und Immigration und der Steigerung der Theaterpreise verschwindet das vertraute Publikum, das das intime Volkstheater zu seiner Vollendung verlangt. Um das Wiener Theater vor einer Flut Operetten und trivialen Dramen zu retten, unternimmt Anzengruber die Erneuerung des Volksstücks. Dabei geht er davon aus, daß seine Zeit ein gesellschaftlich bewußtes und engagiertes Theater benötigt, in dem aktuelle politische und religiöse Themen zum Ausdruck kommen können. Daß er mit diesen Erneuerungsversuchen verhältnismäßig geringen Erfolg findet, ist nicht nur den gesellschaftlichen Verhältnissen, sondern auch der Art seiner Dramen selber zuzuschreiben. Denn er versucht seine sehr ernsten Absichten mit der Unterhaltung eines Publikums zu vereinigen, das an die Zauberposse und an das Lokalstück gewöhnt ist. Er greift wohlbekannte Themen, Gestalten und Motive auf, verwandelt sie aber derart, daß er das Volksstück in neue Bahnen lenkt. Eine Tendenz zum Epischen macht sich bemerkbar, wobei die dramatische Spannung verloren geht. Seine Gestalten wirken manchmal übertrieben, vertreten also kaum den typischen Fall, den sein gesellschaftlich bewußtes Drama verlangt. Obwohl seine dramatische Sprache seinen Vorgängern, vor allem Nestroy, vieles verdankt, bleibt sie im Grunde gekünstelt, leugnet also die

Verwurzelung des Volkstheaters im wirklichen Volksleben. Andererseits kann man Anzengrubers Erneuerungen auch als Beitrag zur unbewußten Annäherung des Volksstücks an das literarische Drama betrachten, die mit Raimund und Nestroy beginnt und später mit Hofmannsthal und Horváth u.a. fortgesetzt wird. Der Aufsatz kommt also zu dem Schluß, daß Anzengrubers Dramen nur in begrenztem Maße als "Ende einer Tradition" betrachtet werden können.

NOTES — ANMERKUNGEN

Margaret Jacobs: ASPECTS OF DIALOGUE IN VIENNESE COMEDY (pp. 1–11)

1 See David Bain, *Actors and Audience: A Study of Asides and Related Conventions in Greek Drama*, Oxford 1977; Gabriel Conesa, *Le Dialogue Moliéresque. Étude stylistique et dramaturgique*, Paris 1983; Andrew K. Kennedy, *Dramatic Dialogue: The Duologue of Personal Encounter*, Cambridge 1983; Deirdre Burton, *Dialogue and Discourse*, London 1980.
2 Only in the *Quodlibet* does the text make it clear that Salome can step outside the emotion established by the relationship with Titus.
3 Gunther Wiltschko, *Raimunds Dramaturgie*, Munich 1973.

Ian F. Roe: RAIMUND'S "VIELE SCHÖNE WORTE" (pp. 13–24)

1 *Ferdinand Raimunds Lebensdokumente*, ed. Richard Smekal, Vienna 1920, p.49.
2 Friedrich Sengle, *Biedermeierzeit. Deutsche Literatur im Spannungsfeld zwischen Restauration und Revolution 1815–1848*, 3 vols, Stuttgart 1971–80, III, 33; Hans Weigel, *Flucht vor der Größe*, Vienna 1960, p. 56.
3 Weigel, *Flucht vor der Größe*, p. 46.
4 See, for example, *Wke.* III, 242; *Wke.* v/ii, 671.
5 Urs Helmensdorfer, *Ferdinand Raimund, "Das Mädchen aus der Feenwelt oder Der Bauer als Millionär": Text und Materialien zur Interpretation*, Berlin 1966, p. 104.
6 The vocabulary of the later plays does in fact find its way into variant lines for the songs of *Der Bauer als Millionär* in later performances; the lines from the "Aschenlied" sung in Munich in January 1832 — "Wie manches ist gemein / Und trägt des Edlen Schein" (*Wke.* I, 284) — would be more appropriate in *Die gefesselte Phantasie*.
7 See Edith Wagesreither-Castle, "Schillersche Züge in Raimunds Dichterantlitz", *Österreich in Geschichte und Literatur* 19 (1975), 257–288; some of the links suggested are not entirely convincing, in particular that between Franz Moor and the character of Wolf in *Der Verschwender*.
8 Kurt Kahl, *Ferdinand Raimund*, Velber bei Hannover 1967, p. 65.
9 Claude David, "Ferdinand Raimund: *Moisasurs Zauberfluch*", in *Das deutsche Lustspiel*, ed. Hans Steffen, 2 vols, Göttingen 1968–69, I, 130.
10 In *Der Alpenkönig und der Menschenfeind* see the scenes I, 2, 18, 21; II, 1, 5. The use of "wild" and "roh" is particularly common in Schiller's Classical dramas and in poems such as "Das Lied von der Glocke" or "Würde der Frauen": "Es befehden sich im Grimme / Die Begierden wild und roh" (vv. 53–54).
11 Jürgen Hein, *Ferdinand Raimund*, Stuttgart 1970, p. 51.
12 See *Wke.* v/ii, 609, 612, 619, 628, 659.
13 See, for example, letters to Toni Wagner in January and September 1826 (*Wke.* IV, 229, 248).

Peter Branscombe: REFLECTIONS ON RAIMUND'S ARTISTIC RELATIONSHIPS WITH HIS CONTEMPORARIES (pp. 25–40)

1 See *Wke.* v/i, 10, 12, 20, (23), 42, 58, (164), 220.

2 See E. Castle's "Einleitung: Raimund und Toni Wagner", *Wke.* IV, lxvii–lxviii, and the editors' "Vorwort", pp. v–vii. I should like to express my thanks to Mr Geoffrey Hargreaves, Keeper of Rare Books, University of St Andrews Library, for his help in the description of Raimund's Kotzebue edition, and to the University of St Andrews for a grant from the Research Fund to cover the cost of the photographic plates.

3 Katharina Ennöckl was to become Bäuerle's wife in 1829 (*Wke.* v/ii, 968).

4 Originally *Ein Graf* [. . .], but altered at the censor's request.

5 Manuscript in the Handschriftensammlung of the Österreichische Nationalbibliothek, Vienna, shelf-mark S.n. 189. I am grateful to Dr Johann Hüttner for obtaining a photocopy for me of the scenes described in detail.

6 The four documents connected with this dispute are printed in *Wke.* III, 367–370, under the heading "Beschwerde über Steinkellers Eingriffe in die Rechte des Theaterdirektors".

7 For a summary of Steinkeller's involvement with the Theater in der Leopoldstadt, see the editors' "Anmerkungen [. . .] zur Geschichte des Theaters in der Leopoldstadt", *Wke.* v/ii, 1001–1008.

8 Richard Smekal, *Grillparzer und Raimund. Funde und Studien*, Vienna and Leipzig 1920, pp. 217–235.

9 Carl Ludwig Costenoble, *Aus dem Burgtheater. 1818–1837. Tagebuchblätter*, 2 vols, Vienna 1889, II, 300. Cf. *Wke.* v/ii, 874–875 (Anschütz, *Erinnerungen*).

10 I. F. Castelli, *Memoiren meines Lebens. Gefundenes und Empfundenes, Erlebtes und Erstrebtes*, ed. J. Bindtner, 2 vols, Munich n.d. [1914], I, 269.

11 See *Wke.* III, 285–286, 455; IV, 421.

12 E.g. *Wke.* III, 415; IV, 353–354, 453–454, 458, 461, 463.

13 See, for example, *Wke.* II, plate facing p. 216; v/ii, 725 ("Ferdinand Raimunds Selbstbiographie"); VI, xx.

14 *Wke.* I, 537, 539; VI, xviii–xix.

15 The italicized phrase denotes that the account was subsequently settled; see editors' note, *Wke.* IV, 571.

Walter Obermaier: Nestroy und Ernst Stainhauser (S. 41–54)

1 Tagebuch Ernst Stainhausers aus dem Jahre 1835, eingebunden in: *Neuer Oesterreichischer Schneit-Kalender*, WSLB (Wiener Stadt- und Landesbibliothek) Ib 188.299. — Im Haus-, Hof- und Staatsarchiv, Wien, Generalintendanz Hofoper 766/1859, befindet sich eine Akte über Stainhauser. Sie enthält sein Anstellungsdekret als Ökonomie-Controllor der Hofoper, eine Äußerung der Obersten Polizeibehörde über Stainhauser vom 12. Jänner 1859, einen Diktatbrief Nestroys, mit dem er Stainhauser seiner Verpflichtungen am Carltheater enthebt (*Briefe*, 183–184), und einen eigenhändigen Bericht Stainhausers: "Amtirung des Controlor's im k.k. pr. Carl-Theater".

2 Vorstellungen der beiden vereinten k.k.p. Theater an der Wien und in der Leopoldstadt unter der Leitung des Direktors Karl Carl 1844 und 1845 (WSLB Ia 33.210). — Handschriftliches Verzeichnis der in den Jahren 1847 bis 1851 im Carltheater aufgeführten Stücke (WSLB Ib 51.620). — Jahres-Bilanz des k.k.priv. Carltheaters in Wien 1859/60 (WSLB Ib 32.029). — Alle diese tagebuchartigen Aufzeichnungen wurden von Stainhauser eigenhändig geführt.

3 Das Geburtsdatum ergibt sich aus Tagebuch a.a.O., zum 4. September und 16. Dezember, sowie aus dem Wiener Totenprotokoll des Jahres 1893 (Archiv der Stadt und des Landes Wien). — Der im folgenden wiedergegebene Werdegang Stainhausers ist aus verstreuten Tagebuchnotizen (insbesondere Eintragung vom 11. Februar) rekonstruiert worden.

4 Tagebuch a.a.O., Eintragung vom 6. Oktober.

5 Ebd., Eintragung vom 26. September.
6 *Theaterzeitung*, 25. Mai 1833, S.428.
7 Zum Theater in St. Pölten vgl. Alois Haider, "Die Geschichte des Stadttheaters St. Pölten von 1820–1975", phil.Diss., Wien 1978.
8 Tagebuch a.a.O., Eintragungen vom 11. März und 14. April.
9 Ebd., Eintragung vom 23. März.
10 Ebd., Eintragung vom 26. Februar.
11 Das Kremser Gastspiel währte vom 10. bis 12. Februar 1835.
12 Tagebuch a.a.O., Eintragung vom 14. Februar.
13 Ebd., Eintragung vom 4. Februar.
14 Zur Tätigkeit von Prix vgl. auch Hans Jürgen Weisker, "Das wirtschaftliche Verhältnis zwischen Autor und Theater 1790–1857", Inaug.-Diss., München 1931, S.51 f. und S.63–65.
15 *Theaterzeitung*, 28. September 1835, S.772.
16 Tagebuch a.a.O., Eintragungen vom 6.–8. April.
17 Ebd., Eintragung vom 13. November.
18 Ebd., Eintragung vom 17. Juli.
19 "Wenn ich am Abend nur im Theater war, so ist mir schon wohler, so sehr wurde diese Leidenschaft für die Schauspielkunst Herrin meines ganzen Wesens" (ebd., Eintragung vom 23. Juni); zu den "Dichterkränzchen" ebd., Eintragungen vom 19. und 30. November.
20 Ebd., Eintragung vom 12. November.
21 Ebd., Eintragung vom 22. September.
22 Ebd., Eintragung vom 23. Oktober.
23 Ebd., Eintragung vom 2. April.
24 Ebd., Eintragungen vom 21. Mai und 4. September.
25 Ebd., Eintragung vom 17. Juni.
26 Ebd., Eintragung vom 31. Mai.
27 *Theaterzeitung*, 23. Dezember 1835, S.1019.
28 Tagebuch a.a.O., Eintragung vom 21. Dezember.
29 Ebd., Eintragung vom 19. September.
30 Ebd., Eintragung vom 19. Jänner.
31 Ebd., Eintragung vom 26. Juni.
32 Ebd., Eintragung vom 1. April.
33 Außerdem existiert noch ein eigenhändiges vierzehnseitiges Gedicht "Das Vaterhaus" von Stainhauser, das zum Geburtstag Kaiser Franz Josephs I. geschrieben worden war (18. August 1857); WSLB, H.I.N. 25.358.
34 Rudolph Stainhauser, eigenhändiger Brief an Ludwig August Frankl, undatiert (1893), WSLB, H.I.N. 103.804.
35 Tagebuch a.a.O., Eintragungen vom 3. November und 21. April.
36 Ebd., Eintragung vom 17. November.
37 Ebd., Eintragung vom 21. August.
38 Ebd., Eintragung vom 4. Oktober.
39 Stainhauser brachte noch zwei weitere Stücke zur Aufführung. Am 27. Juni 1837 im Theater an der Wien die Posse mit Gesang *Maurer und Ziegeldecker als Gymnastiker, oder die Wette um den Araber* mit Musik von Adolf Müller und am 23. Juni 1838 im Theater in der Josefstadt die Zauberposse *Die Reise nach der blauen Insel*, die er gemeinsam mit Franz Tuvora verfaßt hatte, mit Musik von Heinrich Proch. *Maurer und Ziegeldecker* brachte es bis zum 22. Juli 1837 immerhin auf 8 Aufführungen (*Theaterzeitung*, 22. Juli 1837, S.588).
40 Vgl. dazu etwas ausführlicher Walter Obermaier, "Nestroy und seine Freunde", *Nestroyana* 4 (1982), 92–97 (S. 95–96).

41 Handschriftliches Verzeichnis . . . 1848, a.a.O., Eintragung vom 25. November.
42 Ebd., laufende Eintragungen, und 1847 im Monat Juli.
43 Ebd., Juli 1847.
44 Im Haus-, Hof- und Staatsarchiv (vgl. Anm.1).
45 Ebd.
46 Leopold Rosner, *Fünfzig Jahre Carl-Theater (1847-1897)*. *Ein Rückblick*, Wien 1897, S. 17.
47 Mathilde K., eigenhändiger Brief an Ernst Stainhauser, undat., WSLB, H.I.N. 965.
48 Ebd. auch der eigenhändige Antwortentwurf Stainhausers.
49 Ernst Stainhauser, eigenhändiger Brief an Marie Weiler, Wien 16. Juli 1855, WSLB, H.I.N. 24.757.
50 Ernst Stainhauser, eigenhändiger Brief an Karl Treumann, Wien 16. September 1866, WSLB, H.I.N. 71.316.
51 Handschriftliches Verzeichnis . . . 1848, a.a.O.
52 Zur weiteren Laufbahn Stainhausers vgl. die Register der Akten der Hoftheaterintendanz 1867 und 1869 im Haus-, Hof- und Staatsarchiv in Wien.

W. E. Yates: Das Werden eines Nestroystücks (S. 55–66)

1 Dieses Referat ist die stark überarbeitete Fassung eines Vortrags, der zuerst am 31. Mai 1983 an der Universität Basel gehalten wurde.
2 Friedrich Kaiser, *Theater-Director Carl. Sein Leben und Wirken — in München und Wien, mit einer entwickelten Schilderung seines Charakters und seiner Stellung zur Volksbühne*, Wien 1854, S. 65–66; SW xv, 542–548.
3 *Wiener Bote*. Beilage zu den *Sonntagsblättern* (Redakteur: Ludwig August Frankl), 11. April 1847 (Nr. 15), S. 119.
4 Egon Friedell, *Kulturgeschichte Griechenlands. Leben und Legende der vorchristlichen Seele*, München 1949, S. 70.
5 Seidlitz [= I. Jeitteles] in: *Der Humorist*, 12. April 1847 (Nr. 87), S. 347.
6 Zu Nestroys Bearbeitung englischer Vorlagen s. W. E. Yates, *Nestroy: Satire and Parody in Viennese Popular Comedy*, Cambridge 1972, S. 126–148; Friedrich Walla, "Von 'Einen Jux will er sich machen' bis 'Nur keck!': Johann Nestroy und seine englischen Quellen", *Nestroyana* 3 (1981), 33–52.
7 Helmut Herles, *Nestroys Komödie: "Der Talisman". Von der ersten Notiz zum vollendeten Werk*, München 1974.
8 Zitiert nach Gerd Müller, *Das Volksstück von Raimund bis Kroetz. Die Gattung in Einzelanalysen*, München 1979, S. 33.
9 Vgl. Manfred Draudt, " 'Der unzusammenhängende Zusammenhang': Johann Nestroy und William Shakespeare. Dramatische Konventionen im Wiener Volkstheater und im elisabethanischen *Public Theatre*", *Maske und Kothurn* 26 (1980), 16–58.
10 Wiener Stadt- und Landesbibliothek, Musiksammlung, Signaturen: MH 706 und MH 721.
11 In seiner großen Geschichte der Wiener Vorstadtkomödie versucht Otto Rommel, den Erfolg der verschiedenen Werke Nestroys zu resümieren, wobei *Eine Wohnung ist zu vermieten* in die Rubrik "Ablehnung durch revoltierende Masseninstinkte" eingeordnet wird (Otto Rommel, *Die Alt-Wiener Volkskomödie. Ihre Geschichte vom barocken Welt-Theater bis zum Tode Nestroys*, Wien 1952, S. 961). Die meisten Forscher stimmen damit überein, daß der große Mißerfolg der Premiere auf die Einstellung des Publikums zur Satire zurückzuführen sei. Da das Stück Wiener Typen schildert, die ihr Leben ausschließlich in der österreichischen Hauptstadt und deren Vorstädten und Vororten führen, liegt offensichtlich die Vermutung nahe, daß das Publikum sich von der Satire getroffen fühlte. Diese Meinung ist noch 1982 von Wendelin Schmidt-Dengler vertreten

worden ("Familienfassaden. Zur Funktion der Familie bei Johann Nestroy", *Nestroyana* 4, 83–91 (s. S. 88)). Es wird meistens angenommen, daß der Stein des Anstoßes insbesondere in der boshaften Charakterisierung der von Nestroy selbst gespielten Hauptfigur lag. Es ist immerhin zu bedenken, daß der selbstgefällig-spießbürgerliche Herr von Gundlhuber — ein "Rentier", der in der inneren Stadt wohnt — zu einer wohlhabenden Gesellschaftsschicht gehört, daß das Stammpublikum des Theaters an der Wien hingegen, wie wir aus zeitgenössischen Schilderungen wissen, ein vorwiegend kleinbürgerliches Publikum war, das sich aus Handwerkern, kleinen Geschäftsleuten und Beamten und deren Familien zusammensetzte (vgl. meinen Aufsatz "Zur Wirklichkeitsbezogenheit der Satire in Nestroys Posse 'Eine Wohnung ist zu vermiethen' ", *Maske und Kothurn* 27 (1981), 147–154), so daß es folglich gar keinen Grund hatte, sich mit Gundlhuber zu indentifizieren.

12 Friedrich Reischl, *Wien zur Biedermeierzeit. Volksleben in Wiens Vorstädten nach zeitgenössischen Schilderungen*, Wien 1921, S. 182.

13 Die Zensuränderungen im *Haus der Temperamente* sind in der neuen HKA ausführlich angegeben: s. *Stücke 13*, 225–229.

14 Vgl. Johann Hüttner, "Vor- und Selbstzensur bei Johann Nestroy", *Maske und Kothurn* 26 (1980), 234–248. Dieser Aufsatz führt viele Beispiele aus Stücken der dreißiger Jahre an.

15 Vgl. meinen Aufsatz "Kriterien der Nestroyrezeption 1837–1838", *Nestroyana* 5 (1983–84), 3–11.

Johann Hüttner: DER ERNSTE NESTROY (S. 67–80)

1 Vgl. SW xv, 54, 553–558.

2 Vgl. WA I/20, Apparat zu *Traum ein Leben*, Zeugnisse, passim.

3 Vgl. O. Paul Straubinger, "Prolegomena zu Grillparzer im Urteil seiner Zeitgenossen", *Grillparzer-Forum Forchtenstein* 1969, 106–110 (S. 109).

4 Rio Preisner, *Johann Nepomuk Nestroy. Der Schöpfer der tragischen Posse*, München 1968, S. 87.

5 Franz H. Mautner, *Nestroy*, Heidelberg 1974, S. 218.

6 Mautner, *Nestroy*, S. 232.

7 Preisner, *Johann Nepomuk Nestroy*, S. 91.

8 Mautner, *Nestroy*, S. 200–201.

9 Mautner, *Nestroy*, S. 201.

10 *Theaterzeitung*, 7. März 1836, S. 191.

11 *Theaterzeitung*, 12. Oktober 1836, S. 819.

12 Lt. Theaterzettel vom 25. April 1840, Commissionsrath Firner.

13 Lt. Originalhandschrift Nestroys, Handschriftensammlung der Österreichischen Nationalbibliothek, ser. nov. 9377: "zerschellt".

14 Diese Stelle wurde von Nestroy in der Originalhandschrift großenteils als zensurbedenklich "eingeringelt".

15 In großem Ausmaß in der Originalhandschrift "eingeringelt".

16 Lt. Originalhandschrift "Herzlichkeit".

17 Lt. Originalhandschrift: VON SOLMING (*entzückt vortretend für sich*): Es ist beschlossen [. . .] Die Liebkosungen eines fremden Kindes [. . .].

18 Lt. Originalhandschrift "verschlungen".

19 Lt. Originalhandschrift "charakteristischer".

20 Beispielsweise I, 46 (SW VI, 202–203).

21 II, 17 sagt Herr von Falsch zu von Solming: "Mir hat die Natur nur fünf Sinne gegeben, den sechsten, den Sinn für deine spießbürgerlichen Glückseligkeiten, den hab' ich nicht" (SW VI, 231).

M. A. Rogers: THE SERVANT PROBLEM IN VIENNESE POPULAR COMEDY (pp. 81–92)

1 According to statistics kindly supplied to me by Professor Branscombe, there were very few performances of *Figaro* in the 1790s — whether because of Viennese taste or political events is hard to say.

2 Helmut Olles, "Zerrissenheit bei Raimund and Nestroy", Dissertation, Frankfurt a.M., 1954, p. 147.

W. E. Yates: NESTROY, GRILLPARZER, AND THE FEMINIST CAUSE (pp. 93–107)

1 Barbara Rett, "Liebesgeschichten und Heiratssachen: Frauen im Leben und Werk Nestroys", *Nestroyana* 4 (1982), 78–82 (see especially p. 79).

2 Friedrich Kaiser: *Eine Posse als Medizin.* Original-Posse mit Gesang in 3 Akten, Vienna 1850, p. 62.

3 See "Das Werden eines Nestroy-Stücks" (pp. 55–66, above); also SW xv, 562–564 for an extract from one of Nestroy's contracts, and SW xv, 542–548 for the full text of a standard contract between a dramatist and the impresario Karl Carl.

4 Colin Walker, "Nestroy's 'Judith und Holofernes' and Antisemitism in Vienna", *Oxford German Studies* 12 (1981), 85–110 (quotations from pp. 107–109).

5 Schiller, *Werke*, Nationalausgabe (Weimar, 1943 ff.), xx, 442–443.

6 See [Josef Karl Ratislav,] *175 Jahre Burgtheater: 1776–1951. Fortgeführt bis Sommer 1954*, Vienna n.d., p. 12.

7 *König Lear.* Trauerspiel in fünf Aufzügen, von Shakespeare. Für die Darstellung eingerichtet von C. A. West, Vienna (Wallishausser) 1841, p. 25. "Witz" and "List" were the translations generally in currency: "Witz" is used by Johann Heinrich Voss, father and son (1811, 1819) and by J. W. O. Benda (1825), "List" in the translation by Baudissin, which was reissued in the revised edition of the "Schlegel-Tieck" Shakespeare in 1840 (*Shakespeare's dramatische Werke*, übersetzt von Aug. Wilh. v. Schlegel und Ludwig Tieck, 12 vols, Berlin 1839–1841, xi, 27).

8 See M. Kay Flavell, "Women and Individualism: A Re-examination of Schlegel's 'Lucinde' and Gutzkow's 'Wally die Zweiflerin' ", *Modern Language Review* 70 (1975), 550–566 (p. 563). For a concise factual survey of the emancipation movement in the German-speaking countries see Daniela Weiland, *Geschichte der Frauenemanzipation in Deutschland und Österreich: Biographien — Programme — Organisationen*, Düsseldorf 1983. For a brief summary of the position of women in the German-speaking countries in the nineteenth century see Eda Sagarra, *An Introduction to Nineteenth Century Germany*, London 1980, pp. 234–250.

9 Marie von Thurnberg, *Gedanken über die angeborenen Rechte des Frauengeschlechtes*, Vienna 1846, p. 1. See Irmgard Neck, "Die Rolle der Frau in der Nestroy-Zeit", *Nestroyana* 4 (1982), 73–77 (p. 73).

10 See *Frauenemanzipation im deutschen Vormärz. Texte und Dokumente*, ed. Renate Möhrmann, Stuttgart 1978.

11 Josef Schrank, *Die Prostitution in Wien in historischer, administrativer und hygienischer Beziehung*, 2 vols, Vienna 1886, i, 242.

12 See Tertius Chandler and Gerald Fox, *3000 Years of Urban Growth*, New York 1974, p. 327.

13 *Der Humorist* (ed. M. G. Saphir), 12–13 May 1847 (No. 113/114), pp. 453–454 ("Damen-Salon").

14 See Edward P. Harris, "From Outcast to Ideal: The Image of the Actress in Eighteenth-Century Germany", *German Quarterly* 54 (1981), 177–187.

15 "Briefe an eine junge Schauspielerin", in: *Almanach für Theater, Musik und Poesie auf das Jahr 1811*, Vienna 1810, pp. 53–57; quoted by Roger Bauer, *Laßt sie koaxen, Die*

kritischen Frösch' in Preußen und Sachsen! Zwei Jahrhunderte Literatur in Österreich, Vienna 1977, p. 132. How tenaciously prejudice against the profession as a whole lived on is reflected over a century later in the publication of the work *Komödiantin — Dirne? Der Künstlerin Leben und Lieben im Lichte der Wahrheit* by a Viennese gynaecologist, Bernhard Bauer (Vienna and Leipzig 1927), which traces the history of the actress back to indecent erotic dances in Greek drama (p. 17), describes actresses as being characterized by infantilism (p. 115) and exhibitionism (p. 336), and argues that the opportunity of sexual licence may be one of the major factors that draws them into their profession (p. 280). Bernhard Bauer is at pains to distinguish the artistic impulse from the moral corruption and materialism of prostitution (pp. 398–399), but fundamental to his argument is an acceptance of "die Allmacht der Sexualität und aller erotischen Empfindungen auf das Leben und seine Äußerungen" (p. 279), and particularly of the connexions between sexuality and art (p. 243).

16 See *Die Frauenfrage in Deutschland 1865–1915. Texte und Dokumente*, ed. Elke Frederiksen, Stuttgart 1981.

17 See, for example, the review quoted by Barbara Becker-Cantarino at the beginning of her article "Caroline Pichler und die 'Frauendichtung' ", *Modern Austrian Literature* 12, no. 3–4 (1979), pp. 1–23.

18 Johann Gabriel Seidl, *Ausgewählte Dichtungen*, ed. Karl Fuchs, 3 vols, Leipzig n.d. [1906], I, 85–87.

19 Germaine Greer, *The Obstacle Race: The Fortunes of Women Painters and their Work*, London 1979, e.g. p. 75: "to be [. . .] excellent in art was to be de-sexed".

20 Gutzkow, *Werke*, ed. Reinhold Gensel, 12 vols, Berlin, Leipzig, Vienna, Stuttgart n.d., VIII, 104 ("Vergangenheit und Gegenwart").

21 Marianne Burkhard, " 'Die letzte Schuld des Lebens': Grillparzers 'Sappho' als Tragödie der dichtenden Frau", *Monatshefte* 74 (1982), 122–138. The analysis in this article does not, however, convincingly refute the argument that Sappho's suicide is an unsatisfactory conclusion to the problem of the poetic personality as Grillparzer himself, working from his own experience, recurrently posed it. — The unusual combination of qualities in the characterization of Sappho is also stressed by M. Kay Flavell, "Women and Individualism", pp. 553–554.

22 Egon Friedell, *Kulturgeschichte Griechenlands*, Munich 1949, p. 134.

23 See Eda Sagarra, " 'Echo oder Antwort': Die Darstellung der Frau in der deutschen Erzählprosa 1815–1848", *Geschichte und Gesellschaft* 7 (1981), 394–411 (especially pp. 396 and 406).

24 Barbara Rett, "Liebesgeschichten und Heiratssachen", p. 78.

25 This point is made by Wendelin Schmidt-Dengler, "Familienfassaden: Zur Funktion der Familie bei Johann Nestroy", *Nestroyana* 4 (1982), 83–91 (p. 83).

26 E.g. *Der Feenball* III, 2 (SW I, 590–591); *Robert der Teuxel* II, 5 (GW II, 32–33); *Zu ebener Erde und erster Stock* II, 14 (GW II, 486); *Die beiden Nachtwandler* I, 21 (GW II, 574–575); *Der Treulose* I, 21 (MS) (SW VIII, 172); *Das Mädl aus der Vorstadt* I, 13 (GW III, 534–535). That in each case the female figure involved is a secondary character reflects the position of the actresses in the company, but also corresponds to the reality of the social hierarchy.

Günter Berghaus: Rebellion, Reservation, Resignation: Nestroy und die Wiener Gesellschaft 1830–1860 (S. 109–122)

1 Friedrich Uhl, *Aus meinem Leben*, Stuttgart — Berlin 1908, s. 111.

2 Ernst Wangermann, *The Austrian Achievement 1700–1800*, London 1973, S. 116.

3 Zitiert nach Karl Glossy, "Zur Geschichte der Wiener Theatercensur. I", *Jahrbuch der Grillparzer-Gesellschaft* 7 (1897), 238–340 (S. 241).

4 Friedrich Schlögl, *Vom Wiener Volkstheater. Erinnerungen und Aufzeichnungen*, Wien — Teschen o.J. [1883], S. 145, Anm. 1.
5 Zitiert nach SW xii, 662–663.
6 Friedrich Kaiser, *Unter fünfzehn Theater-Direktoren. Bunte Bilder aus der Wiener Bühnenwelt*, Wien 1870, S. 26.
7 Willibald Alexis, *Wiener Bilder*, Leipzig 1833, S. 222–223.
8 Zitiert nach SW xii, 662–663.
9 Karl Haffner, *Scholz und Nestroy. Roman aus dem Künstlerleben*, hg. von Hans Tabarelli, Wien 1947, S. 252–253.
10 Karl Kraus, "Ein zeitgenössischer Kritiker Nestroys", *Die Fackel* 657–667 (August 1924), 100–120 (S. 106).
11 Saphir über den *Lumpazivagabundus*, zit. nach SW viii, 159.
12 Siehe SW xv, 687 (Aphorismus 71).
13 Siehe *Die Anverwandten* iii, 10 (SW v, 79) und *Freiheit in Krähwinkel* i, 7 (SW v, 141).
14 Siehe *Lady und Schneider* i, 4 (SW v, 221).
15 Einen Einblick gibt Nestroys Briefwechsel mit seinem neuen Zensor Janota in SW xv, 374–382.
16 Ilsa Barea, *Vienna. Legend and Reality*, London 1966, S. 222–223.
17 SW xiii, 651 (*Der holländische Bauer*, Nachlese).

John R. P. McKenzie: NESTROY'S POLITICAL PLAYS (pp. 123–138).

1 E. J. Hobsbawm, *The Age of Revolution: Europe 1789–1848*, London 1962, p.121.
2 Ilsa Barea, *Vienna: Legend and Reality*, London 1966, p. 224.
3 Arthur Scherle, "Johann Nestroy, *Der alte Mann mit der jungen Frau*", in *Kindlers Literaturlexikon*, 12 vols, Zürich 1970–74, i, 950.
4 Fritz Martini, *Deutsche Literatur im bürgerlichen Realismus 1848–1898*, Stuttgart 1962, p. 217.
5 Franz H. Mautner, *Nestroy*, Heidelberg 1974, p. 114.
6 Friedrich Sengle, *Biedermeierzeit. Deutsche Literatur im Spannungsfeld zwischen Restauration und Revolution 1815–1848*, 3 vols, Stuttgart 1971–80, iii, 222.
7 Quoted by Otto Rommel, SW v, 628.
8 "Ein Flugblatt aus dem Jahre 1848" in "Dokumente aus der Nestroyzeit", *Der Strom 2* (Vienna 1912–13), 76–84 (p. 77). See also: Clifford A. Barraclough, "Nestroy the Political Satirist", *Monatshefte für den deutschen Unterricht* 52 (1960), 253–257 (pp. 254–255); Otto Basil, *Johann Nestroy in Selbstzeugnissen und Bilddokumenten*, Reinbek bei Hamburg 1967, pp. 119 and 126; Walter Dietze, "Nachwort" to Johann Nestroy, *Freiheit in Krähwinkel. Posse mit Gesang in zwei Abteilungen und drei Akten*, Leipzig n.d. [1964], 79–92 (p. 88); Ernst Fischer, "Johann Nestroy. Zu seinem hundertsten Todestag", *Sinn und Form* 14 (1962), 430–481 (p. 464); Martin Greiner, *Zwischen Biedermeier und Bourgeoisie. Ein Kapitel deutscher Literaturgeschichte im Zeichen Heinrich Heines*, Göttingen 1953, pp. 46–47; Erwin J. Haeberle, "Nestroy oder der gerade Umweg der Satire", *Die neue Rundschau* 81 (1970), 302–314 (p. 309); Bruno Hannemann, *Johann Nestroy, Nihilistisches Welttheater und verflixter Kerl. Zum Ende der Wiener Komödie*, Bonn 1977, pp. 101–113; Heinz Kindermann, "Nestroy — Revolutionär und Bürger", *Maske und Kothurn* 9 (1963), 132–152 (p. 142); Wolfgang Preisendanz, "Nestroys komisches Theater" in *Das deutsche Lustspiel*, ed. Hans Steffen, 2 vols, Göttingen 1969–70, ii, 7–24 (pp. 19–20); Rio Preisner, *Johann Nepomuk Nestroy: Der Schöpfer der tragischen Posse*, Munich 1968, p. 125; Otto Rommel, "Nestroy als Politiker", in *Alt-Wiener Kalender für das Jahr 1922*, ed. Alois Trost, Vienna 1922, pp. 34–45 (p. 39).
9 Ronald Peacock, "Public and Private Problems in Modern Drama" in *Theatre in the Twentieth Century*, ed. Robert W. Corrigan, New York 1963, pp. 304–320 (p. 305).
10 See Elder Olson, *The Theory of Comedy*, Bloomington 1968, pp. 3–24, especially pp. 7–8.

11 An extreme example of the appropriation of Nestroy, a National Socialist production entitled *Revolution in Krähwinkel*, is described by Hans Eberhard Goldschmidt, "Revolution in Krähwinkel — Wien 1938", *Nestroyana* 2 (1980), 50–57.

12 See Peter Pütz, "Zwei Krähwinkeliaden 1802/1848. Kotzebue, *Die deutschen Kleinstädter*, Nestroy, *Freiheit in Krähwinkel*" in *Die deutsche Komödie. Vom Mittelalter bis zur Gegenwart*, ed. Walter Hinck, Düsseldorf 1977, pp. 175–194 and 385–386 (p. 190).

13 See Mautner, *Nestroy*, p. 98; also Rommel's caution, "Auch muß ausdrücklich davor gewarnt werden, an den Sachgehalt von Couplets den Maßstab der sachlichen Vollständigkeit und Objektivität zu legen. Im Couplet herrscht die Pointe, nicht der Sachstoff" (GW vi, 725).

14 See W. E. Yates, *Nestroy: Satire and Parody in Viennese Popular Comedy*, Cambridge 1972, p. 155.

15 See, for example, Rommel, "Nestroy als Politiker", p. 39: "Was sein Eberhard Ultra sagt, das war auch seine [Nestroys] Meinung."

16 See Mautner, *Nestroy*, p. 281.

17 See Rommel's commentary on the reception of *Die Anverwandten*, SW v, 607–609.

18 See John R. P. McKenzie, "Political Satire in Nestroy's *Freiheit in Krähwinkel*", *Modern Language Review* 75 (1980), 322–332 (pp. 322–323); Pütz, "Zwei Krähwinkeliaden 1802/1848", pp. 191–194; Eda Sagarra, "Krähwinkel, Imperial Village. An Episode in the Viennese Popular Theatre", *German Life and Letters* (New Series) 23 (1969–70), 310–315.

19 Sengle is alone in rejecting the Viennese setting; he accuses commentators of committing a basic error, "daß sie nämlich Krähwinkel und Wien (oder Österreich) ungeprüft *gleichsetzen.* [. . .] Wenn mit Krähwinkel Wien gemeint wäre, hätte auch das Auftauchen des flüchtigen Metternich, den Ultra fingiert, keinen Sinn" (*Biedermeierzeit*, iii, 247).

20 Barea observes, "There is nothing like Dickens's scenes of backyard squalor, not only because Vienna was a small metropolis with no vast slummy areas, but also because local comedy has other laws than a novel" (*Vienna*, p. 171).

21 See Pütz, "Zwei Krähwinkeliaden 1802/1848", pp. 188–189.

22 The fullest account of the controversy is given by Colin Walker, "Nestroy's *Judith und Holofernes* and Antisemitism in Vienna", *Oxford German Studies* 12 (1981), 85–110; see also Rommel's account of the reception of *Judith und Holofernes*, SW iv, 381–384. See also above, pp. 96–97.

23 See Barea, *Vienna*, p. 233.

24 Walker concludes, "I believe that if Nestroy is to be criticized it is above all for insensitivity. He subjected to ridicule members of a buffeted and anxious minority at a critical time in their fortunes. Just as black humour is *particularly* out of place at funerals, anti-Jewish satire had no proper place on the stage of the Carl-Theater in the Leopoldstadt, *especially* in the Vienna of March 1849" (Nestroy's *Judith und Holofernes* and Antisemitism in Vienna", p. 109). For contrary opinions see: Jürgen Hein, "Nachwort" to Johann Nestroy, *Judith und Holofernes und Häuptling Abendwind*, Stuttgart 1981, p. 78; Ulrich Scheck, *Parodie und Eigenständigkeit in Nestroys "Judith und Holofernes": Ein Vergleich mit Hebbels "Judith"*, Berne 1981, pp. 101–102; Hans Weigel, *Johann Nestroy*, Velber bei Hannover 1967, p. 52; W. E. Yates, "Das Vorurteil als Thema im Wiener Volksstück" in *Theater und Gesellschaft: Das Volksstück im 19. und 20. Jahrhundert*, ed. Jürgen Hein, Düsseldorf 1973, pp. 69–79 (p. 74).

25 It is the stereotype nature of such criticism that several commentators find offensive; see, for example, Walker, "Nestroy's *Judith und Holofernes* and Antisemitism in Vienna", pp. 93 and 97.

26 "[. . .] bei seiner vierzigjährigen Wüstenrekognoszierung hat's Wachteln g'regnet und Preßburger Zweiback g'schneit" (*Judith und Holofernes*, sc. 14) (GW v, 231); *Wachteln* are a Bohemian confection; Preßburg (Pozsony, now Bratislava) was the seat of the Hungarian Diet.

27 *Briefe*, 217; see also SW xv, 727 and 728.

28 See, for example, Peter von Matt, "Nestroys Panik", *Tagesanzeiger* (Zürich), Magazin 48, 27 November 1976, pp. 7–17 (p. 15).

29 See Barea, *Vienna*, pp. 227–228; Frank F. Bukvic, "Nestroys *Der alte Mann mit der jungen Frau*", *Österreich in Geschichte und Literatur* 22 (1971), 36–46 (p. 38); Rommel, "Nestroy als Politiker", p. 44.

30 A convincing analysis of the effects the reimposition of theatre censorship had on Nestroy is given by Günter Berghaus, "J. N. Nestroys Revolutionspossen im Rahmen des Gesamtwerks" (Inaugural-Dissertation), Berlin 1977, pp. 238–239.

31 See, for example, Mautner, *Nestroy*, p. 287.

32 Mautner argues the opposite case, "Die äußere Handlung ist also 'politisch' genug; sie bleibt aber durchaus äußerlich und hat mit den wesentlichen Vorgängen nichts zu tun". (Franz H. Mautner, "*Der alte Mann mit der jungen Frau* — eine politische Komödie?" in *Über Literatur und Geschichte. Festschrift für Gerhard Storz*, ed. Bernd Hüppauf and Dolf Sternberger, Frankfurt a.M. 1973, pp. 265–274 (pp. 265–266); see also Norbert Geldner, "Der politische Nestroy", *Nestroyana* 3 (1981), 14–19.

33 See Johann Hüttner, "Vor- und Selbstzensur bei Johann Nestroy", *Maske und Kothurn* 26 (1970), 234–248 (especially p. 242); and Hüttner, "Selbstzensur bei Johann Nestroy", *Die Presse*, Vienna, 13–14 September 1980, "Spectrum" pp. iv–v.

34 See, for example, Hannemann, *Johann Nestroy*, p. 110; Mautner, *Nestroy*, pp. 105–109; Preisner, *Johann Nepomuk Nestroy*, p. 139.

Patricia Howe: END OF A LINE: ANZENGRUBER AND THE VIENNESE STAGE (pp. 139–152)

1 George Steiner, *The Death of Tragedy*, London 1961, p. 121.

2 Reinhard Urbach, *Die Wiener Komödie und ihr Publikum*, Vienna 1973, p. 41.

3 See Otto Rommel, *Die Alt-Wiener Volkskomödie. Ihre Geschichte vom barocken Welt-Theater bis zum Tode Nestroys*, Vienna 1952, pp. 20–21; Urbach, *Die Wiener Komödie und ihr Publikum*, p. 9. The importance of this collaboration is discussed in W. E. Yates, *Nestroy: Satire and Parody in Viennese Popular Comedy*, Cambridge 1972, pp. 42–52, especially p. 46, which refers to Zelter's letter of 20 July 1819: "Die Schauspieler und das Publikum zusammen machen das Stück".

4 See M. A. Rogers, "Dies Österreich ist eine kleine Welt", in *Austrian Life and Literature*, ed. Peter Branscombe, Edinburgh 1978, pp. 72–79.

5 Rommel, *Die Alt-Wiener Volkskomödie*, p. 20.

6 Steiner, *The Death of Tragedy*, p. 116.

7 Steiner, *The Death of Tragedy*, p. 121.

8 See W. E. Yates, "Nestroysche Stilelemente bei Anzengruber", *Maske und Kothurn* 14 (1968), 287–296.

9 Otto Rommel, "Ludwig Anzengruber als Dramatiker", GA ii, 333–607: "Hier hatte Anzengruber eine große Mission zu erfüllen im 'Vierten Gebot', im 'Meineidbauer', in 'Stahl und Stein' — lauter Probleme, die auch Kaiser behandelt hat — wird nicht mehr verziehen" (p. 371).

10 See Edward McInnes, "Ludwig Anzengruber and the Popular Dramatic Tradition", *Maske und Kothurn* 21 (1975), 135–152.

11 Yates, "Nestroysche Stilelemente bei Anzengruber", p. 293.

12 Yates, "Nestroysche Stilelemente bei Anzengruber", p. 292.

13 This development is traced in Peter Szondi, *Theorie des modernen Dramas*, Frankfurt a.M. 1964.

14 Rommel, *Die Alt-Wiener Volkskomödie*, pp. 595–596; Urbach, *Die Wiener Komödie und ihr Publikum*, p. 127.

15 This preference for the general rather than the local is discussed in Ronald Peacock, *Criticism and Personal Taste*, Oxford 1972, p. 115.

INDEX — REGISTER

Dates and letters in brackets after titles of stage works refer to first performances in the following Viennese theatres:
Die in Klammern gesetzten Jahreszahlen und Siglen hinter den Werktiteln beziehen sich auf Ur- und Erstaufführungen in folgenden Wiener Theatern:
Hofburgtheater (B), Bürgertheater (Bü), Carltheater (C), Freihaustheater auf der Wieden (F), Theater in der Josefstadt (J), Kaitheater (K), Hoftheater nächst dem Kärntnertore (Hoftmtheater) (Kä), Theater in der Leopoldstadt (L), Hofopernhaus (neues Opernhaus) (Op), Deutsches Volkstheater (V), Theater an der Wien (W).

163

INTERNATIONALE NESTROY-GESELLSCHAFT
INTERNATIONAL NESTROY SOCIETY

Die Internationale Nestroy-Gesellschaft mit ihrem Sitz in Wien besteht seit 1973 und hat mehr als 220 Mitglieder. Sie arbeitet auf internationaler Grundlage und nimmt Mitglieder aus allen Staaten auf. Die Internationale Nestroy-Gesellschaft hat sich zum Ziel gesetzt,

das dramatische Werk Johann Nestroys zu erschließen und seine Verbreitung und Aufführung zu fördern;

das Leben und Schaffen Johann Nestroys zu erforschen und zu dokumentieren;

die wissenschaftliche Erforschung der literatur- und theatergeschichtlichen Bedeutung Johann Nestroys zu unterstützen;

die Aufarbeitung und Popularisierung der gesamten Epoche des Altwiener Volkstheaters zu fördern.

Die seit 1979 erscheinende Zeitschrift "NESTROYANA. Blätter der Internationalen Nestroy-Gesellschaft" hat internationale Verbreitung gefunden und publiziert Fachbeiträge aus aller Welt.

Anfragen, Bestellungen der Fachzeitschrift "NESTROYANA" und Beitrittserklärungen — im jährlichen Mitgliedsbeitrag von derzeit 200.–öS ist der Bezug der Zeitschrift enthalten — sind zu richten an:

Internationale Nestroy-Gesellschaft
z.Hd. Oberrat Dipl.Ing. Karl Zimmel
Gentzgasse 10/3/2
A–1180 Wien
Österreich

The International Nestroy Society, based in Vienna, was founded in 1973 and has over 220 members. Both its activity and its membership are international. The aims of the Society are:

to advance and encourage knowledge and understanding of the dramatic work of Johann Nestroy and to promote its popularization and performance;

to promote the study and documentation of Nestroy's life and work;

to support scholarly research into Nestroy's place in literary and theatrical history; and

to promote the study and popularization of the whole historical phenomenon of the Viennese popular theatre.

The journal "*Nestroyana*. Blätter der Internationalen Nestroy-Gesellschaft", which has appeared since 1979, has built up an international circulation and publishes specialist articles from all over the world.

Inquiries, orders for the journal *Nestroyana*, and applications for membership (the membership fee, which currently stands at 200 Austrian Schilling per year, includes the annual subscription to *Nestroyana*) should be sent to the Honorary Secretary at the following address:

Internationale Nestroy-Gesellschaft
z.Hd. Oberrat Dipl.Ing. Karl Zimmel
Gentzgasse 10/3/2
A–1180 Wien
Austria